Pennsylvania's Covered Bridges

D1566958

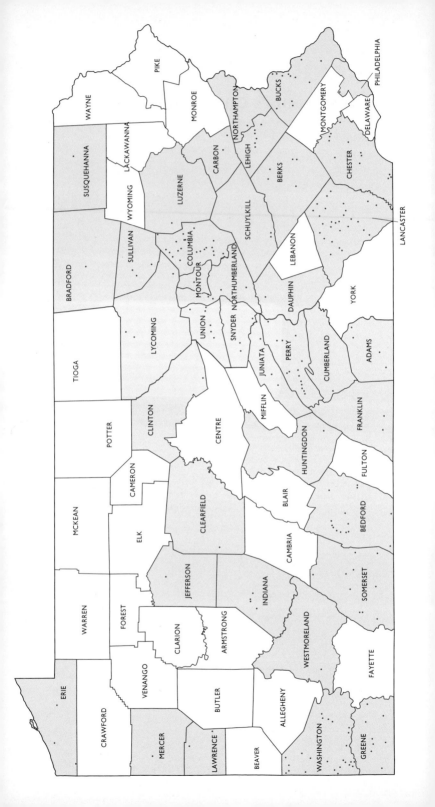

Pennsylvania's Covered Bridges

A COMPLETE GUIDE

SECOND EDITION

Benjamin D. Evans and
June R. Evans

University of Pittsburgh Press

This book is dedicated to the members of the
Theodore Burr Covered Bridge Society of Pennsylvania, Inc.,
for their continued efforts toward the preservation
and restoration of covered bridges.

Title page photograph:
Van Sant / Beaver Dam Bridge, Bucks County

Copyright © 1993, 2001, University of Pittsburgh Press

Manufactured in the United States of America

Printed on acid-free paper

All photographs by Benjamin D. Evans

10 9 8 7 6 5 4 3 2 1

ISBN 0-8229-5764-7

Contents

Preface

Our interest in covered bridges dates back approximately forty years to the time we photographed the Flume Bridge, which spans the Pemigewasset River in Franconia Notch State Park, New Hampshire. It was renewed in fall 1990 when we photographed another New Hampshire bridge about forty miles southeast of the Flume area—the Albany Bridge, located along the Kancamagus Highway. This stretch of highway is considered one of the most scenic in the world, and the photograph of that particular bridge amidst the autumn colors of the White Mountains was very impressive.

Ben received the gift of a new camera from June during the 1990 celebration of our anniversary–Christmas–Ben's birthday, all of which fall within eleven days, and this sparked our interest even further. Shortly after the holiday season, we started to shoot pictures of the covered bridges in our home county, Lehigh. The resulting photographs, and June's interest in the historical aspect of the structures, soon sent us to the library of the local historical society to acquire as much information as possible. Little by little, as we were able to acquire additional printed material on covered bridges in general, we decided to attempt to visit or go "bridging" into the surrounding counties. With relatively few bridges in Berks, Bucks, Carbon, and Northampton Counties, we soon found ourselves in Lancaster, Chester, and Columbia Counties.

By then we had decided that our goal was to develop a photo album complete with as much statistical data as we could accumulate for our own personal satisfaction. As we used the various guides available to us, the most recent having been published in 1989, we found that some of the structures listed were no longer standing, or that directions to the bridges were a little vague or, in a few cases, that the directions were inaccurate. After personally visiting and photographing more than half of the bridges in Pennsylvania, we felt that a more recent guide for the covered bridge enthusiast might be a natural outgrowth of our enjoyable experiences.

The 1993 edition of this book, therefore, was an attempt to provide an up to date listing, complete with photographs, statistical data, anecdotal information, and directions, to every remaining covered bridge in Pennsylvania. Our primary resource for structures that might still be standing was the *World Guide to Covered Bridges*, published by the National Society for the Preservation of Covered Bridges, Inc. We visited the site of every bridge listed for Pennsylvania, and every bridge still standing was photographed by Ben between February 3 and October 31, 1991. Sometimes we found only the remains of the abutments of a bridge, or a few remnants of the deteriorated timbers. If a bridge was not standing intact, we did not include it in this collection. We made every attempt to be accurate in the accumulation of this data. To a very large extent, data such as the year of construction, builder, and length and width of structure were ascertained originally from *The Covered Bridges of Pennsylvania* by Susan Zacher, published in 1982. We found this information to be quite accurate; however, because time has its way of taking a toll even on these lovely, historic structures, some of the bridges that she recorded are no longer in existence. As much data as possible was verified and supplemented by using the *Statewide Covered Bridge Assessment* conducted for the Pennsylvania Department of Transportation in 1990 and 1991 by Ortega Consulting of Media, Pennsylvania.

In the calendar year 2000, when we considered a revision of this book, we began to thoroughly research the changes that had taken place in the 221 structures that we visited in 1991. Upon discovering that there have been changes of some sort in nearly half of the bridges, we decided that it would be necessary to re-visit every bridge to research its status, photograph it again, and personally measure the length (from portal to portal) and width (of the portal opening) of each bridge.

Once again, we have made every effort to validate all of the information represented in this book; however, we do not claim that the information is without error. As we have noticed in the last nine years, some information is subject to change or is still not accessible to us in any available resource. We would, therefore, appreciate any substantiated corrections or additions for use in future updates of this book. We hope that this volume will not only bring the reader pleasure, but provide the inspiration and necessary information to personally visit many of these treasures of our Pennsylvania heritage.

Acknowledgments

To the following people we are sincerely grateful:

Our family, friends and associates who encouraged us to consider the possibility of publishing this guide.

Richard Donovan, Third Vice President of the Theodore Burr Covered Bridge Society of Pennsylvania, Inc., who enthusiastically contributed information from his vast storehouse of covered bridge knowledge every time we called on him.

Tom Walczak, President of the Theodore Burr Covered Bridge Society of Pennsylvania, Inc. who was instrumental in helping to clarify some of our data.

Robert Wilson, Director, and Rebecca Reinhold, staff member, Spatial Science Research Center, Indiana University of Pennsylvania, for their map and computer expertise.

Dan Hall, Bridge Software Development International Ltd., Coopersburg, Pennsylvania, for his bridge engineering expertise.

Trish Kane, Sherburne, New York, member of the Theodore Burr Covered Bridge Society of Pennsylvania, Inc., and the New York State Covered Bridge Society, who provided the National Register of Historic Places information. (She and her husband, Bob, were active in placing the New York covered bridges on the National Register.)

Dan Deibler, Chief, Division of Preservation Services, Bureau for Historic Preservation, Pennsylvania Historical and Museum Commission, for providing the guidelines for covered bridge restoration in Pennsylvania.

Deborah Suciu, Bureau of Design, Pennsylvania Department of Transportation, for providing us with the *Statewide Covered Bridge Assessment* (*SCBA*), conducted for the Department of Transportation by Ortega Consulting, Media, Pennsylvania, which provided verification of much of our statistical data.

The following persons in county offices across the state for their contributions regarding progress on various bridge restorations or locations.: Tina Picket, Commissioner, Bradford County; Richard J. Craig, Bridge Department, Chester County; Lisa Cessna, Executive Director, and Vicki Bryan, her assistant, Washington County Planning Commission; and Dennis Tice, Bedford County Visitors Center.

David Imler, representative of P. Joseph Lehman, Inc., Consulting Engineers, and P. Joseph Lehman, for their warm hospitality and outstanding expertise when we visited the site of the Hewitt Covered Bridge restoration in Bedford County, August, 2000.

The owners of covered bridges located on private property throughout the state for the warm hospitality they extended every time we sought permission to visit a bridge on their property: Halsey Spruance, Director of Public Relations, Laurel Preserve, Brandywine Conservancy, Chester County; Mr. and Mrs. William McCracken, Jefferson County; Kenneth Lehman, Juniata County; Irel Buckwalter, Buck Hill Farms, Lancaster County; Bittenbender Farm, Luzerne County; Carol Strawser, Snyder County; and Meadowcroft Village, Washington County.

Carl Dickson, Curator, Fort Hunter Mansion, for information regarding the proposed restoration of the Everhart Bridge on the Fort Hunter Park property.

Robyn and George Funk, Towanda, Pennsylvania, for assistance in locating the bridge authorities in Bradford County.

The numerous other persons we encountered in our travels who gave us directions, anecdotal information, encouragement, or just pleasant conversation.

Most significantly, we extend our sincere gratitude to Cynthia Miller, Director; Deborah Meade, production editor; Marilyn Prudente, managing editor; and the staff at the University of Pittsburgh Press for their enthusiastic support over the preparation of this second edition of the guide to Pennsylvania's covered bridges.

Pennsylvania's Covered Bridges

Introduction

I. Pennsylvania, Birthplace of the "Kissin' Bridge"

During a trip from town by way of a covered bridge, it was considered quite natural for a young man to steal a kiss from his female companion while passing through the darkened tunnel. Younger brothers or sisters would climb up into the rafters of the structure to watch for couples on their way back from town. It was only fitting that these lovely, covered structures soon acquired the nickname "kissin' bridges."

Timothy Palmer, a carpenter from Massachusetts, is given credit for building the first covered bridge in the United States in 1805. It was located on Market Street in Philadelphia, Pennsylvania, and spanned the Schuylkill River. It was quite a lengthy structure, which would allow a young fella to steal more than a few kisses. With its completion, the age of the covered bridge was born. Shortly thereafter, Theodore Burr built the second covered span in America, a 1,008 foot giant that crossed the Delaware River between Morrisville, Pennsylvania, and Trenton, New Jersey. Following in fairly rapid order were a number of covered spans built across the Delaware between Pennsylvania and New Jersey (along their central and southern borders) and between Pennsylvania and New York (along their borders in the northeast).

The diverse topographic structure of Pennsylvania created a real need for bridges during the formative years. The Appalachian Mountains, which cross the state from the south-central border to the northeastern border, are home to many streams and rivers which challenged westward development. The relatively flat farmland of the Lancaster County area and the rolling hills of the southeastern and southwestern parts of the state had equal numbers of waterways that required crossing. Since the covered span proved its worth over the larger Delaware River, it was only natural to use similar structures within the borders of the state.

The greatest period of bridge building activity took place from the 1820s to the end of the nineteenth century. During this time period, there were at least 1500 covered bridges built in a variety of sizes and truss designs. Records show that at one time, all but three of Pennsylvania's sixty-seven counties had covered bridges in use. Our records show that there are still forty counties in which covered bridges still stand—a grand total of 221 authentic structures. Here, "authentic" does not necessarily mean "historic" (which, incidentally, is also a term subject to debate). In this book, when we discuss authentic bridges, we mean those that are built with authentic bridge trusses. There are many "romantic shelters" scattered across the state that look like covered bridges but do not use authentic covered bridge trusses.

Pennsylvania not only leads the nation as the birthplace of covered bridges, but it has the largest number of "kissin' bridges" still standing. Of those, 151 still carry motorized vehicular traffic. Many of those not open to automobiles have been preserved in park areas or on private property and are still used for two-legged and four-legged traffic.

Since 1991, Pennsylvania has lost three of its historic landmarks—in 1994, the Grimes Bridge in Greene County, and in 1996, the Carmen Bridge in Erie County were lost due to arson. In 1994, the Davis Bridge between Greene and Washington Counties collapsed under the weight of winter snow and ice. While there are plans to restore the Carmen Bridge, the Grimes Bridge has been replaced with a modern span and there are no plans to restore the Davis Bridge. However, on a more pleasant note, a bridge that had been in storage for some time, the Wagner Bridge, has been restored in Columbia County; a new, authentic kingpost truss bridge, the Wren's Nest Bridge, has been built in Greene County; and, as recently as November 2000, we became aware of the Paperdale Bridge in Columbia County. There are also plans to restore the Everhart Bridge (formerly in Perry County) in Fort Hunter Mansion Park, Dauphin County, in the near future. Restoration of this bridge will be accomplished when sufficient funds have been raised. In general, the authors of this guide found Pennsylvania's covered bridges to be in significantly better condition at the beginning of the twenty-first century than they were nine years earlier.

There are primarily two reasons why Pennsylvania still has the largest number of covered spans in existence. First, Pennsylvania reportedly had the largest number of structures built in the nation; and second, people at the state, county, and local level, and in the private sector, had enough concern and foresight to preserve, maintain, and in many cases restore these beautiful pieces of our historic heritage.

II. Locating Covered Bridges

Many times the hunt is half the fun of "bridging." The search for a particular bridge will inevitably take you into some of the most interesting, remote, and often scenic areas of the state. There are very few covered bridges that are still in existence along heavily traveled main roads. Most of them are located on secondary township roads, which are frequently unpaved. It is quite surprising to find that many of our rural roads, maintained by township highway departments, still have dirt or gravel surfaces.

The first resource that we used to locate bridges was the *Pennsylvania Atlas & Gazetteer*, published by DeLorme Mapping Company (1987). It locates all covered bridges with an easy to recognize symbol, but because of the scale of the maps, the actual road on which the bridge is located is sometimes vague. Susan Zacher's book, *The Covered Bridges of Pennsylvania*, published by The Pennsylvania Historical and Museum Commission, was our second resource. The directions contained there, together with the state atlas, helped considerably as we widened our search. On one of our "bridging" excursions we met another bridge enthusiast who had a copy of a detailed county map that was prepared by the Pennsylvania Department of Transportation. We were able to acquire a few maps of the surrounding counties from our local PennDOT office. These proved to be invaluable in our travels to less familiar parts of the state. Realizing that we needed additional county maps for areas we had to traverse, we ordered Type 10, General Highway Maps for the respective counties directly from the state office of the Pennsylvania Department of Transportation. The address in August 2000 was: Pennsylvania Department of Transportation, Sales Store, P.O. Box 2028, Harrisburg, PA 17105; the cost was $3.00 each.

A short time later we acquired a copy of the *World Guide to Covered Bridges* prepared by the National Society for the Preservation of Covered Bridges, Inc. The directions to bridge locations contained in this volume are given in tenths of a mile along specific route numbers or from given locations. These were helpful, except that we were often traveling from a different direction and had to interpret the instructions in reverse, or the directions were given from a town some distance from the bridge, making them difficult to follow.

After utilizing these four pieces of material to locate the bridges, we found that the county maps available from the state department of transportation were the most helpful. Though their dates of preparation ranged from 1978 to 1990 (for maps we acquired in 1991), even the older printings were extremely accurate. However, there are many areas that have recently been developed for residential housing or commercial enterprises, and this has created roads that are not recorded in the older publications. The older printings were gray print on white backing, while newer copies were black and white. Obviously, the newer editions were easier to read. All of the editions have a particular icon which shows the location of covered bridges.

For the serious "bridger," we hope that this guide book will make locating the bridges considerably easier. Using it, together with a copy of the *Pennsylvania Atlas and Gazetteer*, should provide a delightful "bridging safari." Keep in mind, however, that while road names, T or TR (Township Route) numbers, and SR (State Route) numbers are accurate as of our research in 2000, there is no guarantee that they will still be there when you venture forth on your next safari. It appears that road names are the easiest to find. Township Route numbers are sometimes included with the name, and both Township Route numbers (when available) and State Route numbers are located on small, black and white, rectangular signs most evident at road junctions. We have also found that in a few, very rare, cases, the road names as given in the *Pennsylvania Atlas and Gazetteer* are not the same as those we actually found at strategic junctions.

A few typical road signs, in any event, are indicative of a covered bridge in the area:

- Bridge. Weight Limit 3 Tons. 1300 Ft. Ahead
- Covered Bridge Road
- One Covered Bridge→
- → 3 Covered Bridges
- Low Clearance. Bridge Ahead. 11' 6" Clearance.
- Road Closed. Bridge Out
- Covered Bridge Ahead

III. The Structure of Pennsylvania's Covered Bridges

Truss Types Used in Pennsylvania

A bridge is a structure built across a gap in the terrain, most often created by a flowing run, creek, stream, or river. The simplest bridge structure is called a "stringer" bridge, and the most primitive of these consists of a single log laid across the gap from one bank to the other. In order to carry a load of any consequence, two logs were laid some distance from each other with planks joining the two to span the opening. Even this simple structure deteriorated rather quickly when exposed to the elements, hence the need to cover the structure to preserve its supporting framework. This framework, or superstructure, is called a truss, and supports the crossing load on the deck of the bridge.

Records of covered bridges date back to the sixteenth century in Europe; such structures in the United States were first built in the early 1800s. While there have been as many as eighteen distinctively different truss designs used throughout the United States, there have only been seven specific designs, or combinations thereof, used in Pennsylvania. Pennsylvania has one covered stringer type bridge still remaining today, located on private property on the edge of the town of Port Royal in Juniata County, and owned by the Sheaffer family (see more about this bridge under Juniata County).

The stringer bridge is not a truss design by definition. The true truss system consists of massive timbers assembled in a triangle. This is the only two-dimensional figure that cannot be distorted under stress. Each bridge consists of two truss systems, one on either side of the structure. The line drawings that follow illustrate the basic pattern of each truss. There have been many variations to these designs depending upon locale, builder, and materials available. The heavy, solid lines in the drawings represent solid timbers. Fine, dotted lines represent the exterior shape of the side. The heavier, dash lines represent metal rods.

1. The Kingpost Truss

This is the oldest truss design used in bridge construction, initially used under the roadway rather than above. It consists of a stringer, a kingpost (vertical beam), and two diagonals, and is used primarily for short spans of approximately twenty to thirty feet (see the Cox Farm / Lippincott Bridge in Greene County). Pennsylvania has eleven bridges built with this truss. Eight of them are located in Washington County, two in Greene County, and one in Jefferson County. (The last is not a truly historic covered bridge but is listed in the *World Guide to Covered Bridges*—see explanation under Jefferson County.)

2. The Multiple Kingpost Truss

The multiple kingpost design was developed to span longer distances, frequently up to one hundred feet. The design consists of one kingpost in the center with several right angle panels on each side of the center, and all the diagonals pointing toward the center (see the Fischtner Bridge in Bedford County). There are still fourteen remaining multiple kingpost structures scattered throughout the state in seven different counties, and two structures which have a multiple kingpost truss combined with a queenpost truss, described below (see the New Germantown Bridge and the Red Bridge, both in Perry County).

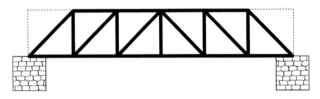

3. The Queenpost Truss

The queenpost truss system followed the kingpost in design chronology. It was also used to span long distances, frequently up to seventy-five feet. The queenpost truss is really an expansion of the kingpost design. Here, a rectangular panel was placed between the two triangles that originally faced the center vertical kingpost timber. The upper horizontal member of that rectangle, however, had to be placed below the horizontal upper chord of the exterior side framework (see the Wilson's Mill Bridge in Washington County). Frequently, additional diagonal timbers were placed between the corners of the central rectangle. There are still forty-one true queenpost trusses remaining in Pennsylvania today, located in or between seven different counties; additionally, five queenpost truss systems are used in conjunction with kingpost structures, located in or between five different counties. Finally, the Rice / Landisburg Bridge, spanning Sherman's Creek in Perry County, has two queenpost trusses used in conjunction with a single Burr arch truss.

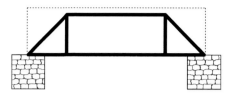

4. The Burr Truss

One of the earliest and most prominent bridge builders in our country was Theodore Burr from Torringford, Connecticut. His career began in New York where he built a bridge spanning the Hudson River in 1804. Burr's truss design soon became one of the more frequently used systems. The Burr arch truss, as the design became known, used two long arches that rested on the abutments on either end, and typically sandwiched a multiple kingpost structure (see the Knapp's Bridge in Bradford County). There are more bridges in Pennsylvania using the Burr truss design than the total of all those using other truss designs—121 located in or between twenty-eight different counties.

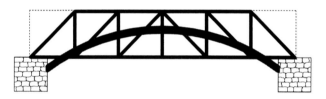

5. The Town Truss

The Town truss was named for its originator, Ithiel Town, who also came from Connecticut. He designed and built his first bridge in 1820. His design is sometimes called the "lattice truss," and a quick glimpse at the pattern formed by its members readily explains the nickname (see the Sauck's Bridge in Adams County). In some areas it became very popular because it used smaller dimension lumber than other trusses, required a limited amount of framing and hardware, could easily be built by unskilled laborers, and could span distances up to 200 feet. The heaviest concentration of Town truss structures is in Bucks County, where each remaining historic span—twelve in all—is of this design. Twenty Town truss systems are still standing in the state and are located in seven different counties. One of these is combined with a queenpost truss (see Schofield Ford Bridge in Bucks County).

6. The Howe Truss

William Howe of Massachusetts patented the Howe truss design in 1840. It is really an elaboration on the multiple kingpost design, whereby two heavy, metal rods are substituted for the vertical timbers. There are also variations on this pattern that add a second diagonal timber to the original, single diagonal of the multiple kingpost, and/or another diagonal timber running in the opposite direction between the vertical rods (see the McConnell's Mill Bridge in Lawrence County). Some accounts indicate that the Howe design provided a bridge that was stronger than any all wood structure; as a result, it became the forerunner of iron bridges. There are 124 Howe truss spans in the United States today. Pennsylvania, however, can claim only five of the Howe truss bridges, located in five different counties.

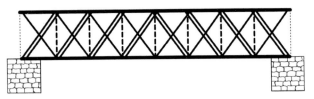

7. The Smith Truss, Type 2

Robert J. Smith of Tippecanoe City, Ohio, designed four truss systems. None became very popular, and only one of them was used in Pennsylvania—the Smith truss, type 2. According to available information, this was also the only one of the four Smith truss types to receive a patent. The patent was granted in 1869, one year after Smith completed the one remaining Smith truss bridge in Pennsylvania—the Kidd's Mill Bridge in Mercer County.

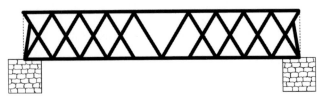

IV. Working to Preserve Pennsylvania's Covered Bridges

There are numerous individual county organizations and groups concerned about the preservation of just one bridge, such as the Bartram Bridge Joint Preservation Board. This is an organization comprised of citizens from both Chester and Delaware Counties concerned about the preservation of a single bridge that lies on their border. For the people in Delaware County, the Bartram Bridge is the only covered bridge they have left.

The Theodore Burr Covered Bridge Society of Pennsylvania was founded in 1959 by a group of Pennsylvania citizens who were concerned about the maintenance and preservation of all the remaining covered bridges in the state. While its base of operation is Lancaster County (the county containing the greatest number of covered bridges at twenty-eight), the Society's concern is for every bridge in the state, from the Van Sant Bridge at the eastern border of Bucks County, to the Erskin Bridge at the western border of Washington County, from the Gudgeonville Bridge at the northern border of Erie County, to the Glen Hope Bridge at the southern border of Chester County.

In the early years of its formation, the Theodore Burr Society convinced state officials that the preservation of our covered bridges was important enough to place a special emphasis on them once a year. Through their efforts, we now annually recognize the importance of our covered bridges with a "See Pennsylvania's Covered Bridges" week. Coincidentally, the authors of this book did some of their most comprehensive research on "bridging" expeditions during this celebratory week. Watch for advertisements of this event in future years. You, too, may want to participate in the celebration of these remarkable treasures of our "Keystone Heritage."

V. The Rehabilitation of Pennsylvania's Covered Bridges

Shortly after starting our visits to covered bridges in 2000, we discovered that a number of bridges have been completely rehabilitated, and many of the restorations utilized building methods that would not have been used originally. The most common practice has been that of placing the rehabilitated structure on steel I-beam stringers in order to provide a sufficient "live load" limit to bring the bridge up to the load limits required on our highways in the twenty-first century.

The Pennsylvania Historical and Museum Commission has been extensively involved in many of these rehabilitations. The Commission is involved in approving all restoration procedures whenever funding for the rehabilitation is provided by either state or federal sources. It is also involved, if requested, in any restorations that are funded totally by local fund raising efforts. The latter is not required, however, even if a structure is placed on the "National Register of Historic Places." In its efforts to oversee and approve these restorations, the Commission follows *The Secretary of the Interior's Standards for Rehabilitation & Illustrated Guidelines for Rehabilitating Historic Buildings*, published in 1992. The following list of "Standards for Rehabilitation" appears on the first page of the Commission's publication, *Standards for Rehabilitation & Guidelines for Rehabilitating Historic Buildings*:

1. A property will be used as it was historically or be given a new use that requires minimal change to its distinctive materials, features, spaces, and spatial relationships.

2. The historic character of a property will be retained and preserved. The removal of distinctive materials or alteration of features, spaces, and spatial relationships that characterize a property will be avoided.

3. Each property will be recognized as a physical record of its time, place, and use. Changes that create a false sense of historical development, such as adding conjectural features or elements from other historic properties, will not be undertaken.

4. Changes to a property that have acquired historic significance in their own right will be retained and preserved.

5. Distinctive materials, features, finishes, and construction techniques or examples of craftsmanship that characterize a property will be preserved.

6. Deteriorated historic features will be repaired rather than replaced. Where the severity of deterioration requires replacement of a distinctive feature, the new feature will match the old in design, color, texture, and, where possible, materials. Replacement of missing features will be substantiated by documentary and physical evidence.

7. Chemical or physical treatments, if appropriate, will be undertaken using the gentlest means possible. Treatments that cause damage to historic materials will not be used.

8. Archeological resources will be protected and preserved in place. If such resources must be disturbed, mitigation measures will be undertaken.

9. New additions, exterior alterations, or related new construction will not destroy historic materials, features, and spatial relationships that characterize the property. The new work shall be differentiated from the old and will be compatible with the historic materials, features, size, scale and proportion, and massing to protect the integrity of the property and its environment.

10. New additions and adjacent or related new construction will be undertaken in a such a manner that, if removed in the future, the essential form and integrity of the historic property and its environment would be unimpaired.

The 114 pages of the *Standards for Rehabilitation & Guidelines for Rehabilitating Historic Buildings* clearly outline "recommended" and "not recommended" procedures to be followed in the entire restoration process. It seems that all efforts are being taken to preserve and restore the historic integrity our state's covered bridges so that those remaining can be seen and enjoyed for many generations to come.

VI. The Guide to Pennsylvania's Covered Bridges

This guidebook contains statistical information and at least one photograph of every bridge still standing in Pennsylvania. Much of the statistical data was gleaned from or verified with data reported in the final copy of the *Statewide Covered Bridge Assessment*. Data for this survey was supplied by contributors across the state—historical groups, conservation groups, the Theodore Burr Covered Bridge Society, the Pennsylvania Historical and Museum Commission, the Pennsylvania Department of Transportation district offices, county engineers, and interested private citizens. Contributions from this diversified group led to some discrepancies in the data reported; therefore, final judgments on the data supplied were made by Ortega Consulting, Media, Pennsylvania, the firm responsible for conducting the survey. To date, however, this appears to be the most accurate data available except for actual measurements taken or other information clarified on our visit to the bridges in 2000. The statistical data listed in this book includes the following.

- **Name.** The name of the bridge, listing the most common name first when a bridge is known or has been known by more than one name. The most common name has been taken from the *SCBA*, or from publication of a name change since the publication of the *SCBA*, or another, more recent posting of a name on or around a bridge.

- **Location.** Location of the bridge, usually based on the nearest town or the township(s) in which or between which the bridge is physically located.

- **Directions.** Directions to the bridge usually given from the nearest town or road junctions as indicated in the *Pennsylvania Atlas & Gazetteer*, published by DeLorme Mapping Co., Yarmouth, Maine, or as actually found on specific road signs at strategic road junctions. In a few, very rare cases, the road names given in the *Atlas* do not match those found at the junctions.

- **Year.** Year of construction as given in the *SCBA* or determined through other valid documentation.

- **Truss.** The truss design used in the construction of the bridge.

- **Waterway.** The run, creek, stream, or river which the bridge spans.

- **In use**. "Yes" indicates usage for all traffic. Other usage is specified. Verified on actual visit to the bridge in 2000.

- **Number of spans.** Data as personally observed and verified in the *SCBA*. A "+" following the number indicates that a pier has been added as additional support.

- **Owner.** Determined from all sources available. See bibliography.

- **Builder.** Information as given in the *SCBA* or other valid documentation.

- **Length.** Measured on actual visit to the bridge in 2000. Outside measurement determined from portal to portal. In the case of a sloping portal, the measurement was taken approximately four feet above the road surface.

- **Width.** Measured on actual visit to the bridge in 2000. Inside measurement determined from one side of the portal to the opposite side of the same portal.

- **Condition.** Recorded as personally observed with untrained eyes, and verified with various articles appearing in statewide covered bridge related publications.

- **Number.** The number originally assigned to the bridge as listed in the *World Guide to Covered Bridges* and modified by the Theodore Burr Covered Bridge Society of Pennsylvania in March, 1996, to replace the first two digits with the state abbreviation. Therefore, the first two letters represent the state; the next two digits represent the county, assigned alphabetically; and the last two digits represent a specific bridge within the county, assigned in the order data was received by the *WGCB* compilers. The original intent of the compilers was to assign the last two digits according to the chronology of the bridge construction date. However, because information on many of the bridges was received after the first edition was compiled, this sequence was broken. A number "2" following the sixth-place bridge number indicates that the bridge has been replaced with primarily new material on the site of the original bridge.

- **Register.** The date on which the bridge was listed in the National Register of Historic Places. A blank in this category simply indicates that registration has not been sought. "Does not qualify" indicates that the bridge does not meet the guidelines established by the National Register, i.e., it is a new bridge, it is not old enough (50 years old), or it has been rebuilt with too much new material.

- **Miscellaneous anecdotal information.** The bridges are arranged in alphabetical order within a specific county. Likewise, all counties are arranged alphabetically. If a bridge is located between two counties, the counties are alphabetized according to the one that occurs first in alphabetical order. The map opposite the title page (and repeated on the final page of this volume) displays the approximate geographic location of each bridge.

Covered Bridge Terminology

abutment—the structure that supports the end of the bridge or accepts the thrust of the Burr arch and supports and retains the bridge approach

approach—the road surface leading to the bridge

bolster beam—a timber between the abutment and truss which extends beyond the abutment. Commonly found in the Town truss

camber—a built in, upward curve of the bridge

chord—the horizontal members, upper and lower, of a truss system extending from end to end

deck—the surface of the bridge that carries the traffic

floor beam—a transverse member between the trusses that supports the decking and live load

gabion—a galvanized wire box filled with stones used to form retaining walls along a stream or bridge approach

parapet—a wall rising above the road level, usually as an upward extension of the wingwall

pier—structure(s) located between the abutments to support a multi-span bridge. Additional support to an existing span. It may be original or added later

portal—the opening at either end of a bridge, the face of that opening

post—a vertical member which is perpendicular or near perpendicular to the bottom chord

runners—lengthwise planks laid over crosswise planks in the tire track area of the bridge deck, probably added sometime after the invention of the automobile to reduce noise from the loose planks

span—the horizontal distance between two supports of the bridge

trunnel, tree-nail—a wooden peg, usually oak, used to fasten timbers in bridge building, sometimes replaced with galvanized steel bolts

wingwalls—extensions of the abutment which contain the fill of the approach

Anderson Farm / Reeser / Mud Run Bridge

Location: On the access road to a pond on private property, approximately 3 miles south of Bermudian, Latimore Township.

Directions: From the junction of US 15 and SR 1005 (Latimore Valley Road), the first crossroad on US 15 south of the county line. Travel southeast on SR 1005 for 2.25 miles to Lake Meade Road (SR 1012), turn left on Lake Meade Road and go 1.45 miles to SR 1007 (Stoney Pond Road to the right, Braggtown Road to the left). Turn right on Stoney Point Road and go 1.6 miles to the entrance of private property. The residents of the home indicate that visitors are always welcome.

Year: Unknown / **Truss:** Burr / **Waterway:** On pond access road
In Use: Yes, private only / **Number of Spans**: 1 / **Owner:** Private
Builder: Unknown / **Length**: 78 ft. 5 in. / **Width**: 14 ft. ½ in.
Condition: Very good / **Number:** PA-01-05 / **Register:**

Originally spanning Mud Run, this bridge was reportedly moved to the Agway chemical plant property, approximately two miles south of Bermudian, when the land was owned by a local farmer named Anderson. The bridge was in that location when we visited it in 1991. However, in 1994, the bridge was moved again— this time to the farm of the elder Mr. Anderson. His ancestors had originally built the bridge. There were plans to build a golf course on the property, which would include the pond access road and the covered bridge. Plans for the golf course were rejected. The property, including the bridge, was placed on the market and purchased for future residency. When we visited the area in June 2000, a large, impressive home had been built on the property, which now includes the pond, the access road, and the covered bridge. The present owners of the bridge have beautifully maintained the bridge, and have made it a focal point of their property. Carriage lights have been installed on each portal, and flourescent lights shine in the interior. The Burr arch no longer rests on abutments, but is attached to the bottom cord of the multiple kingpost. This, in turn, rests on abutments made of poured concrete and topped with stone-and-mortar, extending to short parapets approximately one foot above the bridge approaches. Otherwise, the bridge retains most of its original appearance: barn red, random-width, vertical board siding; white, vertical board portals; and a sheet metal roof.

G. Donald McLaughlin Memorial / Jack's Mountain Bridge

Location: On Jack's Mountain Road (SR 3021), approximately 1.5 miles southwest of Fairfield, Hamiltonban Township. **Directions:** In Fairfield, at the junction of PA 116 West and Miller Street/Fairfield Station Road (SR 3016), follow PA 116 West for 1.1 miles to Jack's Mountain Road. Bear right on Jack's Mountain Road and go 0.6 mile to the bridge.

Year: 1890 / **Truss:** Burr / **Waterway:** Toms Creek
In Use: Yes / **Number of Spans:** 1 / **Owner:** State
Builder: Joseph Smith / **Length:** 75 ft. 2 in. / **Width:** 15 ft. 6 in.
Condition: Excellent / **Number:** PA-01-08 / **Register:** August 25, 1980

This is the only remaining covered bridge in Adams County that is open to vehicular traffic. While it was always referred to as the Jack's Mountain Bridge, its name was officially changed to the G. Donald McLaughlin Memorial Covered Bridge in 1998 in memory of the gentleman who spearheaded the bridge's restoration campaign. It is the only bridge in Pennsylvania that uses traffic lights to control the flow of traffic across the one lane structure. It has been carefully restored using well-concealed I-beams to support its twenty-ton live load limit. The bridge rests on stone-and-mortar abutments, which are capped with concrete and built on concrete foundations. It has moderate length stone-and-mortar wingwalls rising to concrete-capped parapets and concrete curbs to provide additional protection. The bridge is covered with barn red, shiplapped siding on both sides and portals, and the portals are trimmed with white. There is a sheet metal roof and a deck of lengthwise planks laid over crosswise planks set on edge. The very high Burr arch truss system, which sandwiches the multiple kingpost structure in a common design, reaches the narrow lengthwise openings directly under the eaves. As we did our research and took our photographs, we found it very easy to understand the reason for the installation of traffic lights to control passage over the bridge. This is a very heavily used highway. Every means possible should be used to protect and preserve this outstanding restoration.

Heikes / Heike's Bridge

Location: Bypassed by Willow Lane, approximately 2.5 miles north of Heidlersburg, between Tyrone and Huntington Townships.
Directions: In Heidlersburg, at the junction of PA 234 and SR 3001, go north on SR 3001 for 0.9 mile to Oxford Road (SR 1016). Turn left on Oxford Road and go 0.6 mile to Willow Lane, turn right on Willow Lane and go 0.2 mile to the bypassed bridge.

Year: 1892 / **Truss:** Burr / **Waterway:** Bermudian Creek
In Use: No, storage only / **Number of Spans:** 1 / **Owner:** Private
Builder: Unknown / **Length:** 64 ft. 5 in. / **Width:** 14 ft. ½ in.
Condition: Good / **Number:** PA-01-14 / **Register:** August 25, 1980

Although this bridge is being used for storage on a private farm property, the structure has been maintained in fairly good condition. It is in a lovely setting over a quiet stream that divides Tyrone and Huntington Townships. The downstream side and portals are covered with shiplapped siding and the upstream side is covered with clapboard siding. The paint is predominantly barn red with a touch of white trim. The sides are open at approximately mid-wall height for the length of the bridge. This design exposes some of the medium height Burr arch and the multiple kingpost truss system. These side openings are similar to the ones at the Sauck's Bridge, also in Adams County. The Heikes Bridge rests on stone-and-mortar abutments placed on concrete footings. There are relatively long stone-and-mortar wingwalls which rise to concrete-capped parapets only on the Willow Lane side. The deck is covered with lengthwise planking. During our visit in June 2000, we found the bridge in good condition, which is a tribute to its present owners. They obviously have a great deal of respect for the structure and its historic significance.

Sauck's / Sachs Bridge

Location: On an unnamed, unmarked road, approximately 5 miles southwest of Gettysburg, between Cumberland and Freedom Townships.
Directions: Travel approximately 3 miles south of Gettysburg on US 15 Business. At the junction of US 15 Business and Millerstown Road, turn right on Millerstown Road and go 1.6 miles to an unnamed road. Turn left on the unnamed road and go 0.2 mile to the bridge.

Year: 1854 / **Truss:** Town / **Waterway:** Marsh Creek
In Use: Foot traffic only / **Number of Spans:** 1 / **Owner:** County
Builder: David Stoner / **Length:** 101 ft. 2 in. / **Width:** 15 ft. 10 in.
Condition: Excellent / **Number:** PA-01-01 / **Register:** August 25, 1980

This bridge was used for the movement of troops by both the Confederate and Union forces during the military campaign at Gettysburg. At that time it was known as Sauck's Bridge and accomodated a considerable amount of road traffic. In the spring of 1991 there was significant interest in restoring the bridge. In the spring of 1993 the project was undertaken by Gettysburg National Military Park and nine other organizations. A bronze plaque located near the restored bridge states: "In 1938, the Pennsylvania Highway Department determined that the Sachs Bridge was the most historic covered bridge in the state. It was closed to traffic in 1968 and listed in the National Register of Historic Places in 1980. Flood waters swept it from its abutments on June 19, 1996. The county of Adams rehabilitated the bridge by supporting its trusses with steel beams and by raising its elevation three feet." It has been restored on new stone-faced abutments with very long, stone-and-mortar wingwalls and parapets. The horizontal clapboard siding on the sides and portals is positioned in such a way that a good portion of the Town truss structure is visible. The lower one-fourth of the sides are covered, the next four feet are open, the next (approximately) six feet are closed, and there are typical, narrow, lengthwise openings under the eaves. The bridge has a sheet metal roof and wide, diagonal floor planks. It is now painted a deep, barn red, which we assume was its original color. When we visited it in 1991, it was burnt orange. While the change in color and increase in abutment height seem to have removed some of this bridge's original charm, we still consider it to be in a picturesque setting.

Bowser / Osterburg Bridge

Location: Bypassed by Covered Bridge Road (T 575), 0.9 mile northwest of Osterburg, East St. Clair Township. **Directions:** In Osterburg, at the junction of PA 869 and SR 4019, go west on PA 869 for 0.9 mile to Covered Bridge Road. The bridge is just ahead to the left, bypassed by Covered Bridge Road.

Year: 1890 / **Truss:** Burr / **Waterway:** Bobs Creek
In Use: No, closed / **Number of Spans:** 1 / **Owner:** County
Builder: Unknown / **Length:** 97 ft. 2 in. / **Width:** 12 ft. 5 in.
Condition: Good / **Number:** PA-05-22 / **Register:** April 10, 1980

There is little information available about the Bowser Bridge. It was bypassed by a new steel and concrete bridge on Township Route 575 in 1973, and is now closed with a cable across the portals. However, there are no signs posted in the vicinity of the bridge. Similar to many other bridges in Bedford County, it has vertical boards on the lower one-third of the exterior sides and wide, horizontal boards on the interior. The portal gable ends are also covered with horizontal boards. The Burr arch truss system has an additional horizontal brace that runs the length of the bridge between the two arches. The roof is sheet metal, and the deck consists of runners laid over crosswise planking. The structure rests on stone-and-mortar abutments.

This is the first in a series of five bridges that are quite close together. We suggest that they be visited in this order: Bowser, Snook's, Dr. Knisley, Ryot, and Cuppett's. Using this sequence, directions to each bridge will assume that the visitor is coming from the previous bridge.

Claycomb / Reynoldsdale Bridge

Location: At the entrance to Old Bedford Village, approximately 2 miles north of Bedford. **Directions:** Travel along US 220 Business to the entrance to Old Bedford Village, which is 0.85 mile south of the Pennsylvania Turnpike entrance and approximately 2 miles north of Bedford.

Year: 1880 / **Truss:** Burr / **Waterway:** Raystown Branch, Juniata River
In Use: Yes / **Number of Spans:** 1 / **Owner:** County
Builder: Unknown / **Length:** 126 ft. / **Width:** 14 ft. 1 in.
Condition: Good / **Number:** PA-05-12 / **Register:**

This bridge was originally built in 1880 in Reynoldsdale, approximately fifteen miles north of its present location. In 1975 it was rebuilt at the entrance to Old Bedford Village, and a pedestrian walkway was added to the original structure. The typical Burr truss system has been heavily reinforced by steel U-channels which have been added to the timbers that support the deck of the bridge. The entire structure is unpainted; it has been left to weather naturally. The Claycomb Bridge creates a most authentic and attractive entrance to the village and areas to its south and west.

The bridge is covered with vertical, random-width, tongue-and-groove boards on the sides and walkway portals and horizontal boards on the main portals. The roof is constructed of cedar shakes and the deck is of crosswise planking. The bridge rests on poured concrete abutments with concrete, road-high wingwalls. The sides are open directly under the eaves for about one-quarter of the sides' height. During our visit in May 2000, the pedestrian walkway was closed because the uncovered portion had deteriorated. That portion adjoins an additional forty-three foot long, pony truss type extension to the original Reynoldsdale span. The bridge extension is located on the village end of the bridge, and while it is quite sound, the walkway will require some reconstruction before it is safe for pedestrian traffic.

Colvin / Calvin / Shiller Bridge

Location: On Mill Street Extension (T 443), approximately 1 mile southwest of Schellsburg, Napier Township. **Directions:** In Schellsburg, at the junction of US 30 (Pitt Street) and Mill Street Ext., go south on Mill Street Ext. for 0.8 mile to the bridge.

Year: 1880 / **Truss:** Multiple kingpost / **Waterway:** Shawnee Creek
In Use: Yes / **Number of Spans:** 1 / **Owner:** County
Builder: Unknown / **Length:** 70 ft. 7 in. / **Width:** 12 ft. 1 in.
Condition: Excellent / **Number:** PA-05-24 / **Register:**

This is another of the eight Bedford County owned covered crossings that is still in use for vehicular traffic today. After the Hewitt Bridge restoration is completed, there will be nine county owned bridges that still accommodate traffic. The third name, listed above, refers to a Dr. Shiller who owned the bridge at one time. The Colvin Bridge's truss system is classified as a multiple kingpost truss in all accounts except the *Statewide Covered Bridge Assessment*, which lists it as a rare truss type. This bridge is quite unusual compared to most multiple kingpost type truss structures found throughout the state. Except for the centermost vertical timber of the truss, all of the other "verticals" actually lean toward the end approximately fifteen to twenty degrees off vertical. In addition, the diagonal timbers reach only halfway up the verticals. Finally, where the diagonal timbers meet the vertical timbers, there are horizontal beams extending the length of the interior and exterior sides. This is quite noticeable in the photo above.

The siding consists of red, vertical boards on both the portals and the sides. The sides—as in some of the other bridges in this county—are covered on only the lower one-third of the outside and inside. The roof is sheet metal, and the deck has runners laid over crosswise planking. The bridge was completely restored in 1998 and rededicated on June 20. For its restoration, the abutments and wingwalls were rebuilt using poured concrete, beautifully faced with stone-and-mortar. This seems to be the common practice throughout the state for most of the recent restorations. (See the Hewitt Bridge, Bedford County, for a photo of this construction process in progress.) During our visit to Bedford County in May 2000, we were pleased to find that six of the county owned bridges have been restored in the past decade and one, the Hewitt Bridge, was under restoration at the time of our visit.

Cuppett's / Cupperts / New Paris Bridge

Location: Just east of PA 96, approximately 1 mile north of New Paris, Napier Township. **Directions:** From the Ryot Bridge, continue on Dunnings Creek Road for 0.65 mile to the junction with SR 4013 and SR 4026; bear right on SR 4013 for 0.3 mile to PA 96. Turn left on PA 96 and go south for 0.7 mile. The bridge is just to the left on private property.

Year: 1882 / **Truss:** Burr / **Waterway:** Dunnings Creek
In Use: Private, foot traffic only / **Number of Spans:** 1 / **Owner:** Private
Builder: Unknown / **Length:** 70 ft. 9½ in. / **Width:** 12 ft. 1 in.
Condition: Poor / **Number:** PA-05-18 / **Register:** April 10, 1980

This bridge was originally owned by William and Phillip Cuppett, which is reflected in the first of its three names. The unpainted vertical boards on the lower one-third of the exterior follow the curve of the low Burr arches. At the time of our 1991 visit, the material and equipment stored inside the bridge obscured the interior walls; however, on our visit in May 2000, the bridge was completely empty. This improved the bridge's overall appearance, and allowed us to see that the interior is covered (to the same height as the exterior) with wide, unpainted, horizontal boards. The portals are unusual; the gable end is covered with horizontal siding, and the entire gable structure is supported by relatively lightweight, vertical posts. (The photo shows this quite clearly.) The bridge rests on stone-and-mortar abutments and has no wingwalls.

This is the fifth in the series of five bridges located close together in the northwestern part of the county. (See Bowser Bridge.)

Dr. Knisley Bridge

Location: Along Dunning Creek Road (TR 671), approximately 1.4 miles southeast of Pleasantville, West St. Clair Township. **Directions:** From Snook's Covered Bridge, continue through the bridge on Fish Hatchery Road and turn right immediately on Ridge Market Road (TR 554). Travel 0.6 mile to the junction with PA 56, cross PA 56 and the road name will change to Dunning Creek Road (TR 671). Continue on Dunning Creek Road for 0.1 mile. The bridge is to the right of the road on private property.

Year: 1867 / **Truss:** Burr / **Waterway:** Dunnings Creek
In Use: Private, foot traffic only / **Number of Spans:** 1 / **Owner:** Private
Builder: Unknown / **Length:** 86 ft. 6½ in. / **Width:** 12 ft. 10 in
Condition: Fair / **Number:** PA-05-16 / **Register:** April 10, 1980

This bridge was built in the 1860s over Dunnings Creek, along the main road between Bedford and Johnstown. At the time of our visit, the roadway was on private property and not open to the public. The present owners, however, have not posted the property with "No Trespassing" signs. The bridge, like many others in Bedford County, is covered on only the lower one-third of the sides by vertical boards outside and horizontal boards inside. The portals are covered with horizontal boards. The roof is sheet metal, and the deck is a mixture of crosswise and lengthwise planking. The abutments, wingwalls, and parapets were originally stone-and-mortar, but one of the abutments has started to fall away and been reinforced with concrete. The bridge has been reasonably well maintained, is attractively painted, and located in a lovely setting. We did notice, however, that while the condition of the exterior remains good, the interior, especially the deck, is beginning to show signs of deterioration.

This is the third in the series of five bridges that we suggest the "bridger" visit in succession. (See Bowser Bridge.)

Felten's Mill Bridge

Location: Bypassed by SR 2029, approximately 1.5 miles west of Jackson Mills, East Providence Township. **Directions:** From the Jackson's Mill Bridge, continue south through the bridge on Covered Bridge Road and go 0.7 mile to SR 2029. Turn right on SR 2029 and go 0.85 mile to the junction with Memorial Church Road. Turn right into the gravel parking area. The bridge can be seen from the concrete bridge just ahead on SR 2029 or by walking down the gravel road past the parking area to the old mill. The path to the bridge is just to the left of the mill.

Year: 1892 / **Truss:** Burr / **Waterway:** Brush Creek
In Use: Private, foot traffic only / **Number of Spans:** 1 / **Owner:** Private
Builder: W. S. Mullins / **Length:** 106 ft. / **Width:** 12 ft. 10½ in.
Condition: Poor / **Number:** PA-05-03 / **Register:** April 10, 1980

This bridge has been bypassed and is only open for foot traffic. It is covered with vertical boards on the sides and horizontal boards on the portals. The downstream side, however, is open above the lower three feet, which almost completely exposes the Burr truss system to the elements. The upstream side is covered up to the narrow opening under the eaves. The interior of each side is also covered for three feet above the deck. The roof is covered with sheet metal, and the deck consists of runners laid over crosswise planking. The bridge rests on stone-and-mortar abutments and has no wingwalls. The Bedford County tourist folder, "Crossroads of Heritage and Hospitality," lists this bridge as privately owned, but it is not posted with "No Trespassing" signs. We have no reports of any maintenance on this bridge since our first visit to it in 1991. The area surrounding the bridge is heavily overgrown and it appears that there are not many visitors to the bridge.

Fischtner / Palo Alto Bridge

Location: On a private road, in Palo Alto, Londonderry Township.
Directions: In Palo Alto, at the junction of PA 96 and SR 3002, go west on SR 3002 for 0.1 mile. The bridge is just to the left of SR 3002.

Year: 1880 / **Truss:** Multiple kingpost / **Waterway:** Gladdens Run
In Use: Yes, private only / **Number of Spans:** 1 / **Owner:** Private
Builder: Fischtner / **Length:** 56 ft. 1 in./ **Width:** 13 ft. 4 in.
Condition: Fair / **Number:** PA-05-21 / **Register:** April 10, 1980

This bridge is located in a remote, southwestern valley of Bedford County, quite a distance from any other county covered bridge. The Bedford County tourist folder indicates that either Jacob or Johnathon Fischtner built this bridge near Palo Alto, hence its dual identity. It has been reasonably well maintained in the past and is used regularly by the families living on the west side of Gladdens Run, but present family members are aware that the bridge is in need of some refurbishing if it is to continue to carry vehicular traffic for many more years. It is posted by the present owners with "No Trespassing" signs; however, a family member indicated to us that anyone interested in seeing the bridge is always welcome. The bridge has shiplapped siding on the lower one-third of the sides and wider, horizontal boards on the inside, making it very easy to see the multiple kingpost truss structure from the side of the bridge. The portals are covered with shiplapped siding. There is a tarred metal roof and a deck with runners laid over the crosswise planking. The structure rests on stone-and-mortar abutments and has no wingwalls or steel reinforcing.

Hall's Mill Bridge

Location: On St. Paul's Church Road (T 539), approximately 1 mile southeast of Yellow Creek, Hopewell Township. **Directions:** In Yellow Creek, at the junction of PA 26 and Yellow Creek Road (T 557), go north on PA 26 for 0.4 mile to Prices Hill Road (SR 1022). Turn right on Prices Hill Road and go 0.5 mile to St. Paul's Church Road; turn left to the bridge.

Year: 1872 / **Truss:** Burr / **Waterway:** Yellow Creek
In Use: Yes / **Number of Spans:** 1 / **Owner:** County
Builder: Unknown / **Length:** 95 ft. 2 in. / **Width:** 12 ft. 10 in.
Condition: Excellent / **Number:** PA-05-15 (2)
Register: April 10, 1980

According to the tourist folio prepared by Bedford County, this is the seventh bridge built on this site since the 1860s. It was named for the Hall family, who owned the adjacent mill from 1823 through 1933. The Hall's Mill Bridge, like several other bridges in the county, has been extensively restored since our visit in 1991. This was one of the first bridges to benefit from the Pennsylvania Billion Dollar Bridge Fund, and restoration work began in 1993. Work progressed more slowly than expected, however, because deterioration of the original trusses was more extensive than first presumed. The restored bridge was rededicated on June 11, 1994.

This attractive structure now rests on reconstructed concrete abutments that extend to road-level wingwalls, all of which are faced with sandstone. The bridge has white, vertical board siding on the lower one-third of the sides, while the remaining portion is open. The portals are covered with white, horizontal siding trimmed with deep pink. The interior walls are also covered to the same height as the exterior, which seems to be a common practice in Bedford County. The roof is covered with corrugated metal, and the deck has runners laid over crosswise planking. This bridge has a very high Burr arch truss system which is quite noticeable in the photograph on the preceding page. You may also notice the height and width restricting barriers at the beginning of each approach to the bridge. These protective barriers have been built at each of the restored bridges in the county. While detracting from the aesthetic appearance of the bridge, they do much to protect the portals and upper bracing timbers inside.

Herline / Heirline / Kinton Bridge

Location: On Watson Road (SR 4007), approximately 1 mile north of Manns Choice, between Harrison and Napier Townships.
Directions: In Manns Choice, where combined PA 31/PA 96 divide, go east on PA 31 for 1 mile to Watson Road. Turn left on Watson Road and go 0.4 mile to the bridge.

Year: 1902 / **Truss:** Burr / **Waterway:** Juniata River
In Use: Yes / **Number of Spans:** 1 / **Owner:** County
Builder: Unknown / **Length:** 136 ft. 4½ in. / **Width:** 14 ft. ½ in.
Condition: Excellent / **Number:** PA-05-11(2) / **Register:** April 10, 1980

When we visited this bridge in 1991 we found it closed with "No Trespassing" signs posted on the barricades located at each portal. It had been closed to traffic since 1983. In the summer of 1996, the Commonwealth agreed to finance the restoration if the bridge could then be turned over to the county for future maintenance. The contract was awarded to Kee-Ta Quay Construction with the entire project under the supervision of P. Joseph Lehman, Inc., engineer. The restored Herline Bridge, like many other restorations done in recent years, is resting on concealed, heavy, steel stringers. The stringers, in turn, rest on reconstructed abutments that extend to road-level wingwalls. The abutments and wingwalls consist of poured concrete faced with cut stone-and-mortar. All of the historic, covered bridge restorations throughout the state are under the careful scrutiny of the Pennsylvania Historical and

Museum Commission, to make sure that the resulting reconstructions remain as close as possible to the originals.

This fine restoration has barn red, vertical board siding on the sides and horizontal clapboard siding on the white-trimmed portals. It, too, has the clearance barriers located at the beginning of each bridge approach. The Herline Bridge has been finished with a deck of runners laid over crosswise planks and is covered with a corrugated metal roof. We were quite pleased to see that Bedford County now has another restored bridge, especially one that can now carry loads of twelve tons.

Hewitt Bridge

Location: On Covered Bridge Road (TR 305), approximately 0.4 mile south of Hewitt, Southampton Township. **Directions:** In Hewitt, at the junction of PA 326 and Town Creek Road (TR 306), go south on Town Creek Road for 0.3 mile to Covered Bridge Road. Turn left on Covered Bridge Road and go 0.2 mile to the bridge.

Year: 1880 / **Truss:** Burr / **Waterway:** Twin Creek
In Use: No (restoration underway) / **Number of Spans:** 1
Owner: County
Builder: Unknown / **Length:** 88 ft. / **Width:** 13 ft. 10 in.
Condition: Under restoration / **Number:** PA-05-26
Register: April 10, 1980

Located in a remote area, this bridge was under reconstruction at the time of our visit in May 2000. The photo above is a portal view of the bridge as it appeared in 1991, and the information that follows was gathered for the first edition of this book.

The sides are almost completely covered with vertical boards and have only lengthwise openings under the eaves. This is typical of many other bridges in the state, but not typical of this county. The interior does reflect the common style in Bedford County, however, in that the lower three feet are covered. The portals are covered with horizontal boards, the roof is sheet metal, the deck consists of crosswise planking, and the bridge rests on a stone-and-mortar abutment on the west end and a concrete abutment on the east end. There are no wingwalls and no evident steel reinforcements. There is a cable on one end to help support the side which leans slightly.

The second photo of the Hewitt Bridge was taken at the current restoration site and shows one of the new abutments in the process of being faced with stone. Notice the two openings on the face of the abutment which will receive the ends of the long curved Burr arches of the truss structure. The completed reconstruction should be ready to carry vehicular traffic again later in 2000 or early 2001. After seeing a number of other restorations in this county, we expect that this bridge, too, will be a close duplication of the original, historic structure.

Jackson's Mill Bridge

Location: On Covered Bridge Road (T 413), approximately 2 miles south of Breezewood, East Providence Township. **Directions:** In Breezewood, go to the junction of US 30 and SR 2029, just west of I 70. Travel south on SR 2029 for 0.6 mile, turn right on SR 2029 (E. Mattie Road), and go 1.5 miles to Jackson Mill Road. Turn left on Jackson Mill Road and go 0.9 mile to Covered Bridge Road; turn right to the bridge.

Year: 1875 / **Truss:** Burr / **Waterway:** Brush Creek
In Use: Yes / **Number of Spans:** 1 / **Owner:** County
Builder: A. D. Bottomfield and Joe Pee
Length: 96 ft. 5½ in. / **Width:** 12 ft. 3½ in.
Condition: Excellent / **Number:** PA-05-25 / **Register:** April 10, 1980

The bridge was named for M. J. Jackson, owner of a gristmill and sawmill located nearby. In addition to the two original builders listed above, the *Statewide Covered Bridge Assessment* lists Karn Rohm as another possible builder. Notice the unusual, uncovered bridge portion that extends from the roadbed to the east end of the bridge proper. It appears to originally have been two, very short, uncovered kingpost spans. These spans were originally added during an earlier restoration, which was undertaken after the Johnstown Flood of 1889 washed the bridge about two hundred yards downstream to its present location. This unusual appearance has led to the nickname "the grasshopper bridge."

During our visit to the bridge in 1991, there was no physical evidence of attempts to restore this structure. However, after our visit, the summer 1991 newsletter of the Theodore Burr Society indicated that bids were opened on June 18, 1991, for the bridge's restoration. The low bid for the project was $489,000, which was considerably less than replacement with a contemporary structure. The contract for its rehabilitation was awarded to Kee-Ta Quay Construction of Hustontown, PA. Aware that the reconstruction had been completed, we returned to the bridge again in the spring of 1994 and, of course, again on our 2000 research safari.

The Jackson's Mill Bridge is now a striking structure resting on new, stone-faced abutments and wingwalls. There is bright white, vertical board siding on the sides, white horizontal boards trimmed with red on the portals, a deck of lengthwise planking, and a roof of corrugated metal. Even the two "grasshopper" extension spans have been restored. The area around the bridge is also being well maintained.

Ryot Bridge

Location: On Bowser Road (T 549), 0.4 mile east of Ryot, Clair Township. **Directions:** From the Dr. Knisley Bridge, continue on Dunnings Creek Road for 2.4 miles to Bowser Road. Park along Dunnings Creek Road for easy access to both this and another nearby (Cuppett's) bridge.

Year: 1868 / **Truss:** Burr / **Waterway:** Dunnings Creek
In Use: Yes / **Number of Spans:** 1 / **Owner:** County
Builder: Unknown / **Length:** 81 ft. 2 in. / **Width:** 12 ft. 2½ in.
Condition: Excellent / **Number:** PA-05-17 / **Register:** April 10, 1980

This is one of nine bridges in Bedford County that is still being used for vehicular traffic. It was named for the town of Ryot, located just to the west of the bridge. The Ryot Bridge underwent restoration in 1995. The bright white, vertical boards on the sides cover about three-fourths of the bridge's height, and white, horizontal boards with red trim cover the portals. Like many other Bedford County bridges, the lower three feet of the interior sides are covered with horizontal boards. The roof is corrugated metal, and the deck consists of runners laid over crosswise planking. The structure rests on reconstructed stone-and-mortar-faced abutments with road-level, stone-and-mortar wingwalls. The approaches to the bridge include the clearance restriction barriers typical of the county's restored bridges.

This is the fourth of the group of five bridges located in the northwestern part of the county. (See Bowser Bridge)

Snook's Bridge

Location: On Fish Hatchery Road (TR 578), approximately 1 mile north of Spring Meadow, East St. Clair Township. **Directions:** From the Bowser Covered Bridge, continue on Covered Bridge Road for 2 miles to a "T" with Gordon Hall Road (TR 574). Turn right on Gordon Hall Road and go 0.6 mile to Fish Hatchery Road. Turn left on Fish Hatchery Road and go 0.3 mile to the bridge.

Year: 1880 / **Truss:** Burr / **Waterway:** Dunnings Creek
In Use: Yes / **Number of Spans:** 1 / **Owner:** County
Builder: Unknown / **Length:** 80 ft. 6 in. / **Width:** 12 ft. 9 in.
Condition: Excellent / **Number:** PA-05-23 / **Register:** April 10, 1980

When we visited this bridge in 1991, the truss on the south side of the bridge was kept in its upright position by guy cables running from ground anchors to the top of the truss, and two columns of concrete had been poured into corrugated pipe columns placed under the east end of the deck. During our visit in May 2000, we found that this bridge has been beautifully restored in a fashion similar to the other restorations in Bedford County. All of the rehabilitated bridges display a monument with a bronze plaque giving a brief history of the bridge and its dates of reconstruction.

The Snook's Bridge is covered with white vertical boards on the lower two-thirds of the sides and red trim. This is somewhat different from most of the county's bridges. On the inside, however, the lower one-third is covered with horizontal boards, a common practice in Bedford County. The portal gables, which overhang the vertical supports by several feet, are covered with wide, white, horizontal boards. The deck has lengthwise runners laid over crosswise planking, and the roof is covered with corrugated metal. The bridge now rests on refurbished, stone-faced abutments extended to road-level wingwalls, which is typical of most of the restorations throughout the state. The photo clearly shows the height and width clearance barriers that are located at the beginning of the approach to the bridge. This, too, is typical of all the restorations in Bedford County.

Snook's is the second of the group of five bridges that are located close together in the northwestern part of the county. (See Bowser Bridge.)

Turner's / Raystown / Diehl Bridge

Location: On Faupel Road (T 418), midway between New Buena Vista and Manns Choice, Harrison Township. **Directions:** From the junction of PA 31 (Allegheny Road) and PA 96, between Schellsburg and Manns Choice, go west on Allegheny Road for 2 miles to Faupel Road. Turn right and go 0.4 mile to the bridge.

Year: 1892 / **Truss:** Burr / **Waterway:** Raystown Branch, Juniata River
In Use: Yes / **Number of Spans:** 1 / **Owner:** County
Builder: Unknown / **Length:** 86 ft. 4 in. / **Width:** 12 ft 10½ in.
Condition: Fairly good / **Number:** PA-05-19 / **Register:** April 10, 1980

This is another one of the eight county owned covered bridges that still carries vehicular traffic today, and one of only two that has not seen extensive restoration in the past decade. While the Turner's Bridge was scheduled for restoration, allocated monies were redirected to the Hewitt Bridge, which was in greater need of repairs. However, the Turner's Bridge has been fairly well maintained, and there is evidence of recent repairs, including repainting. This bridge, like many others in this county, is covered on the lower one-third of the sides with vertical boards outside and horizontal boards inside. Like the Cuppett's Bridge, the Turner's Bridge has only small, vertical timbers supporting the gable end of the bridge, which is covered with horizontal boards. The roof is made of sheet metal, and the deck has runners laid over crosswise planking. The bridge rests on cut stone abutments that have been reinforced with concrete. There are no wingwalls. Perhaps in the early part of the twenty-first century, the Turner's Bridge, like others near it, will be completely restored.

Dreibelbis Station Bridge

Location: Two miles south of Lenhartsville, Greenwich Township.
Directions: From I 78, take Exit 11 (PA 143) to Lenhartsville. Go south through Lenhartsville for 2 miles to the bridge, which will appear immediately on the side road to the left.

Year: 1869 / **Truss**: Burr / **Waterway**: Maiden Creek
In Use: Yes / **Number of Spans**: 1 / **Owner**: County
Builder: Unknown / **Length**: 189 ft. 11½ in. / **Width**: 16 ft. 4½ in.
Condition: Good / **Number**: PA-06-07 / **Register**: February 23, 1981

This bridge has an interesting, stepped portal with shiplapped siding. The sides, however, are covered with clapboard siding and differ from the other county bridges because of an opening at midwall that runs the entire length of the bridge in addition to the openings under the eaves. The Dreibelbis Bridge, like Wertz's Bridge (also in Berks County), has a high double Burr arch truss system. The deck is constructed of a double layer of lengthwise planking. The structure rests on stone-and-mortar abutments with long wingwalls and parapets on the east end and short, curved wingwalls and parapets on the west. The four parapets are all capped with concrete. Notice, also, the Pennsylvania Dutch hex signs on the portal. These are frequently found on covered bridges and barns in this part of the state.

A Fall 1997 newsletter article in *Pennsylvania Crossings*, the newsletter of the Theodore Burr Covered Bridge Society, indicated that this bridge was being painted by the county. When we visited in May 2000, we did find the bridge in fine condition with a reasonably fresh coat of paint.

Greisemer's Mill Bridge

Location: On Spangsville Road, just north of Spangsville, Oley Township.
Directions: From the junction of PA 73 and SR 2051, between
Pleasantville and Shanesville (Club Road comes in from the north), go
south on SR 2051 (becomes Manatawny Road) for 0.1 mile. Turn right
and go 1.3 miles on Manatawny Road (be sure to stay on Manatawny
Road) until the junction with Spangsville Road. Turn right on Spangsville
Road for 0.3 mile to the bridge.

Year: 1832 / **Truss**: Burr / **Waterway**: Manatawny Creek
In Use: Yes / **Number of Spans**: 1 / **Owner**: County
Builder: Unknown / **Length**: 140 ft. 7 in. / **Width**: 16 ft. 6 in.
Condition: Good / **Number**: PA-06-03 / **Register**: February 23, 1981

According to printed information available, this is the oldest covered span in Berks County. Repairs were done in 1957 and 1971.
Although the *Statewide Covered Bridge Assessment* rated the condition of the Greisemer's Mill Bridge fairly low, we found its outward appearance good during our visits in both 1991 and 2000.
While we have no reports of specific work being done on the
bridge, it still has a newly painted appearance. The sides and portals are covered with horizontal clapboard siding, and there are
no side openings other than those directly under the eaves. The
truss system is comprised of the typical Burr arches sandwiching
a multiple kingpost structure. Located in a lovely, quiet farm setting, the bridge rests on stone-and-mortar abutments and has long
stone-and-mortar wingwalls and parapets. The parapets are capped
with concrete. We did notice that one of the parapet caps had been
repaired since our last visit.

Kutz's Mill / Kutz / Sacony Bridge

Location: On Kutz Mill Road, approximately 2 miles northwest of Kutztown. **Directions**: From I 78, take Exit 12 (Krumsville/Kutztown, PA 737). Go south on PA 737 for 2 miles to Kutz Mill Road (watch carefully for the road, which is just before a highway bridge). Turn right on Kutz Mill Road and go 0.7 mile to the bridge. The bridge is also accessible from Kutztown. From the junction of Main Street and College Boulevard (the beginning of the Kutztown University campus), go north on College Boulevard for 1.9 miles to Kutz Mill Road. Turn right on Kutz Mill Road and go 0.3 mile to the bridge. (College Boulevard bears left at the north end of town, be sure to follow College Boulevard until Kutz Mill Road.)

Year: 1854 / **Truss**: Burr / **Waterway**: Sacony Creek
In Use: Yes / **Number of Spans**: 1 / **Owner**: County
Builder: Bitner and Ahrens / **Length**: 106 ft. 2 in. / **Width**: 16 ft. 10 in.
Condition: Fair / **Number**: PA-06-05 / **Register**: February 23, 1981

This bridge has a rather unusual portal design. In 1991, after visiting over 150 bridges, it was the only one we had seen with this style of portal. Our visits to all of the bridges again in 2000 confirmed that while some bridges have similar portal designs, none in the state are exactly the same. The difference is clearly evident in the photo above.

The Kutz's Mill Bridge is covered with shiplapped siding on both the sides and the portals, and has side openings only under the eaves. The entire structure rests on stone-and-mortar abutments with long stone-and-mortar wingwalls and parapets. The parapets are capped with concrete, and the roof is covered with sheet metal. While we reported in 1991 that this bridge had a steel deck and beams which had been placed there during the second half of this century, we found on our trip in 2000 that it now has a concrete deck. We have no reports on this replacement.

We did find out during our visit in 2000, thanks to a resident who lives adjacent to the bridge, that the bridge had been painted in 1999. However, the painting was completed without any repairs to the superstructure. There is a fair amount of dry rot visible in some of the main portal support timbers. If not replaced in a reasonable amount of time, they will no longer be able to support the portal siding boards. Otherwise, the bridge appears to be quite sound and is used moderately by local residents.

Pleasantville / Oley Turnpike / Manatawny Bridge

Location: On Covered Bridge Road (SR 1030), Manatawny, Oley Township. **Directions**: From the Greisemer's Mill Bridge, travel through the bridge for 0.3 miles to the junction with Church Road (T 612). Turn right on Church Road and go 0.2 mile to a "T" with Covered Bridge Road (name not posted). Turn right on Covered Bridge Road and go 0.3 mile to the junction with Kaufman Road. Continue straight on Covered Bridge Road for 0.8 mile to the bridge. The bridge is also accessible from PA 73, just southeast of Pleasantville. At the junction of PA 73 and Covered Bridge Road, go south on Covered Bridge Road for 0.4 mile to the bridge.

Year: 1852 / **Truss**: Burr / **Waterway**: Little Manatawny Creek
In Use: No / **Number of Spans**: 1 / **Owner**: State
Builder: David Renno, Jonathan Bitner
Length: 141 ft. 10½ in. / **Width**: 17 ft. 5½ in.
Condition: Poor / **Number**: PA-06-01 / **Register**: February 23, 1981

Within nearly every county, the covered bridges are marked by one or more common characteristics. Berks County is no exception. Every bridge in this county includes the Burr truss system, is painted barn red, and has stone-and-mortar wingwalls and parapets. The parapets are capped with concrete, and some of these parapets are very long. Most Burr arches surround a multiple kingpost framework. The truss system for the Pleasantville Bridge, however, is rather unusual. It has one pair of very high Burr arches, and what appears to be another pair of low double Burr arches approximately three feet above the roadbed. These arches sandwich a number of vertical timbers resting on a long horizontal tim-

ber, and pairs of short diagonal supports brace every other vertical. (See interior photo.)

While the bridge itself was built in 1852 by David Renno, it was
not until 1856 that Jonathan Bitner covered it. The *Statewide Covered Bridge Assessment* lists Levi Marks as another documented
builder. Today the bridge is covered with horizontal boards on the
upper half and vertical boards on the lower half. The lower siding
includes an attractive arch pattern. The portals are covered with
horizontal clapboard, the roof is made of shingles, and the bridge
rests on stone-and-mortar abutments with long wingwalls. There
are no side openings except for the typical lengthwise ones directly
under the eaves.

Unfortunately, this bridge has been closed since Fall 1993. The
northwest wingwall, parapet, and part of the abutment were
washed away during a storm in the summer of 1993. In Spring
1995 it was reported that the Pennsylvania Department of Transportation would make repairs to the bridge, after which the Berks
County Commissioners would take over ownership and maintenance. Because the restoration involves several agencies and an
extensive amount of "red tape," it is anticipated at the time of this
writing (May 2000) that repairs to the bridge will begin in the
spring of 2001. Presently, the restoration process still remains in
the design and study phase as required by the various government
agencies involved. Hopefully, by the time this guide comes off the
press, the bridge will again be restored, rededicated, and open to
traffic. It is a lovely, historic structure that should certainly be preserved.

Wertz's / Wertz / Red Bridge

Location: In Berks County Heritage Park, north of Reading, between Bern and Spring Townships. **Directions**: From the US 222 Reading Bypass, take the Reading Airport Exit. Go south for 0.3 mile to Red Bridge Road (see sign for Berks County Heritage Park), turn right, and go 0.7 mile on Red Bridge Road to the parking area. The bridge is down the hill past the C. Howard Heister Canal Center.

Year: 1867 / **Truss**: Burr / **Waterway**: Tulpehocken Creek
In Use: Foot traffic only / **Number of Spans**: 1 / **Owner**: County
Builder: Amandas Knerr / **Length**: 218 ft. 1 in. / **Width**: 17 ft. 2½ in.
Condition: Very good / **Number**: PA-06-06 / **Register**: November 17, 1978

This is the longest single-span covered bridge in Pennsylvania. Also known as the Red Covered Bridge, it was constructed in 1867 at a cost of $7,650. Between the years of 1867 and 1884 it spanned the Union Canal system as well. It is covered with horizontal clapboard siding on both the sides and portals (notice the interesting portal design, similar to several others throughout the state). The truss system consists of high double Burr arches which sandwich the typical multiple kingpost framework. The arches rest on stone-and-mortar abutments, and there are short stone-and-mortar wingwalls capped with concrete. The roof is covered with shakes, and the bridge has narrow openings under the eaves. Another interesting feature is the cable car and gauge house on the west side of the bridge, which is used by the United States Geological Survey to measure the stage and discharge of the creek The bridge has been in very good condition every time we have visited the park, and continues to be in prime condition as of 2000.

Knapp's / Luther's Mill / Brown's Creek Bridge

Location: On Covered Bridge Road, Luthers Mills, Burlington Township.
Directions: In Luthers Mills, from the junction of US 6 and Covered Bridge Road, go north on Covered Bridge Road for 0.1 mile to sign which reads "Covered Bridge 1 Mile." Turn right at the sign and continue to the bridge.

Year: 1853 / **Truss**: Burr / **Waterway**: Brown's Creek
In Use: No / **Number of Spans**: 1 / **Owner**: County
Builder: Unknown / **Length**: 108 ft. 2 in. / **Width**: 14 ft. 3 in.
Condition: Fair / **Number**: PA-08-01 / **Register**: July 24, 1980

Among all the covered bridges in the state, this one is reported to be the highest above its stream bed. There is a drop of more than thirty feet from the bridge to the creek below. Located on a dirt road that serves the farming area outside of Luthers Mills, the bridge's setting makes it even more attractive. It is covered with vertical boards and battens only halfway up the sides, exposing the upper part of the Burr arches and multiple kingpost structure. The portals are covered with vertical boards and battens, the roof with shakes, and the deck with crosswise planking. The entire structure rests on concrete abutments with stone-and-mortar wingwalls that are below road level. The bridge has been closed since 1997 awaiting approval of funds for restoration. The Pennsylvania Historical and Museum Commission and the Bradford County Commissioners are overseeing the project. Estimated costs are in excess of $800,000. It is hoped that bids will be requested by the end of 2000 and the bridge will be reopened by 2002. Improvements will include the installation of steel I-beams to provide safe passage for general traffic, including school buses. In recent years, prior to its closing, school buses were not allowed to cross the bridge.

Cabin Run Bridge

Location: On Covered Bridge Road, approximately 0.7 mile northwest of Smiths Corner, Plumstead Township. **Directions:** In Smiths Corner, at the junction of Stump Road (SR 1010) and Covered Bridge Road, go northwest on Covered Bridge Road for 0.5 mile to the junction with Schlentz Road. Turn right on Covered Bridge Road and go 0.2 mile to the bridge.

Year: 1871 / **Truss:** Town / **Waterway:** Cabin Run Creek
In Use: Yes / **Number of Spans:** 1 / **Owner:** County
Builder: David Sutton / **Length:** 82 ft. 4 in. / **Width:** 16 ft.
Condition: Good / **Number:** PA-09-10 / **Register:** December 1, 1980

Like the covered bridges of most Pennsylvania counties, the bridges of Bucks County share a common feature. In this case, the common feature is a particular truss structure—the Town truss. Every authentic, historic, covered bridge in this county was built with a Town truss. The Cabin Run Bridge has vertical board siding on the sides, portals, and interior portal walls. The sides have no openings. Consequently, the interior is very dark—perfect for a "kissin' bridge." The portals have angular, rather than rounded, openings. The bridge has a shake roof, and rests on stone-and-mortar abutments. The wingwalls and parapets of this bridge are a little shorter than those of most bridges in the county.

Another interesting feature of this bridge, as of several others in the county, is the unique portal extensions. Sided with vertical boards on the interior, the portal extensions flare, or funnel out, from the main truss structure. These flared or funnel-like extensions caused us to look more carefully at all the other bridges in the county, but seemed most noticeable on the Cabin Run Bridge. Wherever they are found, however, these flared extensions can be seen most clearly from the side of the bridge, which appears to bend out at each end of the structure. There may be a specific name for this structural treatment; however, at the time of this writing we have not been able to ascertain what it might be.

Erwinna Bridge

Location: On Geigel Road, just west of Erwinna, Tinicum Township.
Directions: In Erwinna, at the junction of PA 32 and Headquarters Road, go west on Headquarters Road for 0.3 mile to Geigel Hill Road; turn right on Geigel Hill Road and travel for 0.2 mile to the bridge.

Year: 1871 / **Truss:** Town / **Waterway:** Lodi (Swamp) Creek
In Use: Yes / **Number of Spans:** 1 / **Owner:** State
Builder: Unknown / **Length:** 57 ft. / **Width:** 16 ft. 2 in.
Condition: Very good / **Number:** PA-09-04
Register: December 1, 1980

This is the shortest remaining covered span in Bucks County. It is in a quiet rural setting, and has typical vertical board siding which is painted red on the sides and white on the portals. The portals have angular, rather than curved, openings, and the interior is covered with vertical boards. The deck, like the decks of most Bucks County bridges, is heavily reinforced with steel I-beams. The structure rests on stone-and-mortar abutments, each capped with a concrete slab. The wingwalls and parapets are stone-and-mortar, and the parapets are capped with concrete. The roof is covered with cedar shakes.

An article in the Spring 1996 edition of *Pennsylvania Crossings*, a publication of the Theodore Burr Covered Bridge Society, reported that the bridge was to be rebuilt, at an anticipated cost of $240,000, starting February 12, 1996. The construction phase of the project was awarded to Conestoga Construction Co., Lancaster, PA. When the project was completed in the fall of 1996, the bridge was more stable, abutments were strengthened, siding replaced and painted, new cedar shakes placed on the roof, sediment and debris cleaned from the stream under the bridge, and weeds cut around the bridge. While we found the bridge in good condition in 1991, it was exceptionally good in 2000.

Frankenfield Bridge

Location: On Cafferty Road, Sundale, Tinicum Township. **Directions:** In Sundale, at the junction of Cafferty Road and Hollowhorn Road, go southeast on Cafferty Road for 0.3 mile to the bridge.

Year: 1872 / **Truss:** Town / **Waterway:** Tinicum Creek
In Use: Yes / **Number of Spans:** 2 / **Owner:** County
Builder: David Sutton / **Length:** 130 ft. 3 in. / **Width:** 16 ft. 3 in.
Condition: Good / **Number:** PA-09-09 / **Register:** December 1, 1980

Bucks County had restored the Frankenfield Bridge prior to our 1991 visit, and we found it in fine condition. It has similar characteristics to the other covered bridges in the county; however, the deck area is supported with an additional concrete pier located in the center of Tinicum Creek. Consequently, some documentation, including the *Statewide Covered Bridge Assessment*, lists it as a two span structure, and thus, so have we. The Town truss could have originally spanned this distance with a single truss. It also seems that the exceptionally long stone-and-mortar wingwalls and parapets have been repointed in recent years, probably as part of the restoration process that occurred prior to 1991. During our visit in April 2000, we found the bridge still in good condition, except for noticeable damage to the southeast portal siding, and paint, in general, that is slightly faded.

Knecht's / Sleifer's Bridge

Location: On Knecht's Bridge Road, approximately 2 miles northeast of Pleasant Valley, Springfield Township. **Directions:** In Pleasant Valley, at the junction of PA 212 and Old Beth Rd (SR 4101) go east on 212 for 1.1 miles to Slifer Valley Road (SR 4069). Turn right on Slifer Valley Road and go 1.1 miles to Knecht's Bridge Road. Turn right on Knecht's Bridge Road for 0.1 mile to the bridge.

Year: 1873 / **Truss:** Town / **Waterway:** Cooks (Durham) Creek
In Use: Yes / **Number of Spans:** 1 / **Owner:** County
Builder: Unknown / **Length:** 110 ft. 2 in. / **Width:** 15 ft. 10½ in.
Condition: Excellent / **Number:** PA-09-02
Register: December 1, 1980

As we mentioned earlier, the covered bridges in Bucks County have several elements of design and style in common. The most significant characteristic is the use of the Town truss, which appears in every remaining authentic bridge. All of these spans, likewise, do not have the lengthwise side openings under the eaves typical of bridges in other parts of the state. Moreover, only two of the bridges in Bucks County have a window of any kind. All have stone-and-mortar abutments, stone-and-mortar wingwalls and parapets, parapets capped with concrete, and shake roofs. It appears that everything possible has been done to preserve the structures in their original states.

In 1999, Bucks County Commissioners voted to allocate $27,000 annually to protect and preserve the county's covered bridges. A portion of this money is to be used to purchase insurance coverage for the twelve remaining, authentic, historic bridges.

Loux Bridge

Location: On Wismer Road, Plumstead Township, or Carversville Road, Bedminster Township, just southeast of Pipersville. **Directions:** From Wismer, at the junction of Stump Road and Wismer Road, travel northwest on Wismer Road for 1 mile to the bridge. From Pipersville, at the junction of PA 611 and PA 413, go south on PA 413 for 0.6 mile to the junction with Dark Hollow Road. Go left on Dark Hollow Road for 0.2 mile to Carversville Road. Turn right on Carversville Road and go 0.5 mile to the bridge.

Year: 1874 / **Truss:** Town / **Waterway:** Cabin Run Creek
In Use: Yes / **Number of Spans:** 1 / **Owner:** State
Builder: David Sutton / **Length:** 85 ft. 6 in. / **Width:** 15 ft. 8½ in.
Condition: Good / **Number:** PA-09-11 / **Register:** December 1, 1980

The most impressive thing about this bridge is its spectacular setting. Located in a relatively remote section of the county, Cabin Run Creek flows past a beautiful, large, old farmhouse just north of the bridge. A concrete plaque in the wingwall identifies the bridge as "Cabin Run." Local residents do not know why. It may have been named for the creek over which it is built, but another bridge in the county is also called the Cabin Run Bridge, according to the name plate on its gable end. The Loux Bridge has basically the same features as the other bridges in the county, except that it is the only one painted white on both the sides and the portals.

Periodicals from the Theodore Burr Covered Bridge Society indicate that the bridge was closed in January 1996 for six months to allow for repairs and restoration. At an estimated cost of $344,000, the bridge "received a facelift"—a new roof, rafters, painted siding, strengthened abutments, and removal of sediment from the streambed. The funds were supplied by the state, and the work done by Nyleve Bridge Corp., Emmaus, PA. The bridge was reopened on July 5, 1996 without ceremony. While some of the attractive post and rail fencing around the south side of the bridge is no longer standing, the bridge, itself, is in fine condition.

Mood's / Branch Bridge

Location: On Blooming Glen Road, on the northeast edge of Perkasie, East Rockhill Township. **Directions:** In Perkasie, go north on North Fifth Street to the junction with Blooming Glen Road (traffic light at the junction). Turn right on Blooming Glen Road and go 0.4 mile to the bridge.

Year: 1874 / **Truss:** Town
Waterway: Perkiomen Creek (northeast branch)
In Use: Yes / **Number of Spans:** 1 / **Owner:** State
Builder: Unknown / **Length:** 120 ft. 3 in. / **Width:** 16 ft.
Condition: Very good / **Number:** PA-09-07
Register: December 1, 1980

This bridge is located on a road that carries a considerable amount of traffic. Consequently, it is maintained in good condition. Reportedly repaired in 1962, it has also had extensive repairs in the mid-1990s. In the fall of 1996, a Perkasie newspaper reported that work was about to begin on a reconstruction project with an anticipated cost of $277,813, and that the project would take up to 243 days to complete. The work was to include replacement of the deck, siding, paint, and roof, as well as paving of the roadway approaches and stabilization of the abutments.

During our visit in April 2000, we found the bridge fully restored. It now has vertical board siding that is painted red on the sides and white on the portals. The deck is made of lengthwise planking and the roof of cedar shakes. The structure rests on stone-and-mortar abutments with stone-and-mortar wingwalls and parapets. The parapets are capped with concrete. Like most of the Bucks County bridges, it is in very good condition.

Pine Valley / Iron Hill Bridge

Location: On Old Iron Hill Road, at the northwest edge of New Britain, New Britain Township. **Directions:** In New Britain, at the junction of US 202 and Keeley Avenue, go northwest on Keeley Ave. for 0.5 mile to the bridge. (Keeley Avenue merges with Old Iron Hill Road after approximately 0.25 mile. Continue straight on Old Iron Hill Road to the bridge.)

Year: 1842 / **Truss:** Town / **Waterway:** Pine Run Creek
In Use: Yes / **Number of Spans:** 1 / **Owner:** County
Builder: David Sutton / **Length:** 80 ft. 9 in. / **Width:** 15 ft. 7 in.
Condition: Very good / **Number:** PA-09-12
Register: December 1, 1980

This bridge is one of the oldest in the county, and has primarily the same characteristics as the other Bucks County bridges. When the Pine Valley Bridge was built in 1842, records show that it cost $5,553. Covered with random-width vertical boards on the sides, portals, and inside portal walls, the bridge has a shake roof and rests on stone-and-mortar abutments. There are stone-and-mortar wingwalls and parapets, and the parapets are capped with concrete. Like the other bridges in the county, the Pine Valley Bridge has no side openings. We have no reports on improvements to the bridge since our 1991 visit, but we did find the bridge in very good condition in April 2000.

Ralph Stover State Park (Boxed Pony) Bridge

Location: On Stover Park Road, in Ralph Stover State Park, Plumstead Township. **Directions:** In Smiths Corner, at the junction of Stump Road and Covered Bridge Road, go northeast on Stump Road 0.8 mile to a "T". Turn right for 0.05 mile to the first left turn; turn left into the parking lot. The bridge is straight ahead.

Year: Unknown / **Truss:** Howe / **Waterway:** Tohickon Creek
In Use: Foot traffic only / **Number of Spans:** 2 / **Owner:** State
Builder: Unknown / **Length:** 179 ft. 9 in. / **Width:** 14 ft. 6 in.
Condition: Excellent / **Number:** PA-09-P1 / **Register:**

This bridge has been included in this collection only because it is novel and unique in Pennsylvania and is listed in the *World Guide to Covered Bridges*. It is not included on the list of Pennsylvania bridges compiled by the Theodore Burr Covered Bridge Society of Pennsylvania, Inc., or in Susan Zacher's *The Covered Bridges of Pennsylvania*. It was included, however, in the *Statewide Covered Bridge Assessment*. As the photo shows, the entire truss structure is closed with vertical boards and battens, but the *World Guide* lists it as a two-span Howe truss, boxed pony bridge. (A pony truss bridge is one that is less than full height and one for which only the truss structure is covered.) The roofs on the two sides consist of wide boards with battens, the deck has open crosswise planking, and the entire structure rests on high, stone-and-mortar abutments and a center pier. The bridge has stone-and-mortar wingwalls and parapets, and appears to have been used for vehicular traffic at one time. It is now open only for foot traffic but is heavily used in that capacity, especially during the warm weather months.

When we visited the park in April 2000, we found that the bridge is being very well maintained. In fact, the maintenance seems considerably better than it was in 1991. The bridge has been recently painted, and all the siding and roofing materials seem to be intact. The area of the park in which the bridge is located has also been improved.

Schofield Ford / Twining Ford / Solly's Bridge

Location: In Tyler State Park, at Schofield Ford/Twining Ford, between Northampton and Newtown Townships. **Directions:** Just southeast of Rushland, at the junction of PA 232 and Swamp Road (SR 2036) go southeast on Swamp Road for 1.8 miles to Schofield Covered Bridge Parking Lot Road. Turn right and go 0.3 mile to the parking area. The trail to the bridge is straight ahead.

Year: 1836 / **Truss:** Town combined with queenpost
Waterway: Neshaminy Creek
In Use: Foot traffic only / **Number of Spans:** 2 / **Owner:** State
Builder: Unknown / **Length:** 164 ft. 9 in. / **Width:** 15 ft. 9 in.
Condition: Excellent / **Number:** PA-09-13 (2)
Register: Does not qualify

Until October 7, 1991, a short walk of approximately a quarter mile from the Tyler State Park parking area brought one to this lovely bridge, used only for two- and four-legged foot traffic. However, a television news report on that date indicated that this charming bridge had been destroyed by fire, and that: "The remains of the structure have fallen into the Neshaminy Creek." We, like many others, were quite distressed at the loss of this structure.

The embers of the charred remains were hardly cold, however, when friends and neighbors of this exceptional structure began to talk about rebuilding it. During the next six years, wave after wave of activity occurred. Supporters worked on fund raising, practiced bridge building techniques, and poured in physical energy and effort. By September 6, 1997, an exact duplicate of the original structure had been built, using the same abutments and piers on which the first Schofield Ford Bridge was erected in 1836. The rebuilt bridge was dedicated to the volunteers and contributors who made the reconstruction possible. The most amazing fact about this entire process is expressed in this quote taken from graphic displays adjacent to the approaches to the bridge: "Local volunteers came out in force, and within six years the rebuilt bridge—a gleaming replica of the original, made entirely of native Pennsylvania hemlock and white oak—was re-opened to the public. More than 800 volunteers donated time, talent, and dollars to the project. They reconstructed the bridge in just under three weeks, placing more than 3,000 pegs into the wooden posts and beams."

Another very unusual feature of this bridge needs illustration. Look carefully at the photo of the bridge's interior. It shows the only instance of a queenpost truss system supporting a Town truss  system in the state of Pennsylvania. The queenpost truss is substantially attached everywhere it makes contact with a diagonal of the Town truss by the placement of oak trunnels (tree-nails, or pegs).

Look, too, through one of the bridge's four, diamond shaped windows at the lovely, serene view of the Neshaminy Creek which the bridge spans at Schofield Ford.

Sheard's Mill / Thatcher Bridge

Location: On Covered Bridge Road, Thatcher, between Haycock and East Rockhill Townships. **Directions:** In Thatcher, at the junction of Thatcher Road (SR 4043) and Covered Bridge Road, go south on Covered Bridge Road for 0.2 mile to the bridge. Or, from the junction of PA 563 and Old Bethlehem Road (SR 4101), near the southwest end of Lake Nockamixon, go north on Old Bethlehem Road for 1.2 miles to the junction with Thatcher Road. Turn left on Thatcher Road and go 0.5 mile to Covered Bridge Road; turn left on Covered Bridge Road and travel 0.2 mile to the bridge.

Year: 1873 / **Truss:** Town / **Waterway:** Tohickon Creek
In Use: Yes / **Number of Spans:** 1 / **Owner:** State
Builder: Unknown / **Length:** 134 ft. 8 in. / **Width:** 15 ft. 10 in.
Condition: Good / **Number:** PA-09-06 / **Register:** December 1, 1980

This bridge is located next to an old abandoned mill, which was at one time owned by a man named Sheard. In 1991, when we visited the bridge, we felt that the exterior covering of the bridge was in need of some repair, but its basic structure appeared to be reasonably sound. Still open to traffic on a slightly used secondary road, this bridge is a typical Bucks County structure covered with vertical boards on the sides, portals, and inside portal walls. The Sheard's Mill Bridge has a shake roof, rests on stone-and-mortar abutments, and has long stone-and-mortar wingwalls and parapets. The parapets are capped with concrete. While we have no documentation regarding recent repairs to the bridge, we found it in better condition during our April 2000 visit.

South Perkasie Bridge

Location: In Lenape Park, Perkasie. **Directions:** The entrance to Lenape Park is in the southern part of Perkasie, on West Walnut Street. The bridge is just to the left of the park drive as you enter the park.

Year: 1832 / **Truss:** Town / **Waterway:** Relocated in park on dry land
In Use: Foot traffic only / **Number of Spans:** 1 / **Owner:** Private
Builder: Unknown / **Length:** 93 ft. / **Width:** 14 ft. 3 in.
Condition: Very good / **Number:** PA-09-05 / **Register:** December 1, 1980

The South Perkasie Bridge is the oldest remaining covered bridge in the county. Through the efforts of the local historical society, the structure was saved after being condemned for traffic. It was moved to its present location over dry land in 1958, where it is being maintained by the Perkasie Historical Society. It has all the typical characteristics of the other covered county spans. A rather interesting, original sign appears over the portal: "$5 Fine for Any Person Riding or Driving Over This Bridge Faster Than a Walk or Smoking Segars On."

Uhlerstown Bridge

Location: On Uhlerstown Hill Road, Uhlerstown, Tinicum Township.
Directions: In Uhlerstown, at the junction of River Road (PA 32) and Uhlerstown Hill Road, go west on Uhlerstown Hill Road for 0.4 mile to the bridge. Access to the canal tow path that passes under the bridge is available from Tinicum Park, between Erwinna and Uhlerstown, or from the Delaware Canal Park Office, below Upper Black Eddy. Distance to the bridge from Tinicum Park parking area is approximately 1.5 to 1.75 miles. Distance to the bridge from the park office parking area is approximately 2 miles.

Year: 1832 / **Truss:** Town / **Waterway:** Tinicum Creek
In Use: Yes / **Number of Spans:** 1 / **Owner:** County
Builder: Unknown / **Length:** 101 ft. 4 in. / **Width:** 15 ft. 11 in.
Condition: Good / **Number:** PA-09-08 / **Register:** May 26, 1994

This bridge crosses the Delaware Canal at Lock Number 8. A large home is adjacent to the bridge (see photo) and may have originally been part of either the canal boat building company, the lock controls, or the toll gate building. The bridge was named for Michael Uhler, who owned a canal boat-building yard near this location. The sign on the portal of the bridge indicates that the length is 101 feet; other documented data lists the length as 110 feet. On our visit in April 2000, we measured the bridge from portal to portal and found the length to be 101 feet, 4 inches. The bridge is typical of the other Bucks County covered bridges, except for a long, narrow window located in the center on each side. Considerable efforts have gone into preserving this structure, and some of the old canal lock remains. Access to the restored canal lock areas, however, is limited because of the private homes located adjacent to the east end of the bridge and canal. On our "bridging" excursions, we have frequently sought the permission of property owners to enter their premises for research or photography. With the exception of this location, we have always been well received and given the opportunity to do whatever was necessary. Many home owners have even been able to contribute information that was helpful in our research and preparation of material for this book. We simply caution every "bridger" to always seek permission to enter private property areas.

Van Sant / Beaver Dam Bridge

Location: On Van Sant Road, approximately 1 mile east of Buckmanville, just west of Washington Crossing State Park, Solebury Township.
Directions: In Highton, at the junction of PA 232 and Street Road (SR 2101), go southeast on Street Road for 0.3 mile to Lurgan Road (also SR 2101). Turn left on Lurgan Road for 1 mile to Van Sant Road, turn left on Van Sant Road and go 0.5 mile to the bridge.

Year: 1875 / **Truss:** Town / **Waterway:** Pidcock Creek
In Use: Yes / **Number of Spans:** 1 / **Owner:** County
Builder: G. Arndt and P. S. Naylor
Length: 86 ft. 5 in. / **Width:** 15 ft. 9 in.
Condition: Fairly good / **Number:** PA-09-03
Register: December 1, 1980

This is a typical Bucks County covered bridge. It has vertical board siding on both the sides and portals. All of the county bridges have gable type roofs, but differ in the style of the portal opening. This bridge has a curved opening at the top of the portal, and the inner sides of the portal area are closed with vertical boards. The roof is covered with shakes, and the structure rests on stone-and-mortar abutments that have been reinforced with concrete and have stone-and-mortar wingwalls and parapets. The parapets, again, are capped with concrete. We have no reports of any work having been done on this bridge since our visit in 1991, and, comparing it to the other structures in the county, we would have to rate its condition lower than any of the others. While the truss structure is still quite sound and does not pose a danger to those who use it, we noticed that there are a number of holes between the cedar shakes on the roof which will eventually allow moisture to reach the deck boards and possibly the truss itself. The north end of the bridge seems to lean slightly off-square. Respect for this structure also seems to be lacking. There is an extensive amount of graffiti on the inside.

Buck's / Harrity Bridge

Location: In Beltzville State Park, Franklin Township. **Directions:** At the junction of US 209 and Beltzville State Park Road, just northeast of the PA Turnpike entrance, go north on Beltzville State Park Road and follow the signs to the park. After passing the park boundary sign, enter the park on the second road to the right. Pass the Park Office to the first road on the right, turn right and then left at the next road which leads to the parking area. The bridge is just to the right of the parking area.

Year: 1841 / **Truss:** Multiple kingpost / **Waterway:** Dry creek gulch
In Use: Foot traffic only / **Number of Spans:** 1 / **Owner:** State
Builder: Paul Buck / **Length:** 87 ft. 5 in. / **Width:** 11 ft. 11 in.
Condition: Very good / **Number:** PA-13-01 / **Register:**

When the Beltzville Dam was built in 1970 to create a lake and state park recreation area, the Bucks Bridge was located along the Pohopoco Creek, which is the water source for the lake. If it had been left in its original location, the bridge would have been flooded upon the completion of the dam. Consequently, the U.S. Corps of Engineers moved the bridge to its present location over dry land in the park's recreation area. The structure is a typical example of the multiple kingpost truss design. It is covered with horizontal, shiplapped siding on only the lower third of the sides and on the portals. The roof is covered with cedar shakes and the deck with runners laid over crosswise planking.

During our visit in April 2000, we found several improvements to the bridge. In 1991 it was resting on stone abutments which appeared to have been laid dry and had no wingwalls. It now rests on concrete abutments. Decorative, short, stone-and-mortar para-pet-like structures have been built at each end, resting on the poured concrete abutments. The entire structure has received new, shiplapped siding, painted barn-red, and the bridge has a new, cedar shake roof. The appearance was quite remarkable in comparison to what we recalled from our earlier visit.

Little Gap Bridge

Location: On Covered Bridge Road, Little Gap, Towamensing Township.
Directions: In the village of Little Gap, on Covered Bridge Road.

Year: 1860 / **Truss:** Burr / **Waterway:** Aquashicola Creek
In Use: Yes / **Number of Spans:** 1 / **Owner:** County
Builder: Unknown / **Length:** 92 ft. 4 in. / **Width:** 18 ft.
Condition: Good / **Number:** PA-13-02 / **Register:** December 1, 1980

According to a plaque located on the interior of the Little Gap Bridge, this bridge was built with a Burr truss system which sandwiches a Howe truss. This differs from the typical design, in which a Burr truss system sandwiches a multiple kingpost truss. Some restoration of this bridge was done prior to 1991, including the addition of steel beams to support the deck. The bridge is covered with vertical tongue-and-groove boards on both the sides and portals, and the portals have been extended beyond the original truss system. The sides are open for approximately three feet immediately under the eaves, and there is also a large window which was added as part of the portal extension on the end where the road curves. Earlier reports regarding this bridge indicate that a slate roof had been added in about 1935. However, during our visit in April 2000, we ascertained that the roof now consists of asphalt shingles. The bridge rests on concrete abutments with short stone-and-mortar wingwalls which rise a little above road level to form low parapets.

In 1996, publications of the Theodore Burr Covered Bridge Society reported that in January of that year, flooding caused the Little Gap Bridge to lose some of its siding. During our visit in 2000, the only missing board we noticed was one short siding board located under the window on the southwest side of the bridge. Otherwise, the bridge facade, which encases a primarily steel bridge, is in good condition.

Gibson's / Harmony Hill Bridge

Location: On Harmony Hill Road (T 391), between East Bradford and West Bradford Townships. **Directions:** In Downingtown, from the junction of US Business 30 and US 322, go east on US 322 for approximately 2.3 miles to Harmony Hill Road. Turn left on Harmony Hill Road to the bridge.

Year: 1872 / **Truss:** Burr / **Waterway:** Brandywine Creek (east branch)
In Use: No / **Number of Spans:** 1 / **Owner:** County
Builder: Edward Hall & Thomas Schull
Length: 98 ft. 4 in. / **Width:** 14 ft. 2½ in.
Condition: Poor / **Number:** PA-15-10 / **Register:** December 10, 1980

Although most counties' covered bridges have something in common, the only thing the Chester County bridges have in common is their truss design, and that is true only of the ones owned by the county or state. The truss design used for all such bridges was the Burr arch truss. Located in a lovely setting, but at an intersection with very heavily traveled US Route 322, this bridge has an interesting step portal. The bridge crosses the east branch of Brandywine Creek at a location called Gibson's Ford. The cost of its construction in 1872 was $2,600. Built on stone-and-mortar abutments, it has the typical eastern Pennsylvania stone-and-mortar wingwalls, which are coated with white stucco on the side facing the road. In addition to the typical lengthwise, narrow openings under the eaves, the bridge has only one other window located on the south side. The sides and portals are covered with white clapboard siding, the roof is covered with shakes which are overgrown in places with moss; and the truss structure consists of high double Burr arches sandwiching multiple kingposts.

This bridge is presently closed because of extensive damage caused by the hurricanes of 1999. A local resident tells that siding was torn from the bridge by a large tree that floated downstream. No information regarding anticipated repairs is known at the time of this writing.

Glen Hope Bridge

Location: On Hickory Hill Road (T 344), Elk Township. **Directions:** In Hickory Hill, from the junction of Lewisville Road (PA 472) and Hickory Hill Road (T 344) go south on Hickory Hill Road for 1.7 miles to the bridge.

Year: 1889 / **Truss:** Burr / **Waterway:** Little Elk Creek
In Use: Yes / **Number of Spans:** 1 / **Owner:** County
Builder: Menander Wood and George E. Jones
Length: 78 ft. 1 in. / **Width:** 16 ft.
Condition: Good / **Number:** PA-15-02 / **Register:** December 10, 1980

In the 1993 edition of this book, the 1991 photograph displayed only the charred skeleton truss structure that remained after the bridge suffered arson. The bridge had been set on fire, supposedly by college students, prior to the winter of 1990–1991. By the next summer, however, work to restore the bridge had begun. By 1992 the bridge was completely restored. The siding of unpainted boards and battens has been left to weather naturally, the portals are covered with white, shiplapped siding, and the roof is finished with cedar shakes. The stone-and-mortar abutments, wingwalls, and parapets appear to be the original ones, and the parapets are capped with concrete. The deck, likewise, appears to be the original, and consists of runners laid over crosswise planking. The deck has been reinforced, however, with eight crosswise steel I-beams. The Burr arch truss, too, is original to the bridge. The truss is rather low, and of angular shape, rather than the more common smooth, curved arch. The photo on this page displays a beautifully restored historic landmark.

Hayes Clark Bridge

Location: In the Laurel Reserve, property of the Brandywine Conservancy. Permission to see the bridge (as well as directions) must be obtained from the conservancy in Chadds Ford, Pennsylvania.

Year: 1971 / **Truss:** Queenpost / **Waterway:** Doe Run
In Use: Foot, horse, and cattle / **Number of Spans:** 1+ / **Owner:** Private
Builder: Buck and Doe Run Valley Farms
Length: 86 ft. 3 in. / **Width:** 18 ft.
Condition: Good / **Number:** PA-15-07 (2) / **Register:**

 Originally a Burr truss structure, this bridge was built in 1884 by Menander Wood and Denithorne and Pollitt of Phoenixville. The total cost of the original structure was $2,526. The original bridge, however, was destroyed by fire in 1963.

 This is the first of the "twin bridges" also described under Speakman No. 2 Bridge and is only one-quarter mile away from its twin. Since it is located in the Laurel Reserve, anyone wishing to see this bridge must obtain permission from the Brandywine Conservancy. Except for age and width, the two bridges are truly twins, except that the Hayes Clark Bridge is several feet wider than Speakman No. 2. Neither of the twins has windows, but they both have long, narrow openings under the eaves. The Hayes Clark Bridge, like its twin, has jagged, upward projecting stones along the top of the parapets.

Kennedy Bridge

Location: On W. Seven Stars Road (T 522), East Vincent Township.
Directions: In Kimberton, from the junction of Kimberton Road and
Hares Hill Road (SR 1045), go north on Hares Hill Road approximately
0.7 mile to W. Seven Stars Road. Turn left on W. Seven Stars Road and
go 0.3 mile to the bridge.

Year: 1856 / **Truss:** Burr / **Waterway:** French Creek
In Use: Yes / **Number of Spans:** 1 / **Owner:** County
Builder: Lex Kennedy and Jesse King
Length: 120 ft. 5 in. / **Width:** 14 ft.
Condition: Good / **Number:** PA-15-13 (2) / **Register:** January 21, 1974

Although the *Statewide Covered Bridge Assessment* lists Alex King and
Jesse King as the builders of this bridge, a plaque on the inside of
the bridge has the following information: "Built in 1856 by Lex
Kennedy & Jesse King . . . Rehabilitated in 1979 . . . Destroyed by
fire on May 10, 1986 . . . Rehabilitated in 1987." The present bridge
is a duplicate of the original. It was named for a local farmer,
Alexander Kennedy, and was originally built at a cost of $2,149.
The photo on this page illustrates the unusual portal design. The
Kennedy Bridge also has a long, horizontal window, which is similar in style to the windows in the Rapp Bridge. The Kennedy is
the second of three covered bridges still remaining across French
Creek. The restored structure appears to have been placed on its
original stone-and-mortar abutments, which are built on a concrete foundation. The bridge has stone-and-mortar wingwalls and
parapets, and the parapets are capped with concrete. The 1987
rehabilitated structure is roofed with cedar shakes.

Knox / Valley Forge Bridge

Location: In Valley Forge National Historical Park, on Yellow Springs Road (SR 1016), just west of PA 252, Tredyffrin Township.
Directions: Just east of the village of Valley Forge, at the junction of PA 23 and PA 252, go south on PA 252 approximately 1 mile to the junction with SR 1016 (Yellow Springs Road). The bridge is immediately to the left.

Year: 1865 / **Truss:** Burr / **Waterway:** Valley Creek
In Use: Yes / **Number of Spans:** 1 / **Owner:** State
Builder: Robert Russell / **Length:** 66 ft. 9 in. / **Width:** 14 ft.
Condition: Good / **Number:** PA-15-15 / **Register:** October 15, 1966

The original bridge built on this site in 1851 was destroyed by the flood of 1865; consequently, this second structure was built later that year. It is one of the most unusual bridges we have seen in the southeastern part of Pennsylvania. The truss design, built primarily of oak timbers, is a Burr arch, but remains comparatively low to the ground for the entire span of the bridge. The Knox Bridge has white, horizontal siding divided by mid-wall openings that run the length of each side. The deck consists of runners laid on crosswise planking, and is reinforced by steel girders since the bridge is heavily traveled.

The entire structure was repaired again during the mid-1990s (with funds provided by the state) at a cost of nearly $193,000. Repairs included new decking, siding, fire-retardant cedar roof shingles, painted steel support beams, new traffic signs, and fresh paint inside and out. The bridge was reopened, completely restored, in September 1996.

There is some question as to the origin of the Knox name; some believe the bridge was named for Philander C. Knox, the U.S. Senator from Pennsylvania, and others claim it was named for General Henry Knox, who was an officer quartered at nearby Valley Forge during the time of the Revolutionary War.

Larkin Bridge

Location: In Marsh Creek State Park, Upper Uwchlan Township.
Directions: In Ludwigs Corner, from the junction of PA 100 and PA 401, go south on PA 100 for 1.5 miles to Font Road (SR 4045). Turn right on Font Road for approximately 0.5 mile to Milford Road (SR 4045). Turn left on Milford Road and go approximately 1.7 miles, nearly to the end of the road. The bridge, surrounded by high weeds, can be seen approximately 0.25 mile to the left in a field.

Year: 1881 / **Truss:** Burr / **Waterway:** Branch of Marsh Creek
In Use: No / **Number of Spans:** 1 / **Owner:** State
Builder: Menander Wood and Ferdinand Wood
Length: 77 ft. 4 in. / **Width:** 14 ft. 1 in.
Condition: Very poor / **Number:** PA-15-11
Register: December 10, 1980

This bridge's name, Larkin, comes from its original location near the Jesse Larkin gristmill. However, the state moved this bridge prior to 1972, when the Marsh Creek Dam was built. It is significant that the bridge was moved, since its former location in the valley is now covered by water. In its new location, though, the bridge was placed on concrete abutments with no approaches, so in order to get on to the deck of the bridge, one must crawl up from the abutments. Perhaps the state ran out of funds, or simply has not put a high priority on finishing the reclamation of the bridge. Publications of 1998 indicated that the bridge was to be moved to Hickory Park as part of a trail system. However, no action on this proposal has yet taken place, and the bridge continues to deteriorate in its present location. While it was in fairly sound condition in 1991, the Larkin Bridge is now missing much of its roof. Part of the tarp which was covering the leaking roof has been blown away, allowing the bridge to be further damaged by inclement weather. The weed growth around the bridge has increased considerably in the past nine years. The bridge is barely visible from the closest road access.

Linton Stevens Bridge

Location: On King Row Road (T 310), Elk Township. **Directions:** In Hickory Hill, from the junction of Lewisville Road (PA 472) and Hickory Hill Road (T 344), go southeast on Lewisville Road approximately 0.4 mile to King Row Road (T 310), turn left on King Row Road and go north 0.8 mile to the bridge.

Year: 1886 / **Truss:** Burr / **Waterway:** Big Elk Creek
In Use: Yes / **Number of Spans:** 1 / **Owner:** County
Builder: J. Denithorne & Son / **Length:** 114 ft. 7 in. / **Width:** 16 ft.
Condition: Excellent / **Number:** PA-15-03
Register: December 10, 1980

Linton Stevens was the postmaster of the town of Hickory Hill. The first bridge over Big Elk Creek at this location was only a foot bridge, and it was followed by an iron bridge which was damaged by the flood of 1884. The bridge standing on this location today was built in 1886 to replace the damaged iron bridge. The sides are covered with board and batten siding, horizontal clapboard covers the portals, and the roof is constructed of shakes. The bridge rests on stone-and-mortar abutments, and has stone-and-mortar wingwalls and parapets capped with concrete.

The bridge was closed in the spring of 1996 because of flood damage to the underpinnings. The reconstruction took place during 1996 and 1997, and the bridge was reopened in August 1997. The repairs included the addition of concrete reinforcements to the original stone-and-mortar abutments. In addition, five heavy, lengthwise I-beams were placed under a steel deck which supports two-by-eight inch grooved planks across the width of the structure. The Linton Stevens Bridge is now in excellent condition, except for recent damage to the siding caused by the hurricane flood waters of 1999. Its location in a rather remote, secluded area of the county provides road access to six families who live north of the bridge.

Rapp's / Rapp's Dam Bridge

Location: On S. Rapp's Dam Road (SR 1049), East Pikeland Township.
Directions: In Phoenixville, from the junction of PA 23 and PA 29, go west on PA 23 for 2.2 miles to Rapp's Dam Road. Turn left approximately 0.3 mile to S. Rapp's Dam Road; turn left to the bridge.

Year: 1866 / **Truss:** Burr / **Waterway:** French Creek
In Use: Yes / **Number of Spans:** 1 / **Owner:** State
Builder: Benjamin D. Hastman / **Length:** 118 ft. 8 in. / **Width:** 14 ft. 6 in.
Condition: Good / **Number:** PA-15-14 / **Register:** January 18, 1973

Named for George A. Rapp and his sons, who operated a sawmill and gristmill just south of the bridge, the structure is a high double Burr arch truss sandwiching the typical multiple kingpost framework. The Rapp's Bridge has a cedar shake roof and cross plank flooring. The wide cedar clapboard siding is unpainted except for the portal ends, where the siding is painted white. Notice the attractive trim on the portal gable end with the boxed cornice return.

An interesting feature is the very long, horizontal, eye-level windows on the sides of the bridge, each of which has a small roof projection protecting the opening. These windows are in addition to the typical lengthwise openings immediately under the eaves.

Periodicals of the 1990s indicate that the bridge portals have been damaged many times by high trucks. Consequently, PennDOT has changed the height limit from 12 feet to 10 feet. While repairs were made to the portals and siding in the late 1990s, flood damage of 1999 has again done minimal damage to some of the siding near the bottom of the bridge.

Rudolph and Arthur Bridge

Location: On Camp Bonsall Road (T 307), between New London and Elk Townships. **Directions:** From the junction of Lewisville Road (PA 472) and Camp Bonsall Road (T 307), approximately 0.7 mile southeast of Peacedale, go east on Camp Bonsall road 0.7 mile to the bridge.

Year: 1880 / **Truss:** Burr / **Waterway:** Big Elk Creek
In Use: Yes / **Number of Spans:** 1 / **Owner:** County
Builder: Menander Wood and Richard Meredith
Length: 99 ft. 5 in. / **Width:** 16 ft. 5 in.
Condition: Good / **Number:** PA-15-01 / **Register:** December 10, 1980

This particular bridge was built near the site of the paper company operated by the Rudolph and Arthur families. The contractor for the bridge itself was Menander Wood, who built the structure for $1,440. The mason was Richard T. Meredith, who laid the stone-and-mortar abutments, wingwalls, and parapets for $890. The bridge is covered with white, vertical board and batten siding on both the sides and the portals and has a shake roof. It has no windows but is open under the eaves on both sides. It is an attractive structure in a lovely, rural setting. Local residents tell of heavy damage done to the bridge siding in the floods of the 1999 hurricane season. However, repairs were made soon after the flood waters receded.

Sheeder-Hall / Hall's / Sheeder Bridge

Location: On Hollow Road (SR 1033), East Vincent Township.
Directions: In Sheeder, from the junction of Pughtown Road (SR 1028) and Hollow Road (SR 1033), go south on Hollow Road for 0.3 mile to the bridge.

Year: 1850 / **Truss:** Burr / **Waterway:** French Creek
In Use: Yes / **Number of Spans:** 1 / **Owner:** State
Builder: Robert Russell & Jacob Fox
Length: 100 ft. / **Width:** 14 ft. 5½ in.
Condition: Good / **Number:** PA-15-12 / **Register:** April 23, 1973

The bridge appears to be in good condition and carries a considerable amount of traffic. The narrow clapboard siding is painted red but is peeling. It has a shake roof and lengthwise plank flooring laid on top of crosswise planking. It is set on stone-and-mortar abutments with a center concrete support, probably added in recent years. The deck is also reinforced with four steel I beams. It is in a lovely rural setting on the French Creek which is fished quite heavily.

Speakman No. 1 Bridge

Location: On Frog Hollow Road (SR 3047), between East Fallowfield and West Marlborough Townships. **Directions:** In McWilliamstown (Hephzibah), from the junction of Strasburg Road (SR 3062) and Frog Hollow Road (SR 3047), go south on Frog Hollow Road approximately 1.8 miles to the bridge.

Year: 1881 / **Truss:** Burr / **Waterway:** Buck Run
In Use: Yes / **Number of Spans:** 1 / **Owner:** State
Builder: Menander Wood and Ferdinand Wood
Length: 93 ft. 2½ in. / **Width:** 16 ft. 2 in.
Condition: Good / **Number:** PA-15-05 / **Register:** December 10, 1980

Located in a lovely remote valley of the county, this bridge at one time served the Jonathan Speakman gristmill, hence its name. Constructed at a cost of $2,000, it has vertical red board and batten siding, narrow lengthwise openings under the eaves, a cedar shake roof, and stone-and-mortar abutments and wingwalls. The flooring is constructed of runners laid on crosswise planking. One of the parapets is missing, possibly removed intentionally after being hit by a vehicle. The undercarriage of the bridge is supported with three iron or steel I beam structures set on concrete foundations in the middle of the stream. While the exterior condition of the bridge is quite good, the interior is being defaced with an extensive amount of graffiti. The bridge is only one and one-half miles, as the crow flies, from the Speakman No. 2 Bridge.

Speakman No. 2 / Mary Ann Pyle Bridge

Location: In the Laurel Reserve, property of the Brandywine Conservancy. Permission to see the bridge (as well as directions) must be obtained from the conservancy in Chadds Ford, Pennsylvania.

Year: 1881 / **Truss:** Queenpost / **Waterway:** Buck Run
In Use: Foot, horse, and cattle / **Number of Spans:** 1 / **Owner:** Private
Builder: Menander Wood and Ferdinand Wood
Length: 82 ft. 5 in. / **Width:** 14 ft. 7 in.
Condition: Good / **Number:** PA-15-06 / **Register:** December 10, 1980

This is the second of the "twin bridges" in the Laurel Reserve, which is private property of the Brandywine Conservancy and not open to the public. Anyone wishing to see either of the bridges must obtain permission from the Brandywine Conservancy, which is located in Chadds Ford, Pennsylvania. Speakman No. 2 and Hayes Clark bridge are the only queenpost truss designs in the county. Both were originally built by James B. Pyle, a local landowner, and this one was named for his daughter, Mary Ann. Prior to ownership by the Brandywine Conservancy, the last owner of record was the King Ranch, and so the bridges have been used primarily in the operation of the private farm acreage. Speakman No. 2 was last painted red with vertical board and batten siding, cedar shake roof, and stone-and-mortar abutments, wingwalls, and parapets. The parapets are unusual in appearance because of the jagged, upward projecting stones along the top. The bridge was built at a total cost of $1,938—$1,183 for the woodwork and $755 for the masonry. The location is in a lovely, quiet, pastoral setting.

Since 1991, the siding on the south side of the bridge has been replaced and repainted, and a wooden support post has been placed on a concrete foundation about one-third of the bridge length from the west end of the deck.

Bartram's / Goshen Bridge

Location: Bypassed by Goshen Road, approximately 1 mile west of Echo Valley, between Newtown Township, Delaware County and Willistown Township, Chester County. **Directions:** In Newtown Square, at the junction of PA 3 and PA 252, go west on PA 3 for 0.8 mile to Boot Road. Turn right on Boot Road and go 1.2 miles to Goshen Road. The bridge is just to the left, bypassed by Goshen Road.

Year: 1860 / **Truss:** Burr / **Waterway:** Crum Creek
In Use: Closed, ornamental gate / **Number of Spans:** 1
Owner: Counties
Builder: Ferdinand Wood / **Length:** 80 ft. 6 in. / **Width:** 14 ft. 7 in.
Condition: Excellent / **Number:** PA-15-17/PA-23-02
Register: December 10, 1980

Bartram's is the only covered bridge that Delaware County can claim. Although the rest of the bridge is covered with horizontal siding, the portal end siding follows the pitch of the roof. It is the only bridge in Pennsylvania with this unusual siding treatment on the portal ends. There is one horizontal window on each side of the bridge with a typical awning-type roof over the opening. The sides also have a typical narrow, lengthwise opening under the eaves.

Bypassed with a highway in 1941, this bridge has been the focus of preservation attempts by a local historical society based in

Delaware County. During our visit in 1991, we felt that the society had been somewhat successful, evidenced by the fact that that the bridge was still standing. However, the Bartram's Bridge was still in considerable need of repairs. It was completely closed to all traffic, with large, wrought iron gates over the portal openings. The Burr arch was exposed where it meets the abutment because of missing siding boards. Moss was beginning to cover the shingled roof, and the roof was beginning to sag.

At the time of our visit in May 2000, we were greatly impressed with the improvements to the bridge. On October 27, 1996 the reconditioned bridge was rededicated by the Bartram Bridge Joint Preservation Board. It has freshly painted, new clapboard siding, a new cedar shake roof, an installed fire alarm system, and an installed fire sprinkler system. The bridge is now completely closed by a locked, ornamental, wrought iron gate. While the gate completely eliminates the possibility of internal vandalizing of the bridge, it limits access through the bridge to everyone. It is the only Pennsylvania bridge that is closed in this manner.

Mercer's Mill / Mercer's Ford Bridge

Location: Approximately 2.5 miles south of Christiana, in Sadsbury Township, Lancaster County and 1.5 miles south of Atglen, in Fallowfield Township, Chester County. **Directions:** From Lancaster County on SR 2009, approximately 1.5 miles south of Christiana, turn southeast on an unnamed road to follow the course of the East Branch of the Octoraro Creek (look for sign along road "Entering Scenic Octoraro Creek"). Continue approximately 1 mile to the bridge. From Chester County on PA 41, approximately 2 miles south of Atglen, at the junction with Highland Road, go southwest on Highland Road for 1.2 miles to junction with Bailey Crossroads. Turn right (northwest) on Bailey Crossroads for 1.4 miles to the bridge.

Year: 1880 / **Truss:** Burr / **Waterway:** Octoraro Creek (East Branch)
In Use: Yes / **Number of Spans:** 1 / **Owner:** Counties
Builder: B. C. Carter / **Length:** 102 ft. 7 in./ **Width:** 15 ft. 10½ in.
Condition: Excellent / **Number:** PA-15-19 / PA-36-38
Register: December 11, 1980

This bridge has the widest "clear roadway" of any in the Lancaster County area—fourteen feet, five inches. Although similar in most respects to the other bridges in the area, the portal ends are slightly different because of their curved, rather than angular, openings. The sides have vertical board and batten siding, and the portal gable ends are covered with shiplapped siding. The bridge rests on stone-and-mortar abutments with stone-and-mortar wingwalls and parapets. The parapets are capped with concrete. Reports since early 1991 indicate that the Mercer's Mill Bridge received new siding and paint during 1991, and that further repairs were made in 1996. From all outward appearances, it is in excellent condition.

Pine Grove Bridge

Location: On Forge Road (SR 2006), East Nottingham Township, Chester County, and Ashville Road (SR 2006), Little Britain Township, Lancaster County. **Directions:** On Forge Road, at the southeast edge of Pine Grove, Lancaster County.

Year: 1884 / **Truss:** Burr / **Waterway:** Octoraro Creek
In Use: Yes / **Number of Spans:** 2 / **Owner:** State
Builder: Elias McMellen / **Length:** 199 ft. 9 in. / **Width:** 14 ft. 2 in.
Condition: Good / **Number:** PA-15-22/PA-36-41
Register: December 11, 1980

The first bridge on this site was built in 1816, but was destroyed by a storm. A second one, built in 1846, was swept away by ice. The bridge standing today was built in 1884. It is the longest in the Lancaster County area and one of the longest in the state. The Pine Grove Bridge and the Herr's Mill Bridge are the only two-span bridges in the county. The dam located above the bridge on the Octoraro Creek is used to impound water for the Octoraro recreation area, and there has been considerable grading done on the terrain below the dam area. When we visited in 2000, the power company (located on the Lancaster County side of the bridge) was doing extensive construction on the downstream (Chester County) side of the bridge. Theodore Burr Covered Bridge Society publications of 1999 indicate that the bridge is on the 4 or 5 year plan for restoration.

McGees Mills Bridge

Location: On Covered Bridge Road (T 322), McGees Mills, Bell Township. **Directions:** In McGees Mills, at the junction of PA 219 and Covered Bridge Road, just south of PA 36. Go east on Covered Bridge Road for 0.1 mile to the bridge.

Year: 1873 / **Truss:** Burr
Waterway: Susquehanna River (West Branch)
In Use: Yes / **Number of Spans:** 1 / **Owner:** County
Builder: Thomas A. McGee / **Length:** 121 ft. 8 in. / **Width:** 11 ft. 9½ in.
Condition: Very good / **Number:** PA-17-01 / **Register:** April 17, 1980

This is the only remaining covered bridge in Clearfield County. In 1982, it was dedicated by NSDAR (National Society of Daughters of the American Revolution) chapters from Dubois, James Alexander, Punxsutawney, and Susquehanna; the Chinclacamoose Chapter, Daughters of American Colonists; the Clearfield County Historical Society; and the Clearfield Heritage Foundation. It has been heavily reinforced in a variety of ways—heavy steel mending plates at the joints of the Burr arches, angle irons and mending plates on other wooden timbers, and a five-foot high wall of laminated two-by-twelve inch planks banded together with steel plates that run the entire length of the bridge interior. In outward appearance, this is the most extensively reinforced covered bridge in the state. The sides are covered nearly to the eaves with random-width vertical boards, and the portals are covered with horizontal clapboard. The roof is covered with cedar shakes, and the deck consists of very narrow, lengthwise two-by-eight inch planks set on edge. This extremely substantial structure rests on cut stone-and-mortar abutments with concrete reinforcement and also has well preserved cut stone-and-mortar wingwalls with moderate height parapets.

On March 19, 1994, under the weight of a twenty inch snowfall and an additional three inches of ice, the roof of this impressive structure collapsed. This caused the closing of the bridge until repairs could be undertaken. By spring of 1995, covered bridge publications indicated that repairs were under way. On October 11, 1995, a rededication ceremony for the bridge was held. During our visit in May 2000, we found the bridge in very good condition.

Logan Mill / Logan Mills Bridge

Location: On Logan Mills Road, approximately 3 miles northeast of Tylersville, Logan Township. **Directions:** In Tylersville, where PA 880 makes a ninety degree turn, go north on PA 880 for 2.4 miles to Logan Mills Road; turn right (south) on Logan Mills Road and go 0.4 mile to the bridge.

Year: 1874 / **Truss:** Queenpost / **Waterway:** Big Fishing Creek
In Use: Yes / **Number of Spans:** 1 / **Owner:** State
Builder: Unknown / **Length:** 60 ft. 6 in / **Width:** 11 ft. 7 in.
Condition: Fairly good / **Number:** PA-18-01 / **Register:** August 6, 1979

This is the last remaining covered bridge in Clinton County. It is covered with vertical board and batten siding on the sides, though some of the battens are missing, and it has horizontal siding on the portals. The roof is covered with sheet metal, and the deck is covered with crosswise planking. The structure rests on stone-and-mortar abutments with only one stone-and-mortar wingwall remaining below road level on one side. The bridge has a rather low queenpost truss system, which might make this bridge weaker than those with Burr or multiple kingpost trusses. The Logan Mill Bridge is reinforced with wooden timbers placed vertically on a poured concrete foundation in the streambed. There is no additional steel reinforcing. The state, however, has placed a three-ton load limit on the bridge. We did not see any noticeable change in the bridge between our visit in 1991 and the one in 2000. The bridge still appears to be in fairly good condition, and is used on a regular basis for vehicular traffic, especially by the local farming population. A local fisherman told us that there has been some highway survey activity near the bridge in recent months. He wondered if a new bridge in the vicinity might be a possibility in the future.

Creasyville Bridge

Location: On Creasyville Bridge Road (TR 683), approximately 6.7 miles northeast of Sereno, between Pine and Jackson Townships.
Directions: From the Jud Christie bridge (also in Columbia County), continue northeast on Sereno Road (SR 4031) for 0.7 mile to junction with SR 4039. Continue straight, past the junction with Sones Hollow Road where Sereno Road (SR 4031) becomes Creasyville Hollow Road (TR 710). Continue north on Creasyville Hollow Road for 0.6 mile until you find a road on the left with the bridge in sight. Turn left to the bridge.

Year: 1881 / **Truss:** Queenpost / **Waterway:** Little Fishing Creek
In Use: Yes / **Number of Spans:** 1 / **Owner:** County
Builder: T. S. Christian / **Length:** 44 ft. 7 in. / **Width:** 14 ft. 2 in.
Condition: Good / **Number:** PA-19-36 / **Register:** November 29, 1979

The Creasyville bridge, together with two other bridges—the Sam Eckman bridge and the Jud Christie bridge—is located in the most northern part of Columbia County and is easily found by locating the other bridges along Sereno Road: first Sam Eckman, then Jud Christie, and finally Creasyville. The distance from Sam Eckman to Creasyville is only 3.2 miles.

This is one of the shorter bridges still standing in Columbia County. It was built near Iram Derr's sawmill at a cost of $301.25 in 1881 and was probably known at that time as the Derr Bridge. The structure rests on concrete abutments with concrete wingwalls and is covered with vertical board siding. Its deck consists of runners laid over crosswise planking. It was in better condition when we visited it in 2000 than it had been on our 1991 bridging safari. The new sheet metal roof and paint applied by the township maintenance crew in 1998 have made considerable improvements in its appearance.

Davis Bridge

Location: On Shakespear Road, northwest of Slabtown, Cleveland Township. **Directions:** In Slabtown, at the junction of PA 42 and Ideal Park Road (SR 2001), go north on PA 42 for 1 mile to the junction with Queen City Road (T 377). Turn left (west) on Queen City Road for 0.9 mile to Shakespear Road. The bridge is just to the right on Shakespear Road.

Year: 1875 / **Truss:** Burr / **Waterway:** Roaring Creek (North Branch)
In Use: Yes / **Number of Spans:** 1 / **Owner:** County
Builder: Daniel Kostenbauder / **Length:** 87 ft. 4 in. / **Width:** 14 ft. 6 in.
Condition: Good / **Number:** PA-19-16 / **Register:** November 29, 1979

Just as there are three bridges grouped together in the northern part of Columbia County there are three bridges located in the same general area in the southern part of the county. The Davis bridge belongs to this southern group, along with the Furnace Bridge and the Parr's Mill Bridge. They are all located within two and one-quarter miles of each other.

Built at a cost of $1,248, the Davis Bridge was named for a farmer who lived nearby. It rests on poured concrete abutments with wingwalls of similar material. The Burr arches sandwich a multiple kingpost truss. The bridge has vertical board and batten siding on the portals, with vertical boards on the sides, and a sheet metal roof. The deck has runners on crosswise planking. We have no reports of improvements made to this bridge since 1991, but it still appears to be in good condition. The Davis Bridge is another testament to the longevity of these historic gems.

East Paden (Twin) Bridge

Location: In Twin Bridges Park, east of Forks, Fishing Creek Township.
Directions: In Forks, at the junction of PA 487 and SR 1020, go east on SR 1020 for 0.3 mile to the Twin Bridges Park, just off the road to the right.

Year: 1884 / **Truss:** Queenpost
Waterway: Huntingdon Creek (overflow)
In Use: Foot traffic only / **Number of Spans:** 1 / **Owner:** County
Builder: W. C. Pennington / **Length:** 72 ft 8 in. / **Width:** 14 ft. 4 in.
Condition: Good / **Number:** PA-19-11 / **Register:** November 29, 1979

This is a "twin bridge," meaning that it is one of two bridges that stand nearly portal to portal along the same road. In this case, one of the bridges is over the main stream (Huntingdon Creek) and the other (the East Paden Bridge) spans the overflow of the waterway. This is reportedly the only set of twin covered bridges in the United States. Both bridges were built for $720 and named after John Paden, who operated a sawmill nearby. The *World Guide to Covered Bridges* and a plaque at the portal of West Paden state that the twins were built in 1850. However, the *Statewide Covered Bridge Assessment* and the pamphlet, *Covered Bridges of Columbia and Montour Counties, Pennsylvania*, list the building year as 1884.

When the state road bypassed the bridges in 1963, efforts of the Theodore Burr Society of Pennsylvania and its president, Vera Wagner, convinced the state to turn the structures over to the county. Columbia County created the Twin Bridges Park recreation area, and both bridges are now used as picnic pavilions. The bridges are not really twin in design; East Paden Bridge is the shorter of the two, and has a queenpost design that spans a dry creek bed that is the overflow for Huntingdon Creek. West Paden Bridge has a Burr truss, and spans Huntingdon Creek. Poured concrete fencepost walls were added between the bridges during their preservation in 1962. A 1994 article in the Theodore Burr Covered Bridge Society newsletter indicated that a roof beam, snapped under the weight of the winter snows, had been repaired. The cost of the repairs was $10,000.

In the first photo, the bridge in the foreground is East Paden, and West Paden is in the background. In the second photo, the camera angle highlights the noticeable Burr arch truss of West Paden, and points through to the queenpost truss of East Paden. It appears that wingwalls existed at the south end of East Paden at one time. It is obvious that maintenance continues on both structures. They appeared to be in fine condition when we visited them in 2000.

Fowlersville Bridge

Location: In Briar Creek Park, Briar Creek Township.
Directions: Entrance to the park is along Lake Road (SR 1017), approximately 0.8 mile south of Evansville. The bridge is located near the picnic area toward the end of the park road. It is not visible from the entrance.

Year: 1886 / **Truss:** Queenpost / **Waterway:** Small spring-fed run
In Use: No / **Number of Spans:** 1 / **Owner:** County
Builder: Charles King / **Length:** 40 ft. 1½ in. / **Width:** 14 ft. 4 in.
Condition: Excellent / **Number:** PA-19-05
Register: November 29, 1979

The Fowler family moved to this area and became quite prominent after the Revolutionary War. The Fowler Bridge was originally built over the West Branch of Briar Creek near Fowlersville at a cost of $397. It was moved to the park in 1986 after a new bridge was constructed over Briar Creek.

The Fowlersville Bridge has vertical board siding and rests on concrete abutments without wingwalls. It has a metal roof and is decked with runners on crosswise planking. The bridge adds an interesting touch to the picnic area of Briar Creek Park. During our visit to the park in 2000, we found that there were considerable improvements made to the park in the past nine years. The bridge itself has been well maintained; and while we have no reports of specific improvements, it appears to be in excellent condition.

Furnace / Esther Furnace Bridge

Location: On Esther Furnace Road (T 373), northwest of Slabtown, Cleveland Township. **Directions:** From the Davis bridge, continue on Queen City Road (T 377) for 1 mile to "T". Turn right for 0.2 mile to Esther Furnace Road; turn right for 0.2 mile to the bridge.

Year: 1882 / **Truss:** Queenpost
Waterway: Roaring Creek (North Branch)
In Use: Yes / **Number of Spans:** 2 / **Owner:** County
Builder: C. W. Eves / **Length:** 99 ft. 6 in. / **Width:** 12 ft. 6 in.
Condition: Good / **Number:** PA-19-20 / **Register:** November 29, 1979

This is the second of the three bridges grouped closely together in the southern part of the county. (The other two bridges are the Davis bridge and the Parr's Mill bridge.) The Furnace bridge will be just about 1.35 miles from the Davis bridge.

This bridge, built at a cost of $1,044.75 in 1881, is situated near the site of the Esther iron smelting furnace, which was built in 1817. It is a two-span queenpost structure supported with a center concrete pier. The sides and portals are covered with vertical boards. One end has the original stone wingwalls, one of which is broken. The other end has poured concrete wingwalls. The deck consists of runners over crosswise planking. In addition to the typical openings under the eaves, there is one window at each end where the road curves, apparently to enable one to watch for approaching traffic.

We have no documentation of specific repairs in the past nine years; but the bridge still appears to be in good condition.

Hollingshead Bridge

Location: On Old Reading Road, Catawissa, Catawissa Township.
Directions: In Catawissa, from the junction of PA 42 and PA 487, go south on PA 42 for 0.5 mile to Mountain Road (T 403). Turn left on Mountain Road and go 0.5 mile to Old Reading Road. The bridge is just to the left.

Year: 1850 / **Truss:** Burr / **Waterway:** Catawissa Creek
In Use: Yes / **Number of Spans:** 1 / **Owner:** County
Builder: Peter Ent / **Length:** 116 ft. 10½ in./ **Width:** 15 ft. 5 in.
Condition: Excellent / **Number:** PA-19-34
Register: November 29, 1979

The cost of this bridge in 1850 was $1,180, and it was named for Henry Hollingshead, who owned a nearby mill. The Burr arches sandwich a multiple kingpost structure, and the bridge rests on stone-and-mortar abutments and has stone-and-mortar wingwalls and parapets. The parapets are capped with concrete. The Hollingshead Bridge has vertical board siding painted red, horizontal board portals, also painted red, a metal roof, and a deck of runners laid over widely spaced crosswise planking.

Covered bridge society publications of 1998 indicated that the bridge was scheduled for extensive repairs during the spring of 1999. Summer 1999 issues of the same newsletter indicated that work was underway and expected to be completed by the end of the year. A contract for $410,211 was awarded to Lycoming Supply, Inc., Williamsport, PA. During our visit to the bridge in April 2000, we found that the repairs are complete. The bridge has been beautifully restored. It is again open, and accommodates a considerable amount of traffic.

Johnson Bridge

Location: On Cleveland Road (T 320), just east of Knoebels Grove Amusement Park, Cleveland Township. **Directions:** From Knoebels Grove Amusement Park, follow Pine Swamp Road (T 337) east for 0.7 mile to Cleveland Road. Turn right (south) for 0.1 mile to the bridge.

Year: 1882 / **Truss:** Queenpost / **Waterway:** Mugser Run
In Use: Yes / **Number of Spans:** 1 / **Owner:** County
Builder: Daniel Stine / **Length:** 61 ft. / **Width:** 13 ft. 5 in.
Condition: Very good / **Number:** PA-19-37
Register: November 29, 1979

This bridge was built near the farm of Adam M. Johnson, who also owned and operated a boot and shoe store in the area. The original cost of the bridge was $799. When we visited the bridge in 1991 it was covered with random-width board and batten siding, but most of the battens were missing. During our visit in 2000, however, we found the bridge in very good condition. It appears that some work has been done on the siding, although we have no documentation to indicate specific repairs. The bridge rests on concrete abutments and has short stone-and-mortar wingwalls on one end and concrete wingwalls on the other, with parapets that rise just a bit above road level. The roof is sheet metal, and the deck has runners laid over crosswise planking.

Josiah Hess / Laubach Bridge

Location: On Covered Bridge Road (T 563), east of Forks, Fishing Creek Township. **Directions:** In Forks, at the junction of PA 487 and SR 1020, go east on SR 1020 for 1.4 miles to Covered Bridge Road. The bridge is just to the left on Covered Bridge Road.

Year: 1875 / **Truss:** Burr / **Waterway:** Huntingdon Creek
In Use: No / **Number of Spans:** 1 / **Owner:** County
Builder: Joseph Redline / **Length:** 106 ft. 3 in. / **Width:** 15 ft. 3 in.
Condition: Fair / **Number:** PA-19-10 / **Register:** November 29, 1979

This is a typical Columbia County covered bridge. It is covered with vertical board and batten siding; most of the battens are missing. It rests on stone-and-mortar abutments with wingwalls. The wingwalls do not extend to parapets above the road on the north end. The southeast wingwall has a parapet above the road. The southwest wingwall is broken away. The bridge has a sheet metal roof and a deck of runners laid over crosswise planking. The Burr truss sandwiches a multiple kingpost truss. There is a long center window on the east side and short windows at the southwest and southeast ends. The bridge also has lengthwise openings under the eaves, which is common for the bridges in this county. While the bridge was open to traffic during our visit in 1991, it was closed to traffic in 2000. We have no documentation concerning the closing of the bridge.

Jud Christian / Jud Christie Bridge

Location: On Ardens Hill Road (TR 685), approximately 5.4 miles northeast of Sereno, between Pine and Jackson Townships.
Directions: From the Sam Eckman bridge, continue northeast on Sereno Road (SR 4031) for 1.9 miles to Arden Hill Road (TR 685). The bridge is immediately to the right (east) on Arden Hill Road.

Year: 1876 / **Truss:** Queenpost / **Waterway:** Little Fishing Creek
In Use: Yes / **Number of Spans:** 1 / **Owner:** County
Builder: William L. Manning / **Length:** 56 ft. 3 in. / **Width:** 12 ft. 9 in.
Condition: Good / **Number:** PA-19-25 / **Register:** November 29, 1979

This is the second of the three most northern bridges in the county—along with the Sam Eckman Bridge and the Creasyville Bridge—and can be found only 1.9 miles further north than the Sam Eckman Bridge

This bridge was built at a cost of $239 in 1876, and was named for a nearby farmer and lumberman, Jud Christian. The portal, however, displays the bridge's name as Jud Christie. This bridge, like those nearest to it, has a relatively short queenpost structure. It has board and batten siding and a sheet metal roof. The wingwalls extend only to road-level. The decking, like that of many Columbia County bridges, is made of runners laid over crosswise planking.

Happily, like so many others, the Jud Christian Bridge was in better condition when we visited it in 2000 than it had been in 1991. It had a new sheet metal roof and paint, applied by the township maintenance crew in 1998. This has made a considerable improvement in its appearance.

Kramer Bridge

Location: On Turkey Path Road, just southwest of Rohrsburg, Greenwood Township. **Directions:** North of Orangeville, approximately 1 mile, at the junction of PA 487 and Rohrsburg Road (SR 4041), go north on Rohrsburg Road for 2.7 miles to Utt Road (T 595). Turn left (west) on Utt Road for 0.5 mile to Turkey Path Road, (T 572). Turn left to the bridge.

Year: 1881 / **Truss:** Queenpost / **Waterway:** Mud Run
In Use: Yes / **Number of Spans:** 1 / **Owner:** County
Builder: C. W. Eves / **Length:** 50 ft. 2½ in. / **Width:** 13 ft. 10 in.
Condition: Fair / **Number:** PA-19-23 / **Register:** November 29, 1979

This is a short queenpost structure, built by C. W. Eves in 1881 at a cost of $414.50. It was named for Alexander Kramer, a local farmer, who also bid on its construction. The original shake roof is covered with sheet metal. The sides are covered with board and battens, but most of the battens are missing. The deck consists of runners laid over crosswise planking, and there are small stone parapets topped with concrete.

During our visit in 2000, we felt that a coat of paint and some repairs to the missing battens would do much to improve this bridge's appearance. However, it is still in fair condition and still carries vehicular traffic.

Paperdale Bridge

Location: On the property of Mr. and Mrs. Elwood Erney, approximately 6 miles north of Benton, Sugarloaf Township. **Directions:** Just north of Benton, where PA 239 goes northwest from PA 487, go north on PA 487 for 5.3 miles to Laubach Road. Turn left on Laubach Road and go 0.4 mile to a private driveway on the left; turn left onto private driveway and go 0.1 mile to a private home. Acquire permission to see the bridge which is located at the end of the lane to the right of the home.

Year: c. 1890s / **Truss:** Queenpost
Waterway: Dry land, formerly spanned Raven Creek
In Use: No, storage only / **Number of Spans:** 1 / **Owner:** Private
Builder: Unknown / **Length:** 46 ft. 2½ in. / **Width:** 13 ft. 1 in.
Condition: Useable for storage / **Number:** PA-19-46 / **Register:**

This bridge has not been documented in any of our printed sources. However, after contacts with covered bridge enthusiasts and long time residents of the town of Benton, located just south of Sugarloaf Township, we can relate the following. For approximately sixty years the Paperdale Covered Bridge spanned Raven Creek, just east of Stillwater on Paperdale Road, and carried traffic to the settlement of Paperdale and the paper mill just east of the bridge. In the late 1950s the bridge was replaced by a "modern" steel and concrete structure. A contractor by the name of Laubach acquired the bridge, had it dismantled and rebuilt on his forested tract of land about eight miles north of its original location. There it was used as a picnic pavilion adjacent to a recreation home utilized by Laubach and his wife. Around 1970, Elwood

Erney and his wife purchased the tract of land formerly owned by the Laubachs. After acquiring the land, Elwood elevated the bridge and supported the bottom chord on cement block piers to prevent further deterioration. He continues to use it to store lumber harvested from his forested acreage. Because of the absence of siding, the truss structure can readily be identified. There is no deck, nor are there abutments, wingwalls, or parapets. The portals are covered with unpainted, random-width boards and the roof consists of sheet metal. The fact that this bridge is still standing, despite the absence of siding on the sides, once again displays the durability of these historic structures.

Parr's Mill Bridge

Location: On Parr's Mill Road (T 328), northwest of Slabtown, Cleveland Township. **Directions:** From the Furnace Bridge, continue through the bridge for 0.4 mile to the junction with Rider Road (T 344). Bear left on Esther Furnace Road for 0.4 mile to crossroads. The bridge is straight ahead across the intersection 0.1 mile.

Year: 1865 / **Truss:** Burr / **Waterway:** Roaring Creek (North Branch)
In Use: Yes / **Number of Spans:** 1 / **Owner:** County
Builder: F. L. Shuman / **Length:** 84 ft. / **Width:** 13 ft.
Condition: Good / **Number:** PA-19-29 / **Register:** November 29, 1979

This is the third of the three bridges in the southern part of the county that are located within two and one-quarter miles of each other. This one is located just 0.9 mile beyond the Furnace bridge.

This bridge was built in 1865 at a cost of $1,275. In 1875, Washington Parr purchased the Willow Grove Grist Mill nearby; from then on, it was known as Parr's Mill Bridge. The Burr arches sandwich a multiple kingpost truss. The bridge is covered with vertical board siding on the portals on the east side and with shiplapped siding on the west side. The roof is sheet metal, and the deck is covered with runners laid over diagonal crosswise planking. The bridge rests on a concrete abutment on the north end and a stone-and-mortar abutment on the south end.

There has been no documentation regarding repairs to this bridge since 1991, but we found it in good condition in 2000.

Patterson / Paterson Bridge

Location: On Hartman Hollow Road, between Orangeville and Rohrsburg, Orange Township. **Directions:** Approximately 1 mile north of Orangeville, at the junction of PA 487 and Rohrsburg Road (SR 4041), go north on Rohrsburg Road for 1.7 miles to Hartman Hollow Road. The bridge is just to the left on Hartman Hollow Road.

Year: 1875 / **Truss:** Burr / **Waterway:** Mud Run
In Use: Yes / **Number of Spans:** 1 / **Owner:** County
Builder: Frank Derr / **Length:** 82 ft. / **Width:** 14 ft 6½ in.
Condition: Good / **Number:** PA-19-26 / **Register:** November 29, 1979

Built at a cost of $804, this bridge was named after the Patterson sawmill, which was located nearby. Covered with board and batten siding and a sheet metal roof, it has small windows at the east end near the junction with SR 4041 and on the west end where the road curves. The bridge rests on stone-and-mortar abutments, which have been reinforced in recent years with concrete. It has short wingwalls which are slightly raised above road-level, and the deck is covered with runners in the center laid over crosswise planking. The bridge is still used quite heavily for vehicular traffic, and, except for some peeling paint, we found the bridge in good condition.

Rupert Bridge

Location: In the village of Rupert, between the town of Bloomsburg and Montour Township. **Directions:** Traveling south on PA 42, just south of the junction with US 11, the bridge can be seen to the east in the village of Rupert.

Year: 1847 / **Truss:** Burr / **Waterway:** Fishing Creek
In Use: No / **Number of Spans:** 1+ / **Owner:** County
Builder: Jesse M. Beard / **Length:** 185 ft. 4 in. / **Width:** 17 ft. 11½ in.
Condition: Under restoration / **Number:** PA-19-33
Register: November 29, 1979

The village in which this bridge is located was settled by, and named for, Leonard Rupert. Rupert established a ferry across the river, and his home became a popular stopping-off place for travelers. The bridge was built at a cost of $1,637 in 1847. The following description of the bridge is based on information gathered for the 1993 edition of this guide.

The Burr arches, which sandwich a multiple kingpost truss, are reinforced with steel U-channels. The arches rest on very high stone-and-mortar abutments, and there are stone-and-mortar wingwalls and parapets. The bridge is covered with horizontal siding on the portals; the vertical board siding on the sides is badly deteriorating near the abutments. The roof is sheet metal, half of which is placed directly over the original cedar shake roof. The deck is constructed of runners laid over crosswise planking. The volume of traffic present while we were visiting the bridge in 1991 indicates that this is one of the most heavily used bridges in the county. It is also Columbia County's longest remaining covered bridge.

Periodicals of the Theodore Burr Covered Bridge Society reported the closing of the Rupert bridge sometime prior to 1996. We became aware of it around 1994. By the fall of 1999, work was underway to make extensive repairs to the bridge—steel I-beams, two concrete piers, new deck, flooring, siding, running boards, and timber truss work where needed. At the time of our visit in April 2000, we found work well underway. The two new piers had been completed, but the bridge was still closed to the public. It is expected that work will be completed sometime in 2001.

Sam Eckman Bridge

Location: Just west of Sereno Road on T 645, approximately 3.5 miles northeast of Sereno, between Pine and Greenwood Townships.
Directions: In Sereno, at the junction of PA 42 and PA 442, go north on PA 42 approximately 1.1 miles to the junction with Sereno Road (SR 4031). Go northeast on Sereno Road for 2.4 miles to the bridge on T 645, immediately to the left (west). Sereno Road is an unimproved, gravel road in places. Be sure to remain on Sereno Road (SR 4031).

Year: 1876 / **Truss:** Queenpost / **Waterway:** Little Fishing Creek
In Use: Yes / **Number of Spans:** 1 / **Owner:** County
Builder: Joseph Redline / **Length:** 65 ft. 5 in. / **Width:** 14 ft. 9 in.
Condition: Good / **Number:** PA-19-08 / **Register:** November 29, 1979

This is the first of the three bridges that can be found near each other in the northern part of the county. The other two—Jud Christian and Creasyville—are a little further north along Sereno Road.

Sam Eckman, for whom this covered span was named, was a local farmer who operated both a shingle mill and a birch oil factory near the site of the bridge. The cost of construction in 1876 was $498. The structure has vertical board siding and a new corrugated sheet metal roof. The east end of the bridge is built on a poured concrete abutment, while the west end abutment is of stone-and-mortar. The bridge is decked with runners laid over crosswise planking.

This bridge, like the other two northern Columbia County bridges, has been painted and re-roofed with sheet metal during 1998. Except for a few missing siding boards on the upstream side (possibly due to flooding in the 1999 hurricane season), the bridge is in good condition. The new paint, alone, has made a considerable improvement to the bridge's appearance since our 1991 visit.

Shoemaker Bridge

Location: On Shoemaker Bridge Road (TR 853), just northwest of Sereno, Pine Township. **Directions:** In Iola, from the junction of PA 42 and Legion Road (SR 4024), go west on Legion Road 0.15 mile to Maple Ridge Road (TR 619), turn right and go 0.45 mile to Shoemaker Bridge Road (TR 853), bear right on Shoemaker Bridge Road for 0.5 mile to the bridge.

Year: 1881 / **Truss:** Queenpost / **Waterway:** West Branch Run
In Use: No / **Number of Spans:** 1 / **Owner:** County
Builder: T. S. Christian / **Length:** 48 ft. 1 in. / **Width:** 14 ft.
Condition: Poor / **Number:** PA-19-06 / **Register:** November 29, 1979

This bridge was named for a local farmer and lumberman, Joseph Shoemaker. One of the bridge's wingwalls is shorter than the other, because the road curves sharply at the foot of the mountain. The bridge is covered with vertical board and batten siding on both the sides and portals. The sides contain lengthwise openings under the eaves, and there is a narrow window at the end where the road curves, which provides a view of oncoming traffic. The deck consists of crosswise planking, and the structure rests on stone-and-mortar abutments with stone-and-mortar wingwalls. One diagonal of the queenpost truss is reinforced with steel U-channels on both the inside and outside.

During our visit in 2000, we found the bridge closed and in poor condition. Periodicals of the Theodore Burr Covered Bridge Society in the fall of 1996 indicated that the bridge had been closed. At the time of this writing, we are not aware of any plans to restore and/or reopen the bridge.

Snyder Bridge

Location: On Rarig Road (TR 361), just east of Slabtown, Locust Township. **Directions:** In Slabtown, at the junction of PA 42 and Ideal Park Road (SR 2001), go east on Ideal Park Road for 1.2 miles to Rarig Road. The bridge is 0.1 mile to the left on Rarig Road.

Year: 1876 / **Truss:** Queenpost
Waterway: Roaring Creek (North Branch)
In Use: Yes / **Number of Spans:** 1 / **Owner:** County
Builder: Unknown / **Length:** 60 ft. 2 in. / **Width:** 15 ft. 2 in.
Condition: Good / **Number:** PA-19-14 / **Register:** November 29, 1979

Some accounts of this bridge list the truss system as a Burr design. The Theodore Burr Society of Pennsylvania lists it as a queenpost truss. A visit to the bridge confirms, at least in our opinion, the fact that it is a queenpost truss. The date of construction is also a point of contention. The *Statewide Covered Bridge Assessment* lists the year 1900, the Columbia County covered bridge brochure indicates that it is "unknown," and the *World Guide to Covered Bridges* lists the year 1876. The abutments are poured concrete as are three wingwalls; one wingwall is missing. The floor is covered with runners on closely spaced crosswise planking. At the time of our visit in 1991, the south side was covered with vertical board siding, and the north side had vertical boards on the bottom two-thirds and horizontal siding for the top one-third. During our visit in 2000, we found that both sides are now covered with vertical board siding, some, obviously, has been replaced since 1991. The portals are both covered with vertical siding. The bridge is painted in typical barn red with white trim, and has the familiar Columbia County openings under the eaves. We considered the bridge to be in good condition during our 2000 visit.

Stillwater Bridge

Location: On Wesley Street, Stillwater, Fishing Creek Township.
Directions: South of the village of Stillwater, at the junction of PA 487 and SR 1022, go north on PA 487 for 1.5 miles to Wesley Street. On the right side of PA 487, across from the U.S. Post Office, turn right on Wesley Street to the bridge.

Year: 1849 / **Truss:** Burr / **Waterway:** Big Fishing Creek
In Use: No, foot traffic only / **Number of Spans:** 1 / **Owner:** County
Builder: James McHenry / **Length:** 157 ft. 2 in. / **Width:** 16 ft. 5 in.
Condition: Poor / **Number:** PA-19-21 / **Register:** November 29, 1979

This bridge was built at a cost of $1,124 by James McHenry, whose family was among the first to settle in the Stillwater area. Its high Burr arches sandwich a multiple kingpost truss. It has an unusual portal at the east end, curved wingwalls, and an angled portal opening. The deck has an unusual diagonal herringbone planking pattern.

In 1991, we found the sides covered with vertical board and batten siding but many missing battens. The portals were covered with horizontal clapboard siding. In April 2000, we found little change other than slight deterioration. There has been no apparent repair or restoration work done on the structure. The bridge, which was barricaded on the west end in 1991, is now barricaded on both ends.

Wagner Bridge

Location: At the entrance of the Foxtail housing development, on the west edge of Bloomsburg. **Directions:** Traveling north on PA 42, from the junction with US 11, look to the right for the Foxtail development. The bridge is located in an open area to the left of the road leading into the development.

Year: 1856 / **Truss:** Queenpost / **Waterway:** Dry gulch
In Use: No / **Number of Spans:** 1 / **Owner:** Private
Builder: Unknown / **Length:** 50 ft 2 in. / **Width:** 14 ft. 1 in.
Condition: Good / **Number:** PA-19-15 / **Register:** November 29, 1979

This bridge originally spanned Roaring Creek, near Slabtown. It was built in 1856 and reportedly had a length of 62 feet and a queenpost truss. At some time prior to 1991, it was removed from its original location and placed in storage. The developers of the Foxtail housing development had the bridge rebuilt near the entrance to Foxtail in 1995. This is approximately eight to ten miles north of its original location. It is now located to the side of the main street into the development where it is resting on steel I-beams. There are no abutments, wingwalls or parapets. There is no road leading to or from it. It is simply there, resting over a small, dry, depression, with the name "Foxtail" highlighted on its side. With its queenpost truss structure completely reassembled and re-sided, and a reasonably recent coat of barn red paint, the bridge appears to be in excellent condition. The lack of approaches, abutments, wingwalls, or parapets, however, make it appear unfinished.

Wanich Bridge

Location: On Covered Bridge Drive, north of Bloomsburg, between Hemlock and Mt. Pleasant Townships. **Directions:** At the junction of PA 42 and Covered Bridge Drive, approximately 4 miles north of Bloomsburg on PA 42, go east on Covered Bridge Drive for 0.2 mile to the bridge.

Year: 1884 / **Truss:** Burr / **Waterway:** Little Fishing Creek
In Use: Yes / **Number of Spans:** 1 / **Owner:** County
Builder: George Russell, Jr. / **Length:** 99 ft. / **Width:** 15 ft. 11½ in
Condition: Good / **Number:** PA-19-18 / **Register:** November 29, 1979

This bridge was named for a local farmer, John Wanich. It rests on stone-and-mortar abutments with stone-and-mortar wingwalls and parapets. The deck consists of runners laid over a herringbone deck pattern. The Burr truss sandwiches a multiple kingpost truss. Notice the typical openings under the eaves. In addition, there is one window on the north side and one on the south. They are both positioned at mid-wall height and in such a way that anyone on the bridge can see approaching traffic.

In 1991, we found this bridge covered with horizontal siding on the sides, vertical boards on the portals, and a sheet metal roof. However, in April 2000, we found it had been recovered with vertical boards on both the sides, and the portals had been painted the typical barn red color. The two parapets on the east end of the bridge have been replaced with concrete. Finally, a second window on the bridge's north side had been removed. We have no specific reports regarding improvements to the bridge, but these changes speak for themselves.

West Paden (Twin) Bridge

Location: In Twin Bridges Park, east of Forks, Fishing Creek Township.
Directions: In Forks, at the junction of PA 487 and SR 1020, go east on SR 1020 for 0.3 mile to the Twin Bridges Park, just off the road to the right.

Year: 1884 / **Truss:** Burr / **Waterway:** Huntingdon Creek
In Use: Foot traffic only / **Number of Spans:** 1 / **Owner:** County
Builder: W. C. Pennington / **Length:** 100 ft. / **Width:** 15 ft. 2 in.
Condition: Good / **Number:** PA-19-12 / **Register:** November 29, 1979

This is the second of the twin bridges mentioned in the discussion of the East Paden Bridge. The Burr arches of the truss structure sandwich a multiple kingpost truss, which is a typical arrangement. This bridge, like the East Paden Bridge, is covered with vertical board siding, painted barn red, and trimmed with white. Both bridges rest on stone abutments, and wingwalls are evident only at the end of the Burr structure between the bridges. The roofs of both bridges are covered with sheet metal roof material. Both structures are quite well maintained by the county, which now owns both bridges and maintains the Twin Bridges Park.

Knoebels Grove Bridge

Location: In Knoebels Grove Amusement Park.

Year: 1975 / **Truss:** Queenpost
Waterway: Roaring Creek (South Branch)
In Use: Foot traffic only / **Number of Spans:** 1 / **Owner:** Private
Builder: Dick Knoebel / **Length:** 46 ft. / **Width:** 14 ft 2½ in.
Condition: Good / **Number:** PA-19-B/PA-49-A / **Register:**

This bridge is listed in *Romantic Shelters*, a supplement to the 1989 *World Guide to Covered Bridges*. It is not included in the *WGCB* itself, the Burr Society list, nor the *Statewide Covered Bridge Assessment*.

Dick Knoebel is the fourth generation of Knoebels directly involved with Columbia County covered bridges. His great-grandfather was the builder of the Wagner Bridge in 1874; in 1936, Dick's grandfather, H. H. Knoebel, purchased a covered bridge over West Creek, near Benton. That bridge was moved and rebuilt by Hartman and Lawrence Knoebel, Dick's uncle and father, respectively. This bridge, situated one hundred feet downstream from the birthplace of the resort and the Lawrence L. Knoebel Bridge, was built in 1975 at a cost of $10,000. The main roof beams measure fourteen inches by sixteen inches by fifty-one feet long. They were hand hewn in 1865 for the Berninger Grist Mill, which was dismantled in 1974.

This bridge has a cedar shake roof, vertical board siding (only halfway up each side), and lengthwise deck planking. It is included with this collection because of the significant efforts of the Knoebels in the construction and preservation of covered bridges in the Columbia County area.

Krickbaum / Kreigbaum / Kriegbaum Bridge

Location: On All Saints Road (T 459, Columbia County; T 462, Northumberland County), 1 mile north of Bear Gap, Northumberland County. **Directions:** Approximately 1 mile northwest of Bear Gap, at the junction of PA 54 with SR 2018 (road to the west at the junction) and All Saints Road (T 462—road to the east at the junction), go east on All Saints Road for 0.7 mile to the bridge.

Year: 1876 / **Truss:** Queenpost
Waterway: Roaring Creek (South Branch)
In Use: Yes / **Number of Spans:** 1 / **Owner:** Counties
Builder: George W. Keefer / **Length:** 62 ft. 2 in. / **Width:** 14 ft. 2 in.
Condition: Good / **Number:** PA-19-32/PA-49-12
Register: August 8, 1979

Named after William Krickbaum, who owned a grist mill nearby, the cost of this bridge's construction in 1876 was $732. The sides are covered with vertical board and batten siding, and the portals are covered with vertical boards. All of the siding is painted barn red. The bridge rests on a stone and mortar abutment on the Northumberland County side and a poured concrete abutment on the Columbia County side. There are stone and mortar wingwalls, a sheet metal roof, and a deck of runners laid over crosswise planking. We have no reports of work done since our 1991 visit, but the bridge continues to carry vehicular traffic and appears to be in good condition.

Lawrence L. Knoebel Bridge

Location: At the entrance to Knoebels Grove Campground, adjacent to Knoebels Grove Amusement Park, between Cleveland Township, Columbia County, and Ralpho Township, Northumberland County.

Year: 1875 / **Truss:** Queenpost
Waterway: Roaring Creek (South Branch)
In Use: Yes / **Number of Spans:** 1 / **Owner:** Private
Builder: J. J. McHenry / **Length:** 38 ft. 6 in. / **Width:** 13 ft. 5 in.
Condition: Fairly Good / **Number:** PA-19-39/PA-49-13
Register: August 8, 1979

This bridge was originally located over West Creek, near Benton, Columbia County. It was built there in 1875 at a cost of $348. In 1936, it was sold to H. H. Knoebel and his sons for $40 when road relocation bypassed it. It was then carefully dismantled, moved fifty miles to the Grove, and reconstructed.

The bridge rests on cement block abutments laid on concrete footers. It is covered with a shake roof, vertical board and batten siding, and has a deck of lengthwise planking. The bridge provides a picturesque entrance to the campground, and there is a covered sidewalk on the downstream side. During our visit to the bridge in 2000, it seemed to be in the same condition as we observed in 1991 even though it is used quite heavily each camping season.

Richards / Reichard Bridge

Location: On Jepko Road (T 805, Northumberland County; no obvious markings in Columbia County), approximately 2.5 miles north of Bear Gap, Northumberland County. **Directions:** From the Northumberland County side of the Krickbaum bridge, travel through the bridge, and turn left on Happy Valley Road (T 302, Columbia County). Go 0.6 mile to junction (no road name visible), turn left, and continue 0.5 mile to an iron bridge. (You will pass a road entering from the right.) After an additional 0.4 mile, go straight on Bear Hollow Road (T 800, Northumberland County) for another 0.4 mile. Cross a concrete and iron bridge, travel to a "T", turn left to the covered bridge.

Year: 1852 / **Truss:** Multiple kingpost with queenpost
Waterway: Roaring Creek (South Branch)
In Use: Yes / **Number of Spans:** 1 / **Owner:** Counties
Builder: Obediah S. Campbell
Length: 63 ft. 8½ in./ **Width:** 13 ft. 4 in.
Condition: Fair / **Number:** PA-19-41/PA-49-07
Register: August 8, 1979

The information available on this bridge varies to some extent. The date of its construction ranges: 1852 in Zacher's *The Covered Bridges of Pennsylvania* and the *Statewide Covered Bridge Assessment*; "before 1871" in the Columbia County Historical Society's publication, *The Covered Bridges of Columbia County*; 1875 in the 1989 edition of the *World Guide to Covered Bridges*; and 1880 in the pamphlet printed by the Columbia-Montour Tourist Promotion Agency, Inc. The reports of the truss design also vary: queenpost in the *WGCB*, queenpost with modified Howe in Zacher's book, and multiple kingpost in the *SCBA*. Our personal observation and photograph, included herein, brought us to the conclusion that it is a modified multiple kingpost overlaid with a queenpost truss. (There are no metal rods evident, which would be present in a Howe truss.)

The bridge is built on skew, with offset portals and crosswise planking laid on a slight diagonal. It rests on concrete abutments, has concrete wingwalls and parapets, and is covered with vertical board siding. During our visit in 1991 we considered the bridge to be in good condition; however, since then there has been some deterioration. There are some loose siding boards, and the paint is peeling. While this is not detrimental to the bridge's continued use, repair of the loose boards and a coat of paint would definitely increase the life of this historic structure.

Ramp Bridge

Location: On Covered Bridge Road (T 387), approximately 2 miles southeast of Newburg, Hopewell Township. **Directions:** In Newburg, at the junction of PA 641 and PA 696 South, go east on PA 641 for 1.2 miles to Covered Bridge Road, turn right on Covered Bridge Road, and go 0.8 mile to the bridge.

Year: 1870 / **Truss:** Burr / **Waterway:** Conodoguinet Creek
In Use: Yes / **Number of Spans:** 1 / **Owner:** County
Builder: Unknown / **Length:** 128 ft. 6½ in. / **Width:** 16 ft. 5 in.
Condition: Fairly good / **Number:** PA-21-11
Register: August 25, 1980

This is the only remaining authentic covered bridge standing within Cumberland County. Its typical Burr truss system is adequately strong without additional steel reinforcement. It is covered with vertical boards and battens on the sides and horizontal clapboard siding on the portals. In addition to the lengthwise openings under the eaves, there is one window in the side near the end where the road curves. The roof is corrugated metal, and the deck is covered with runners laid over crosswise planking. In 2000, the area around the bridge was heavily overgrown with weeds and trees.

Stoner / Bowmansdale Bridge

Location: On the Messiah College campus, Grantham, between Upper Allen Township, Cumberland County and Monaghan Township, York County. **Directions:** At the northeast end of Grantham, at the junction of West Lisburn Road (SR 2004) and Grantham Road, go south on Grantham Road for 0.25 mile to a "T" on the Messiah College campus. Turn right at the "T" and go 0.4 mile, passing all the parking areas, to a "Y" intersection. Turn left at the "Y" and follow the road for 0.1 mile to the bridge. Turn right over the bridge to the athletic field parking area.

Year: 1867 / **Truss:** Burr / **Waterway:** Yellow Breeches Creek
In Use: Yes / **Number of Spans:** 1 / **Owner:** Private
Builder: Unknown / **Length:** 106 ft. 5½ in. / **Width:** 18 ft. 7½ in.
Condition: Good / **Number:** PA-21-13/PA-67-04 / **Register:**

This bridge was originally built in 1867 near Bowmansdale, just north of Grantham. In 1971, Mr. and Mrs. Jacob S. Stoner acquired the bridge and donated it to Messiah College, where it was rebuilt by the college students. The rebuilt bridge was completed in 1972, but can no longer be considered an authentic historic structure because of the extensive reconstruction. However, it is a lovely structure in a beautiful setting and the only remaining covered bridge connecting Cumberland and York counties. It is covered with vertical board and batten siding on both sides and portals, and has a shake roof. A concrete deck is laid over three heavy, lengthwise, concrete beams. In addition to the typical openings under the eaves, the Stoner Bridge has one long, narrow window on one side and two on the other. The bridge rests on concrete abutments that extend to long concrete wingwalls. These are topped with stone and mortar parapets that rise approximately two and one-half feet above road level. The bridge is used extensively by students traveling between the main classroom portion of the campus (on the Cumberland County side) and the southern, athletic field portion of the campus (on the York County side). During our visit in June 2000, we found the bridge in fine condition.

Henninger Farm / Henninger / Stroup Bridge

Location: Bypassed by Matter Road, 4.7 miles northeast of Elizabethville.
Directions: In Elizabethville, at the junction of US 209 and PA 225, go north on PA 225 for 2.3 miles to the junction with Rakers Mill Road (SR 1006). Turn right (east) on Rakers Mill Road and go 2 miles to Henninger Road, turn left on Henninger Road, and go 0.3 mile to Matter Road. Turn left on Matter Road and go 0.1 mile to the bypassed bridge on the left.

Year: Unknown, c.1850 / **Truss:** Burr / **Waterway:** Wisconisco Creek
In Use: Foot traffic only / **Number of Spans:** 1 / **Owner:** Township
Builder: Unknown / **Length:** 72 ft. 1½ in. / **Width:** 15 ft. 9 in.
Condition: Very good / **Number:** PA-22-11
Register: December 18, 1978

Until the Hurricane Agnes flood of 1972, there were nine covered bridges spanning the Wisconisco Creek in Dauphin County. This is the only remaining one, and it was bypassed by a new highway in the early part of 1991. Local covered bridge enthusiasts have preserved it, and the area surrounding it is being made into a recreational area.

The sides and portals are covered with white vertical boards, and the deck is lengthwise planking. The roof is new metal which has been painted red. The only side openings are the typical lengthwise ones under the eaves. The Henninger Farm Bridge rests on stone and mortar abutments that have been reinforced with concrete. It also has stone and mortar wingwalls and parapets that taper from approximately one and one-half feet at the portal to road level as they span out. Notice the interesting Burr arch truss in the photo. Unlike the usual Burr arch trusses which sandwich multiple kingposts, this does not. It is only on the inside of the multiple kingpost truss and has additional straight beams which follow the curve of the arch. These appear to be part of the original structure. During our visit in April 2000, the bridge still appeared to be in very good condition. Since that visit, we have learned that the bridge was the victim of arson later in 2000. We have unconfirmed reports that there is an interest in rebuilding the bridge.

Gudgeonville / Gudgeonville Road Bridge

Location: On Gudgeonville Road, approximately 3 miles east of Girard, Girard Township. **Directions:** From I 90, Exit 4 (PA 98), go south on PA 98 for 1.3 miles to Luther Road. Turn right on Luther Road and go 0.3 mile to Keefer Road. Turn right on Keefer Road and go 0.2 mile to Beckman Road, turn left on Beckman Road, and go 1.3 miles to Gudgeonville Road. Turn left on Gudgeonville Road and go 0.7 mile to the bridge.

Year: 1868 / **Truss:** Multiple kingpost / **Waterway:** Elk Creek
In Use: Yes / **Number of Spans:** 1 / **Owner:** Township
Builder: William Sherman / **Length:** 85 ft. 9 in. / **Width:** 14 ft. 1 in.
Condition: Good / **Number:** PA-25-03 / **Register:** September 17, 1980

This structure is nestled in a deep valley across Elk Creek, which has very high banks of a rather unusual, silt-like material that gives the appearance of solid rock walls. The bridge's sides and the inward, sloping portals are covered with unpainted, vertical board siding. The roof is made of metal, and the deck consists of runners laid over crosswise planking. The structure rests on cut stone abutments with wingwalls that do not reach road level. The truss timbers on one side of the bridge are charred, which gives one the impression that arson may have been attempted. During our visit in May 2000, we found that the bridge was structurally sound. A recently replaced sheet metal roof indicates that the bridge is being maintained. However, the general appearance of the bridge, especially the extensive amount of graffiti, was most disappointing.

Harrington / Sherman / Keepville Bridge

Location: On Barney Road, approximately 3 miles south of Cherry Hill, Conneaut Township. **Directions:** Approximately 2 miles west of Albion, at the junction of US 6 North and PA 215, go west on US 6 North for 1 mile to Barney Road, turn left on Barney Road, and go 1.5 miles to the bridge.

Year: 1870 / **Truss:** Multiple kingpost
Waterway: West Branch, Conneaut Creek
In Use: Yes / **Number of Spans:** 1 / **Owner:** Township
Builder: William Sherman / **Length:** 85 ft. / **Width:** 14 ft.
Condition: Fair / **Number:** PA-25-02 / **Register:** September 17, 1980

The Harrington Bridge has been heavily reinforced with four large, steel I-beams. These rest on poured concrete abutments which extend to create short, road-level wingwalls. The multiple kingpost truss structure is covered with vertical boards only on the bridge's sides. The gable portion of the sloping portal is framed, but it has no siding. The roof is covered with shakes, and the deck consists of crosswise planking resting on edge. The structure has no posted weight limit. While we have no documentation of maintenance on the structure since 1991, it is clearly being maintained. We noticed only one missing siding board in 2000, while there were a number missing at the time of our previous visit. The roof, however, does have some holes where the shakes are beginning to deteriorate. This will allow moisture to reach the truss and deck which will eventually lead to deterioration. It, like the Gudgeonville bridge, has a considerable amount of graffiti. This may indicate a lack of respect for these historic structures.

Waterford / Wattsburg Road Bridge

Location: On South East Street, just east of Waterford, Waterford Township. **Directions:** In Waterford, at the junction of US 19 and East First Street, go east on East First Street for 0.3 mile to South East Street. Turn right on South East Street and go 0.9 mile to the bridge.

Year: 1875 / **Truss:** Town / **Waterway:** Le Boeuf Creek
In Use: Yes / **Number of Spans:** 1 / **Owner:** Township
Builder: Charles Phelps and James Phelps
Length: 85 ft. 11 in / **Width:** 15 ft. 1 in.
Condition: Fairly poor / **Number:** PA-25-04 / **Register:** September 17, 1980

This is the only Town truss type covered bridge in Erie County, and also the only painted bridge in the county. A sign mounted on the gable end of the portal says "OLD KISSING BRIDGE built in 1875 by Phelps Bros." The sides and portals are covered with vertical boards painted barn red. The roof is covered with shakes, and the deck is covered with runners laid over crosswise planking set on edge. The abutments are poured concrete. Unlike the other bridges in this county, the Waterford Bridge has lengthwise openings under the eaves. There is an unusual, blue, metal pipe structure on the exterior of the bridge's southeast side; it may be connected to pipelines that run through the area. The framework supporting this pipework is of a kingpost design.

On our visit to the bridge in May 2000, we considered it to be in fairly poor condition, although it is still being used for vehicular traffic. There are holes in the deteriorating cedar shake roof that expose the truss and deck to inclement weather. The paint is peeling, and the side of the bridge (where energetic youth can reach it via the pipe structure previously mentioned) is covered with graffiti. Our feeling, in general, is that the bridges in this county are not being properly preserved as important, historic structures.

Martin's Mill / Martins Mill / Shindle Bridge

Location: On West Weaver Road (T 341), Antrim Township.
Directions: In Upton, at the junction of PA 16 and Letzburg Road (SR 9001, opposite PA 995 North), go south on Letzburg Road for 1.6 miles to West Weaver Road. Turn right on West Weaver Road and go 1.1 miles to the junction with Worleytown Road, cross Worleytown Road, and continue 1.1 miles to the bridge.

Year: 1839 / **Truss:** Town / **Waterway:** Conococheague Creek
In Use: Yes, 4 times a year / **Number of Spans:** 2
Owner: Private
Builder: Jacob Shirk / **Length:** 206 ft. / **Width:** 14 ft. 8½ in.
Condition: Very good / **Number:** PA-28-01
Register: February 15, 1974

This bridge is reported to be the longest remaining Town truss type covered bridge in Pennsylvania. It was reconstructed after the Hurricane Agnes flood of 1972. At the time of our visit in 1991, the bridge had been closed to all traffic since 1986, was heavily covered with graffiti, and appeared to be in very poor condition. In the past nine years, through the efforts of the Martin's Mill Covered Bridge Society, much has been done to improve the structural integrity of the bridge and its overall appearance. In 1993, Greencastle Metal Works installed four steel frames to brace the bridge, and Geesaman-Rock Construction, Inc., Zullinger, PA, was contracted to shore it up and level it. The anticipated cost was

$37,000, and of that figure, $18,000 was provided by the state, $7,000 came from the association treasury, and the rest was borrowed from a local bank to be paid off with donations and fundraisers. Also in 1993, the central stone pier was rebuilt, and volunteers stripped and repainted the entire structure. A rededication ceremony was held on August 13, 1995. In the spring of 1998, the Department of Community and Economic Development allocated a $58,000 grant to the Society to divert water from the bridge pier and abutments, and to stabilize the banks and surrounding trees with gabions. The stabilized trusses, rebuilt center pier, new cedar shake roof, new siding, new portals, and new paint of the restored bridge marks a striking improvement since 1991. The bridge is now open for vehicular traffic only four times a year—Memorial Day, July 4, Labor Day, and the second week of December.

Witherspoon Bridge

Location: On an unmarked road, approximately 5 miles southeast of Mercersburg, Montgomery Township. **Directions:** Approximately 2.6 miles southeast of Mercersburg, where PA 416 and PA 16 divide, continue east on PA 16 for 1.3 miles to Anderson Road (SR 9081 / T 328). Turn right on Anderson Road and go 1.2 miles to an unmarked road, turn left, and go 0.1 mile to the bridge.

Year: 1883 / **Truss:** Burr / **Waterway:** Licking Creek
In Use: Yes / **Number of Spans:** 1 / **Owner:** County
Builder: S. Stouffer / **Length:** 86 ft. 5 in. / **Width:** 13 ft. 11 in.
Condition: Good / **Number:** PA-28-02 / **Register:**

The Witherspoon Bridge is the only remaining covered bridge in Franklin County still used for vehicular traffic on a daily basis. The bridge's sides are covered with vertical board and batten siding, the portals with horizontal boards, and the roof with sheet metal. The deck consists of crosswise planks laid diagonally. The structure rests on stone and mortar abutments, and has relatively long stone and mortar wingwalls that rise to moderately high, concrete-capped parapets. The bridge is not only in good condition, but is located in a lovely setting in the southwestern part of the county.

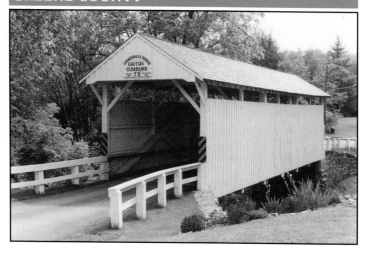

Carmichaels Bridge

Location: On Old Town Road (T 684) in Carmichaels, Cumberland Township. **Directions:** In Carmichaels, at the intersection of E. George Street (PA 88) and Vine Street (SR 1021), go east on Vine Street for 1 block to Market Street. Turn left (north) on Market Street and go 0.2 mile to Old Town Road; turn left to bridge.

Year: 1889 / **Truss:** Queenpost / **Waterway:** Muddy Creek
In Use: Yes / **Number of Spans:** 1 / **Owner:** County
Builder: Unknown / **Length:** 64 ft. 8 in. / **Width:** 13 ft. 8 in.
Condition: Excellent / **Number:** PA-30-21 / **Register:** June 22, 1979

This is one of eight covered bridges still standing within the boundaries of Greene County. Every one of the eight bridges is still in use for vehicular traffic. All are either painted white or left unpainted, and all are built with either a kingpost or queenpost truss design. The Carmichaels Bridge is covered with white, vertical board and batten siding on both the sides and portals. It has a roof of cedar shakes and a deck of lengthwise runners laid over crosswise planking. The structure rests on cut stone-and-mortar abutments that extend to road-level wingwalls. One of the abutments has been reinforced with concrete. The queenpost truss is reinforced with additional diagonal timbers and five steel I-beams under the deck. During our visit to Greene County in 1991 we considered this bridge to be in good condition; upon our return in 2000 we found it in excellent condition. Its improved state is attributed to the extensive refurbishing of the bridge, which was completed in time for the Washington–Greene County Covered Bridge Festival held in Fall 1998. The bridge was rededicated during this festival.

Cox Farm / Lippincott Bridge

Location: On an unnamed road (T 568), Lippincott, Morgan Township.
Directions: In the west end of Lippincott, just south of PA 221, on T 568.

Year: 1940 / **Truss:** Kingpost / **Waterway:** Ruff Creek
In Use: Yes / **Number of Spans:** 1 / **Owner:** County
Builder: Unknown / **Length:** 31 ft. 10 in. / **Width:** 12 ft 7½ in.
Condition: Fair / **Number:** PA-30-25 / **Register:** June 22, 1979

The Cox Farm Bridge, like most of the other Greene County covered bridges, is located on a fairly heavily traveled township road in an open, rural area. The roof is covered with sheet metal, the deck is covered with cross wise planking, and the sides and portals are covered with white, shiplapped siding. The interior walls are covered with similar siding from the portal to the diagonal timbers of the kingpost truss (the lower three and one-half feet of the interior walls). The structure rests on one abutment of stone-and-mortar reinforced with concrete, and one which is completely concrete. The abutments are extended to form short, concrete wingwalls and parapets that rise approximately one and one-half feet above road level. The kingpost truss structure is heavily reinforced with five steel I-beams, but only carries a three-ton load limit. On our visit in May 2000, we found the gable end of one of the portals badly damaged, and since there were no apparent improvements to the bridge, we considered it to be only in fair condition.

King Bridge

Location: On King Sister Hill Road (TR 371), approximately 1 mile south of Kuhntown, Wayne Township. **Directions:** In Kuhntown, at the junction of SR 3013 and Bells Run Road (TR 472), go south on SR 3013 for 1.1 miles to King Sister Hill Road; turn right to the bridge.

Year: 1890 / **Truss:** Queenpost / **Waterway:** Hoovers Run
In Use: Yes / **Number of Spans:** 1 / **Owner:** County
Builder: Unknown / **Length:** 56 ft. 3 in. / **Width:** 14 ft. 8 in.
Condition: Fair / **Number:** PA-30-24 / **Register:** June 22, 1979

This bridge is covered with unpainted, random-width vertical board siding on both the sides and the portals. The roof is covered with sheet metal and the deck with crosswise planking. The structure rests on cut stone abutments which are extended to form short wingwalls slightly higher than road level. The King Bridge has typical, narrow, lengthwise openings under the eaves, and there are no evident steel reinforcements. The bridge carries vehicular traffic up to a three-ton limit. There has been some maintenance work done on the bridge since our visit in 1991. In May 2000, we found that some of the missing siding boards had been replaced, and only one board on one of the portal gables was missing.

Neddie Woods / Nettie Woods Bridge

Location: On Woods Road (TR 582), approximately 1 mile north of Oak Forest, Center Township. **Directions:** Just south of East View, at the junction of PA 18/PA 21 and Oak Forest Road (SR 3013), go south on Oak Forest Road for 1.8 miles to Woods Road (TR 582). The bridge is just to the right on Woods Road.

Year: 1882 / **Truss:** Queenpost / **Waterway:** Pursley Creek
In Use: Yes / **Number of Spans:** 1 / **Owner:** County
Builder: Lisbon Scott / **Length:** 45 ft. 5½ in. / **Width:** 15 ft. 4 in.
Condition: Fairly good / **Number:** PA-30-26 / **Register:** June 22, 1979

The Neddie Woods covered bridge is another bridge located in the open countryside of Greene County. It is covered with unpainted, vertical board siding on both the sides and portals, the roof is made of corrugated sheet metal, and the deck is covered with crosswise planking. The only side openings are fairly wide, lengthwise ones immediately under the eaves. The structure is reinforced with five steel I-beams and rests on cut stone abutments that appear to have been laid dry. The stone abutments extend to moderately long wingwalls and interesting, low, step-like parapets that rise along the sides of one approach. The bridge has a posted load limit of four tons. While some of the siding has been slightly damaged by high water and natural weathering, the bridge still remains in fairly good condition.

Scott Bridge

Location: On Covered Bridge Road, approximately 1.4 miles east of Rutan and 3 miles west of Rogersville, Center Township.
Directions: Approximately 1.4 miles east of Rutan and 3 miles west of Rogersville, at the junction of PA 21 and Covered Bridge Road (TR 424) go south on Covered Bridge Road for 0.1 mile to the bridge.

Year: 1885 / **Truss:** Queenpost / **Waterway:** Ten Mile Creek
In Use: Yes / **Number of Spans:** 1 / **Owner:** County
Builder: William Lang / **Length:** 48 ft. 5 in. / **Width:** 14 ft. 10 in.
Condition: Fair / **Number:** PA-30-28 / **Register:** June 22, 1979

This bridge is covered with unpainted, vertical boards on both the sides and portals. There is a roof of sheet metal and a deck of runners laid over crosswise planking. One side window is cut into the center of the queenpost truss structure in addition to the typical, lengthwise openings under the eaves. The structure has been reinforced with steel I-beams and rests on cut stone abutments. While there were no dramatic differences in this bridge between 1991 and 2000, there was evidence that it is being maintained. Some of the deteriorating or missing siding had been replaced with new lumber.

Shriver Bridge

Location: On Turkey Hollow Road (TR 454), approximately 2 miles south of Rogersville, Center Township. **Directions:** Just west of Rogersville, at the junction of PA 18 and PA 21, go south on PA 18 (Golden Oaks Road) for 0.5 mile to the junction with Hargus Creek Road (SR 3011). Turn left on Hargus Creek Road for 0.9 mile to Turkey Hollow Road (TR 454); turn left on Turkey Hollow Road for 0.1 mile to the bridge.

Year: 1900 / **Truss:** Queenpost / **Waterway:** Hargus Creek
In Use: Yes / **Number of Spans:** 1 / **Owner:** County
Builder: Unknown / **Length:** 46 ft. 5 in. / **Width:** 15 ft. 2½ in.
Condition: Fairly good / **Number:** PA-30-29 / **Register:** June 22, 1979

Another of the queenpost truss structures located in the open countryside of Greene County, this bridge is covered with random-width, unpainted, vertical board siding on both the sides and the portals. The Shriver Bridge has a sheet metal roof and a deck of crosswise planking. The only side openings are fairly wide, length-wise ones immediately under the eaves. The bridge is reinforced with steel I-beams, and it rests on cut stone abutments that appear to have been laid dry. The wingwalls and relatively low, short parapets are made of similar cut stone material and extend a little above road level. The parapets have a step-like pattern similar to that of the Neddie Woods Bridge.

White Bridge

Location: On Roberts Run Road (T 604), approximately 2.5 miles west of Girards Fort, Greene Township. **Directions:** From I 79 South, Girards Fort/Kirby Exit (Exit 2), at the end of the exit ramp, turn left on SR 2018. Go 1.6 miles to a "T" with SR 2011. Turn right on SR 2011 and go 0.6 mile to Roberts Run Road (T 604), turn right on Roberts Run Road, and go 0.1 mile to the bridge.

Year: 1919 / **Truss:** Queenpost / **Waterway:** Whitely Creek
In Use: Yes / **Number of Spans:** 1 / **Owner:** County
Builder: Unknown / **Length:** 70 ft. 2 in. / **Width:** 14 ft. 11 in.
Condition: Good / **Number:** PA-30-30 / **Register:** June 22, 1979

Most sources list the original construction date of this bridge as 1919. The *Statewide Covered Bridge Assessment*, however, states that the bridge was built in 1900. The White Bridge is located just a short distance from the former site of the Red/Neils Bridge, which was destroyed by arson. The White Bridge has an exceptionally high queenpost truss structure with a 17 ft., 6 in. clearance. In 1991, the posted load limit was ten tons; however, on our return to the bridge in May 2000, we found the posted limit reduced to four tons. There is no evidence of steel reinforcements. The bridge is covered with white, vertical, tongue-and-groove board siding on both the sides and the portals, and the roof is covered with sheet metal. The deck consists of runners laid over diagonal, crosswise planking. The structure rests on cut stone and mortar abutments. There are short, cut stone and mortar wingwalls that rise to fairly high parapets. The bridge has typical, narrow, lengthwise openings under the eaves. The only apparent maintenance required on the bridge when we saw it in 2000 was the need for paint. It is beginning to peel noticeably.

Wren's Nest Bridge

Location: Just west of Aleppo Road, approximately 1.5 miles north of Aleppo. **Directions:** In Aleppo, at the junction of SR 3012 (Green Valley Road) and SR 3001 (Aleppo Road), go north on Aleppo Road for 1.5 miles. The bridge is just to the left at the beginning of a private lane.

Year: 1993 / **Truss:** Kingpost / **Waterway:** Wheeling Creek
In Use: Yes, private only / **Number of Spans:** 1 / **Owner:** Private
Builder: Frederick V. McCracken
Length: 28 ft. 6½ in. / **Width:** 11 ft. 4½ in.
Condition: Good / **Number:** PA-30-33 / **Register:**

The Wren's Nest Bridge appeared in Greene County since we prepared the first edition of *Pennsylvania's Covered Bridges*. It is located in a lovely, quiet valley in the western part of the county. It is not mentioned in *The World Guide to Covered Bridges*, *The Statewide Covered Bridge Assessment*, Susan Zacher's *The Covered Bridges of Pennsylvania*, or the *Pennsylvania Covered Bridge List* prepared by the Theodore Burr Covered Bridge Society. It was, however, called to our attention by several avid "bridgers" of the Theodore Burr Covered Bridge Society. In order to locate the bridge, we had to detour from our 1991 excursion route by a few miles, but it was well worth the effort. The Wren's Nest Bridge is an authentic kingpost truss structure built in 1993 by Frederick V. McCracken. The bridge was commissioned by Richard and Eloise Davison to provide access to their home, which is located beyond Wheeling Creek, opposite Aleppo Road. This relatively new bridge is covered with unpainted, vertical board siding, which has weathered quite a bit. It has a sheet metal roof, and is placed on concrete abutments that extend to short concrete wingwalls. The deck is covered with crosswise planks, and the bridge has no additional steel substructure It makes an appropriate entrance to the Davison's rustic home, which is situated on a hillside several hundred yards from the bridge.

Saint Mary's / Saint Marys / Shade Gap Bridge

Location: On Covered Bridge Road (TR 358), 2.5 miles north of Shade Gap, Cromwell Township. **Directions:** In Shade Gap, at the junction of PA 35 and PA 522, go north on PA 522 for 2.4 miles to Covered Bridge Road. Turn right on Covered Bridge Road to the bridge, which is located directly across PA 522 from St. Mary's Roman Catholic Church.

Year: 1889 / **Truss:** Howe / **Waterway:** Shade Creek
In Use: Yes / **Number of Spans:** 1 / **Owner:** County
Builder: Unknown / **Length:** 64 ft. 8 in. / **Width:** 13 ft. 4 in.
Condition: Very good / **Number:** PA-31-01 / **Register:** March 20, 1980

Of all the bridges we visited in Pennsylvania, this one is in one of the most picturesque settings. It is the only remaining covered bridge in Huntingdon County; consequently, the county has taken extensive measures to preserve it. It is heavily reinforced with steel, which allows it to accommodate up to twenty-three tons. The lower half of the exterior walls are covered with vertical boards, and the matching half of the interior walls are covered with horizontal boards. The exposed upper half of the bridge allows visitors to easily see the Howe truss system. The portals have horizontal boards on the gable ends and vertical boards on the side posts. The structure rests on new, concrete abutments, and the old, stone-and-mortar wingwalls are still standing well below road level. The bridge is well maintained. The only repairs for which we have documentation were completed in 1996. At that time, a large hole in the south side, ripped by flood waters, was mended. The nearest covered bridge is approximately forty miles away in Perry County, but it is worth the time and travel to seek out this lovely structure.

Harmon's Bridge

Location: Bypassed by Donahue Road (T 488), approximately 1.6 miles east of Willet, Washington Township. **Directions:** Just east of Willet, at the junction of PA 954 and Five Points Road (SR 4006), go northeast on Five Points Road for 1.6 miles to Donahue Road. Turn right on Donahue Road and go 0.1 mile to the bridge.

Year: 1910 / **Truss:** Town / **Waterway:** Plum Creek (South Branch)
In Use: Foot traffic only / **Number of Spans:** 1 / **Owner:** County
Builder: John R. Carnahan / **Length:** 45 ft. 9 in. / **Width:** 12 ft. 1½ in.
Condition: Fair / **Number:** PA-32-04 / **Register:** August 3, 1979

There almost always seems to be something that the covered bridges in a given county have in common, and the bridges in Indiana County are no exception. The common feature of the four covered bridges in this county is the shape of each bridge when viewed from the side. All are trapezoidal in shape, having parallel lines along the top and the bottom, but side lines that are nearer at the bottom and slope noticeably outward to the top. This shape should be evident in all the photographs taken in this county. In addition, of the four covered bridges, three have Town truss designs. Although only one covered bridge in Indiana County is being used for vehicular traffic, the county has done a good job of preserving all of the remaining covered structures.

The Harmon's Bridge, just about one-half mile from the Trusal Bridge as the crow flies, is being preserved by the county in a park-like setting. It was bypassed by a new wooden bridge in 1984.

This new bridge, with the exception of the concrete abutments and macadam road surface, is constructed of heavy, laminated, creosote-treated wooden beams, planks, and guardrails. The new bridge bypassing the Trusal Bridge is of similar construction.

The Harmon Bridge is covered with random-width vertical boards on both the sides and portals, has a sheet metal roof and a deck of crosswise planking. It rests on cut stone abutments and has no wingwalls. Both the Harmon's Bridge and the Trusal Bridge are in lovely, pastoral settings. All of the bridges in this county are within easy driving distance of the county seat, Indiana, and are all within fifteen to twenty miles of each other. They are well worth seeking if you are in the central to western part of the state.

Kintersburg Bridge

Location: Bypassed by Musser Road (T 612), Kintersburg, Rayne Township. **Directions:** In Kintersburg, at the junction of Tonoma Road (T 809/SR 1005) and Musser Road, go south on Musser Road for 0.2 mile to the bypassed bridge.

Year: 1877 / **Truss:** Howe / **Waterway:** Crooked Creek
In Use: Foot traffic only / **Number of Spans:** 1 / **Owner:** County
Builder: J. S. Fleming / **Length:** 68 ft. / **Width:** 14 ft.½ in.
Condition: Good / **Number:** PA-32-05 / **Register:** August 3, 1979

This bridge is one of the few Howe truss structures left in the state of Pennsylvania and is the only one in Indiana County. It does, however, have the same trapezoidal shape as the other bridges in the county, and is in a similarly pastoral setting. It, too, has random-width vertical boards on both sides and portals, has a sheet metal roof, and has a deck of lengthwise random-width planking. It rests on cut stone and mortar abutments reinforced with concrete. It also has some additional vertical timbers supporting the deck, located on concrete footings a short distance from each end. The only side openings on any of the Indiana covered spans are the narrow lengthwise ones immediately under the eaves.

Thomas Ford Bridge

Location: On Thomas Covered Bridge Road (T 415), approximately 1 mile east of Thomas, Armstrong Township. **Directions:** Approximately 5.5 miles west of Indiana, at the junction of US 422 and Cheese Run Road (T 408), go west on Cheese Run Road for 1.4 miles. Continue to the left for another 0.7 mile until you reach a "T" with Thomas Covered Bridge Road. Turn left on Thomas Covered Bridge Road and go 0.3 mile to the bridge.

Year: 1879 / **Truss:** Town / **Waterway:** Crooked Creek
In Use: Yes / **Number of Spans:** 1 / **Owner:** County
Builder: Amos Thomas / **Length:** 86 ft. 9 in. / **Width:** 13 ft. 3 in.
Condition: Excellent / **Number:** PA-32-06 (2) / **Register:** August 3, 1979

This is the only covered bridge in the county that is being used for vehicular traffic and the only one that has had restoration work done since our visit in 1991. The restoration, at a cost of $650,819, was completed by June 23, 1998 when the bridge was rededicated. The restored bridge sits a little higher than the original because it, like many other restorations throughout the state, has been placed on new, stone-faced, concrete abutments with road-level wingwalls. Additionally, the bridge has been placed on massive, steel stringers to support the original Town truss structure. Otherwise, with the exception of the slightly longer side boards, it conforms to its original historic design. Like the other bridges in Indiana County, the Thomas Ford bridge has vertical board siding on both the sides and portals, a corrugated metal roof, and a deck of lengthwise planking. The reconstructed span now supports a twenty-ton load. The recently painted structure, with its barn red sides and white portals, should stand long, tall, and proud for many generations to come.

Trusal / Dice's Bridge

Location: Bypassed by Trusal Road (T 406), approximately 1.1 miles east of Willet, Washington Township. **Directions:** Just east of Willet, at the junction of PA 954 and Five Points Road (SR 4006), go northeast on Five Points Road for 1.1 miles to Trusal Road, turn right on Trusal Road and go 0.2 mile to the bypassed bridge.

Year: 1870 / **Truss:** Town / **Waterway:** Plum Creek (South Branch)
In Use: Foot traffic only / **Number of Spans:** 1 / **Owner:** County
Builder: Unknown / **Length:** 41 ft. 5 in. / **Width:** 11 ft. 10 in.
Condition: Fairly good / **Number:** PA-32-03 / **Register:** August 3, 1979

Covered with vertical, random-width boards on both sides and portals, a sheet metal roof, and a deck of lengthwise planking, this bridge rests on stone and mortar abutments that have been reinforced with concrete At the time of our visit in 1991, the bridge had recently been bypassed, and little had been done to the surrounding area. Since then, the county has created a park-like setting surrounding the Trusal Bridge. If one looks off to the east, the Harmon Bridge can be seen just one-half mile away, crossing the same stream.

McCracken Bridge

Location: On Moore Bridge Road (SR 4006), 0.5 mile west of Richardsville, Warsaw Township. **Directions:** In Richardsville, at the junction of SR 4005 and Moore Bridge Road (SR 4006), go west on Moore Bridge Road for 0.5 mile to the Wakefield Springs Farm. The bridge is on the left side of the road. The McCrackens welcome all "bridgers."

Year: 1975 / **Truss:** Kingpost / **Waterway:** Wakefield Springs
In Use: Private, foot traffic only / **Number of Spans:** 1 / **Owner:** Private
Builder: William McCracken / **Length:** 24 ft. 2 in. / **Width:** 9 ft. 11 in.
Condition: Good / **Number:** PA-33-03 / **Register:** Does not qualify

This bridge was completed in 1975 by William McCracken, the present owner of the Wakefield Springs Farm. He used hand-hewn timbers, salvaged from an old barn, to provide the basic kingpost truss members. This bridge is not considered an authentic historic structure. It is not included in *The Covered Bridges of Pennsylvania* by Susan Zacher or in the list of Pennsylvania covered bridges prepared by the Theodore Burr Covered Bridge Society of Pennsylvania. It does, however, appear in the *World Guide to Covered Bridges.* McCracken has done an excellent job of creating a structure very much in the tradition of nineteenth century historical bridges. The sides and portals are covered with vertical board siding, the roof with asphalt shingles, and the deck with crosswise planking. The entire structure is resting on cut stone abutments with cut stone wingwalls. The McCracken Bridge was built across the overflow of a spring running from a lovely, round, brick springhouse (also built by McCracken). Visitors are always welcome at the Wakefield Spring Farm. When we visited in May 2000, Bill told us that a family of groundhogs had set up housekeeping near one of the bridge abutments, which could be a problem. So, unfortunately, an eviction of the family was in his future plans. Otherwise, the bridge is in fine condition.

Academia / Pomeroy Bridge

Location: Just to the right of Mill Hill Road (T 334), southeast of Academia, between Beale and Spruce Hill Townships. **Directions:** Approximately 4 miles south of Port Royal on PA 75 south, at the junction with SR 3013, follow SR 3013 for 1.9 miles to Mill Hill Road. Turn right on Mill Hill Road and go 0.1 mile. The bridge is just to the right.

Year: 1870 / **Truss:** Burr / **Waterway:** Tuscarora Creek
In Use: No, closed / **Number of Spans:** 2 / **Owner:** Private
Builder: James M. Groninger / **Length:** 278 ft. 6½ in. / **Width:** 16 ft. 2 in.
Condition: Poor / **Number:** PA-34-01 / **Register:** August 10, 1979

There are three documented dates for the origin of this bridge—1870 in the *Statewide Covered Bridge Assessment*, 1901 in the *World Guide to Covered Bridges*, and 1902 in Zacher's book, *The Covered Bridges of Pennsylvania*. The bridge is now owned by the Juniata County Historical Society, and is one of the longest covered bridges still standing in Pennsylvania. Its exact length also varies depending on the account—the *SCBA* and Zacher indicate 270 feet, the *WGCB* lists 305 feet. In April 2000, we measured the bridge, portal to portal, at 278 feet, 6½ inches.

The Academia Bridge is covered with unpainted, random-width, vertical board on the sides. There is board and batten siding on the portals; however, most of the battens are missing. The deck is covered with narrow, crosswise planking, and the bridge has a metal roof. The two-span Burr arch truss structure rests on stone-and-mortar abutments and a central stone-and-mortar pier. The bridge also has stone-and-mortar wingwalls and parapets. In addition to the lengthwise openings under the eaves, there is one window on each side of the bridge, located directly above the center pier.

Dimmsville Bridge

Location: Bypassed by SR 2017, just north of Dimmsville, Greenwood Township. **Directions:** Just north of Dimmsville, at the junction of PA 235 and SR 2017, go south on SR 2017 for 0.8 mile to the bridge. The bridge is just south of SR 2017, adjacent to a cleared storage area.

Year: 1902 / **Truss:** Burr / **Waterway:** Cocolamus Creek
In Use: Foot traffic only / **Number of Spans:** 1 / **Owner:** Private
Builder: Unknown / **Length:** 109 ft. 2 in. / **Width:** 15 ft. 3½ in.
Condition: Poor / **Number:** PA-34-02 / **Register:** August 10, 1979

This bridge has been bypassed with a new concrete and steel bridge. During our 1991 visit, we found the area heavily overgrown, and the bridge used only for limited foot traffic. At the time of our April 2000 visit, we noticed that the area around it, at least on one end, has been cleared. The Dimmsville Bridge is covered with vertical boards on both sides and portals. It has a metal roof, and a deck of very narrow crosswise planks. There are rectangular windows in the center on each side, in addition to the lengthwise openings under the eaves. The structure rests on stone-and-mortar abutments with stone-and-mortar wingwalls and parapets that rise just a little above the original road level. Gabions have been placed on the upstream side of the abutments to prevent washout. While the photo does not show it, one end of the structure leans noticeably.

Lehman's / Port Royal / McCulloch's / Mayer's Bridge

Location: On Mayer Road (T 421), Port Royal, Milford Township.
Directions: In Port Royal, at the junction of PA 75 and PA 333, go north on PA 333 for 0.2 mile to Mayer Road. Turn left on Mayer Road to the bridge. The bridge is on private property formerly owned by the Lehmans. Please acquire permission before entering the property.

Year: 1888 / **Truss:** Stringer / **Waterway:** Licking Creek
In Use: Yes, private only / **Number of Spans:** 2 / **Owner:** Private
Builder: Unknown / **Length:** 109 ft. 9 in. / **Width:** 12 ft. 7 in.
Condition: Good / **Number:** PA-34-04 / **Register:** August 10, 1979

From 1969 until a short time ago, this bridge was owned by Kenneth and Lucy Lehman. Recently, James and Susan Sheaffer purchased the Lehman farm property and with it, the Lehman Bridge. It was formerly known as McColloch's Bridge, Mayer's Bridge, and the Port Royal Bridge. After it was toppled by the Hurricane Agnes storm in 1972, the Lehmans had the bridge rebuilt from the original timbers, but not with the original truss design. It is now a two-span, steel supported stringer structure, but Burr type arches are attached to the interior in order to make the bridge appear more authentic. Mr. Lehman related that after the stringer structure was completed, he realized that something was missing. He then asked the contractor to add the Burr type arches to improve the bridge's appearance. The bridge has a lovely setting, and is used regularly as an entrance to the farm property.

East Oriental / Meiser's Mill / Schaeffer Bridge

Location: On private land, east of Oriental, primarily in Snyder County, Perry Township. **Directions:** In Oriental, from the junction of SR 2023 and SR 2024, go east on SR 2024 for 0.4 mile to a concrete bridge. The covered bridge can be seen to the left (north). Continue on SR 2024 across the county line for an additional 0.2 mile to Snapper Road. Turn left on Snapper Road to the first house on the right side of the road. Permission to get close to the bridge must be acquired from the owner.

Year: 1907 / **Truss:** Burr / **Waterway:** Mahantango Creek
In Use: Closed, private / **Number of Spans:** 1 / **Owner:** Private
Builder: Unknown / **Length:** 90 ft. / **Width:** 16 ft. 1 in.
Condition: Poor / **Number:** PA-34-06/PA-55-06
Register: August 10, 1979

Carol Strawser, the owner of ninety percent of the East Oriental Bridge (the portion in Snyder County), would like to do everything possible to restore this structure. Her neighbor in Juniata County, however, shows little interest in his ten percent. The bridge is located near a lovely, old mill which is also on the Strawser property. The bridge has vertical board and batten siding on both sides and portals, a sheet metal roof, and a deck of lengthwise planking laid over crosswise planking. It rests on stone-and-mortar abutments with stone-and-mortar wingwalls, and has no additional steel reinforcements. The only openings are the lengthwise ones under the eaves. When we visited the bridge in April 2000, there was no change in the condition of the bridge, but Ms. Strawser still has hopes of restoring this historic structure.

North Oriental / Oriental / Curry's Corner / Beaver Bridge

Location: On SR 2023, just north of Oriental, Juniata County.
Directions: In Oriental, from the junction of SR 2023 and SR 2024, go north on SR 2023 for 2 miles to the bridge.

Year: 1908 / **Truss:** Queenpost with kingpost
Waterway: Mahantango Creek
In Use: Yes / **Number of Spans:** 1 / **Owner:** State
Builder: Unknown / **Length:** 68 ft. 11 in. / **Width:** 14 ft. 4½ in.
Condition: Good / **Number:** PA-34-05/PA-55-05
Register: August 10, 1979

This bridge was rebuilt in 1987 after it had been damaged by a truck. The rebuilt structure is covered with vertical board and batten siding on both the sides and portals. It has a sheet metal roof, a deck of crosswise planks, steel reinforcing under the deck, and heavy steel guardrails protecting the portals. The structure has a multiple kingpost truss system overlaid by a queenpost truss. It rests on what appear to be new stone-and-mortar abutments laid on a poured concrete footing, and it has low, road-level wingwalls. The sides are completely closed except for the typical lengthwise openings under the eaves. The deck has been heavily reinforced with I-beams. It is obvious that this bridge is well maintained. We considered it to be in good condition at the time our visit in April 2000. However, on June 2, 2000, between 3:00 and 5:00 P.M., an oversized vehicle was driven through the bridge. This act damaged the portal on the north end, loosened all the angle braces and the roof stringers, and completely removed the portal on the south end. After hearing of the damage, we returned to the bridge on June 4 and found it closed until repairs could be completed. Fortunately, these repairs were carried out in a reasonably short period of time. Reports that we received early in July indicated that the bridge is again open to traffic. Hopefully, the person responsible for the damage will be appropriately assessed for the repairs to the bridge.

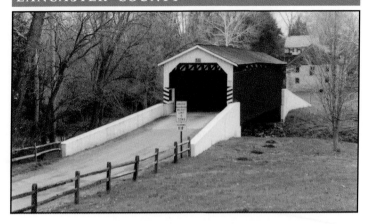

Baumgardner's Mill / Pequea 10 Bridge

Location: On Covered Bridge Road, Marticville, between Pequea and Martic Townships. **Directions:** In the village of Marticville, at the junction of PA 324 and Frogtown Road (T 415), go east on Frogtown Road for 0.5 mile to Covered Bridge Road (T 425). Turn left on Covered Bridge Road and travel for 0.4 mile to the bridge.

Year: 1860 / **Truss:** Burr / **Waterway:** Pequea Creek
In Use: Yes / **Number of Spans:** 1 / **Owner:** County
Builder: Davis Kitch / **Length:** 115 ft. 9½ in. / **Width:** 15 ft. 1 in.
Condition: Good / **Number:** PA-36-25 / **Register:** December 11, 1980

Lancaster County lays claim to more covered bridges than any other county in Pennsylvania. It has twenty-eight covered bridges within its borders and two on the border with Chester County. Like the bridges in many other counties, the bridges in Lancaster have some common characteristics. They all have the familiar triangular-shaped gables above the portals, narrow lengthwise openings under the eaves, and all but one of the bridges use the Burr truss system.

The Baumgardner's Mill Bridge was reconstructed in 1987 and is in fine condition. The mill for which it was named is no longer standing, and though reports indicate that the ruins are still along the banks of Pequea Creek, no trace of them was evident when we visited. The bridge is in a lovely valley below a new, modern home which sits on the hillside above. The photo was taken from the lower part of the new home's driveway. The siding is made up of the typical, vertical boards and battens. The only side openings are the narrow lengthwise ones located under the eaves. The reconstruction of the bridge included the replacement of an older tin roof with wooden shingles. The bridge now rests on concrete abutments with long, concrete wingwalls and parapets.

Bitzer's Mill / Eberly's Cider Mill Bridge

Location: On Cider Mill Road, north of Farmersville, West Earl Township. **Directions:** From the junction of US 222 and PA 322, southwest of Ephrata, go east on PA 322 for 0.9 mile to Cabin Road (T 785). Turn right (south) on Cabin Road to Conestoga Creek Road. Continue straight on Conestoga Creek Road (do not turn right) for 0.4 mile to Cider Mill Road. Turn left for 0.1 mile to the bridge.

Year: 1846 / **Truss:** Burr / **Waterway:** Conestoga Creek
In Use: Yes / **Number of Spans:** 1 / **Owner:** State
Builder: George Fink and Sam Reamsnyder
Length: 98 ft. 9 in. / **Width:** 14 ft. 9½ in.
Condition: Very good / **Number:** PA-36-04
Register: December 10, 1980

Reported to be the oldest state owned bridge in Pennsylvania, the Bitzer's Mill Bridge was nearly replaced by a concrete slab bridge around 1962. Happily, protests of the local residents persuaded the state to restore the covered bridge, instead. The remarkable history of this bridge, however, continued. In the early 1970s there were at least three attempts by arsonists to destroy the bridge, in spite of a slogan carved in the Burr arch which reads: "ETERNITY! Where will you spend it? Your choice. Heaven or Hell." During the mid-1990s the bridge was closed for a period of time, but bridge society publications indicate that is was reopened in the summer of 1997 after a new metal roof was installed. The bridge is now in very good condition, except for some graffiti which has been sprayed on the inside.

The Bitzer's Mill Bridge is similar in style and design to Weaver's Mill Bridge, also in Lancaster County. Both bridges are covered with vertical board and batten siding on the sides and the portals and have sheet metal roofs. Like many other covered bridges, the Bitzer's Mill Bridge has had several names including Fiand's Mill Bridge. It, too, is in a lovely setting.

Bucher's Mill / Cocalico 2 Bridge

Location: On Cocalico Creek Road (T 955), Reamstown, East Cocalico Township. **Directions:** In Reamstown, from the junction of PA 272 and Church Street, go south on PA 272 for 0.5 mile to Conestoga Creek Road (T 746). Turn left (east) on Conestoga Creek Road for 0.1 mile to Cocalico Creek Road. The bridge is just to the right on Cocalico Creek Road.

Year: 1892 / **Truss:** Burr / **Waterway:** Cocalico Creek
In Use: Yes / **Number of Spans:** 1 / **Owner:** County
Builder: Elias McMellen / **Length:** 73 ft. 1 in. / **Width:** 14 ft. 1 in.
Condition: Very good / **Number:** PA-36-12
Register: December 11, 1980

The first bridge on this site was built in 1892; just one year later, the flood of 1893 carried it downstream, even negotiating a horse-shoe bend. All the twisting and turning was too much for the wooden structure, and it was almost damaged beyond repair. It was, however, rebuilt in 1893 by the original builder. By 1966, the old bridge had deteriorated quite extensively, and, although there was talk of tearing it down, the local residents rose up in its defense. Considerable materials and efforts must have gone into its refurbishing because today it stands in very good condition. It has board and batten siding on the sides and portals and a shake roof, and it rests on stone-and-mortar abutments with stone-and-mortar wingwalls capped with concrete. One of the abutments appears to have been reinforced with concrete during its recon-struction. Extensive repairs were made to the bridge in 1997. When we visited the bridge in 2000, it was in very good condition.

Buck Hill / Abram Hess' Mill / Eichelberger's Store Bridge

Location: On the Buck Hill Farm property, just north of the Lancaster Airport. **Directions:** On PA 501, just north of the Lancaster Airport and N. Peters Road, the farm is located on the east side of PA 501.

Year: 1844 / **Truss:** Burr / **Waterway:** Farm pond inlet
In Use: Pedestrian traffic only / **Number of Spans:** 1 / **Owner:** Private
Builder: Theodore D. Cochran / **Length:** 58 ft. / **Width:** 13 ft. 6½ in.
Condition: Good / **Number:** PA-36-15 / **Register:** December 10, 1980

The bridge is located on the Buck Hill Farm, which is the private property of Irel Buckwalter and his sister Mary Ann Hartzell. According to Mr. Buckwalter, the bridge was originally located near the village of Millway, just east of Rothsville, in Warwick Township. His father acquired the bridge sometime during the 1950s or 60s when he learned that it was to be destroyed. Mr. Buckwalter, Sr., then reconstructed the bridge across a small inlet to a pond on his farm property. In recent years, Irel Buckwalter has kept the bridge and its setting in nice condition. He was delighted to have photographs taken of this prize possession.

Colemanville / Martic Forge Bridge

Location: On Pequea Campground Road (T 408), Colemanville, between Conestoga and Martic Townships. **Directions:** In Colemanville, from the junction of PA 324 and Pequea Campground Road, go south on Pequea Campground Road for 0.2 mile to the bridge.

Year: 1856 / **Truss:** Burr / **Waterway:** Pequea Creek
In Use: Yes / **Number of Spans:** 1 / **Owner:** County
Builder: James C. Carpenter (1856 bridge)
Length: 167 ft. 7 in. / **Width:** 15 ft. 2½ in.
Condition: Excellent / **Number:** PA-36-55
Register: December 11, 1980

This bridge is located near the entrance of Susquehannock State Park and is one of the longest bridges in Lancaster County. There are accounts of this bridge having been washed off its abutments twice in its history; each time it was rebuilt in the same location, using as much of the original material as possible. The second time, after the 1972 Hurricane Agnes flood, the bridge was lifted by two cranes and repaired by Amish carpenters. It was rededicated in December 1973. At the time of our 1991 visit, the Colemanville Bridge was again in the process of being completely rebuilt, this time downstream of the original bridge. By September of 1992 the structure was completely finished except for some final refinements to the wingwalls, parapets and surrounding terrain. The bridge was opened to traffic again during the 1992 camping season at the state park. The new structure is a very lovely, substantial replacement of the original. The new Burr arches are more angular than the graceful, double arched curves of the original. The new structure rests on stone-faced, concrete abutments with long, curved, stone-faced, concrete wingwalls and parapets. The siding is composed of the typical Lancaster County boards and battens. While this bridge is in a rather remote part of the county, it is worth traveling the extra miles to see this excellent reproduction. The photograph here shows only one view of this fine structure.

Erb's / Hammer 1 Bridge

Location: On Picnic Woods Road (T 634), Ephrata Township and (T 929), Warwick Township, north of Rothsville. **Directions:** In Rothsville, from the junction of PA 772 and Picnic Woods Road, go north on Picnic Woods Road for 1.3 miles to the bridge.

Year: 1887 / **Truss:** Burr / **Waterway:** Hammer Creek
In Use: Yes / **Number of Spans:** 1 / **Owner:** County
Builder: John G. Bowman / **Length:** 80 ft. 3½ in. / **Width:** 13 ft. 10½ in.
Condition: Very good / **Number:** PA-36-34
Register: December 10, 1980

This bridge was named for the Erb family, who owned a large tract of land in this area, and it is one of the few Lancaster County bridges that was not built near a mill site. The sides of the bridge are covered with barn red, vertical board and batten siding, and the portals are covered with white vertical boards without battens. The structure rests on stone-and-mortar abutments, has stone-and-mortar wingwalls and parapets, and the typical lengthwise openings under the eaves. In 1974 the roof was recovered with wooden shakes. Publications of the Theodore Burr Covered Bridge Society of Pennsylvania indicate that the bridge was closed during 1996 for some repair work. When we visited it in 2000, it was open, beautifully repaired, and in very good condition.

Forry's Mill Bridge

Location: On Bridge Valley Road (T 365), between Rapho and West Hempfield Townships. **Directions:** In Silver Springs, go west on PA 23 for approximately 2.5 miles to Bridge Valley Road (T 365). Turn right (north) on Bridge Valley Road for approximately 0.3 mile to the bridge.

Year: 1869 / **Truss:** Burr / **Waterway:** Chickies Creek
In Use: Yes / **Number of Spans:** 1 / **Owner:** County
Builder: Elias McMellen / **Length:** 102 ft. 1 in. / **Width:** 14 ft.
Condition: Fair / **Number:** PA-36-28 / **Register:** December 11, 1980

This is one of forty-seven bridges in Lancaster County either built or repaired by Elias McMellen. It is named for the Forry family, who lived in the old stone house on the adjoining property. The Forry's Mill Bridge has one concrete abutment and one made of stone-and-mortar. It has the typical vertical board and batten siding and a shake roof. The truss structure is a double Burr arch encasing a multiple kingpost truss. It, too, is in a lovely rustic setting.

Publications of 1994 indicated that substantial damage was done to one wingwall, parapet, and portal side. Repairs, however, which will include a new roof and structural support beams, are to be done over a six year span. These repairs are part of a $203 billion dollar federal transportation bill signed into law in 1998. The bill, the largest in history of it kind, allocated $50 million dollars for the nation's publicly owned covered bridges. This bridge will be one of the first to benefit from these funds. During our visit in 2000, it appeared that the repairs had not yet been started.

Guy Bard / Cocalico 5 / Keller's / Rettews Bridge

Location: On Rettews Road (T 656), northwest edge of Akron, Ephrata Township. **Directions:** In Akron, from the junction of PA 272 and Main Street, go north on PA 272 for 0.9 mile to Rothsville Road. Turn left (southwest) on Rothsville Road (SR 1018) for 0.3 mile to Rettews Road; turn right on Rettews Road for 0.3 mile to the bridge.

Year: 1891 / **Truss:** Burr / **Waterway:** Cocalico Creek
In Use: Yes / **Number of Spans:** 1 / **Owner:** County
Builder: Elias McMellen / **Length:** 73 ft. 10 in. / **Width:** 14 ft. 2 in.
Condition: Fair / **Number:** PA-36-13 / **Register:** December 10, 1980

Although at one time many covered bridges were whitewashed, the Guy Bard Bridge is reported to be the only remaining white bridge in the county. In recent years, the more popular barn red color has replaced the original color on many bridges. Locally known as Guy Bard's Bridge, this structure was named for a leading Pennsylvania jurist who lived nearby. Recent construction has resulted in a large housing development immediately adjacent to the bridge (notice the homes in the background of the photo). It is heavily traveled.

Bridge society publications of 1994 indicated that the non-profit organization, Preservation Pennsylvania, feared that the bridge might be moved to another location and replaced with a new bridge. This would remove it from the old mill structure with which it has been associated. Thus, Preservation Pennsylvania placed the bridge on its list "Pennsylvania at Risk" for 1994. It is also a structure listed on the National Register of Historic Places. In 1996 it was reported that the bridge was to be rebuilt at a cost of $975,000 and moved two road crossings upstream. However, on our 2000 visit, the bridge was still in its original location.

Herr's Mill / Soudersburg Bridge

Location: In Mill Bridge Village, between Paradise and Leacock Townships. **Directions:** In the village of Ronks, on US 30, just west of Soudersburg, go south on Ronks Road for 0.5 mile to the bridge, off the road to the left in the Amish village.

Year: 1891 / **Truss:** Burr / **Waterway:** Pequea Creek
In Use: No / **Number of Spans:** 2 / **Owner:** Private
Builder: Joseph Elliot and Robert Russell
Length: 178 ft. / **Width:** 14 ft. 5½ in.
Condition: Fair / **Number:** PA-36-21 / **Register:** December 10, 1980

Herr's Mill Bridge is located on the Herr's Mill historical site, a restored Amish village which is open to the public as a tourist attraction. The mill is a beautiful, stone structure that dates back to 1728. The bridge is the only remaining two-span bridge in the county, though this is only evident when the exterior structure is examined. An account of this bridge written in *Covered Bridges Today* by Brenda Krekeler (1989) states that the bridge is used by the Amish village for tourists' carriage rides. It has been bypassed by T 696 and is closed to all other traffic by a heavy door. The structure also has an unusual side entrance which, according to one source, connected it to an adjoining road. However, more reliable sources indicate that side doors of this type were used to measure the level of the stream in relation to the bridge, and to provide local fishermen with access to the stream. The sides are covered with vertical boards, and the gable ends of the portals have wooden shingles. There are also several side windows protected by shingled awnings.

Hunsecker's Mill Bridge

Location: On Hunsecker Road (SR 1029), between Manheim and Upper Leacock Townships, northeast of Lancaster. **Directions**: Northeast of Lancaster, at the junction of PA 23 with Snake Hill Road (SR 1029). Go north for 0.2 mile to Hunsecker Road; turn left on Hunsecker Road for 0.7 mile to the bridge.

Year: 1843 / **Truss:** Burr / **Waterway:** Conestoga Creek
In Use: Yes / **Number of Spans:** 1 / **Owner:** State
Builder: Joseph Russell / **Length:** 180 ft. 8 in. / **Width:** 14 ft. 1½ in.
Condition: Excellent / **Number:** PA-36-06 (2) / **Register:**

Like many other Lancaster County bridges, this bridge was swept off its abutments several times by flood waters. Only the persistence of local citizens convinced state officials to replace it each time with another wooden covered bridge. These early replacements required teams of mules and wagons to drag the dismantled structure back to its original abutments, which were raised three feet in order to prevent further loss by flood. The 1869 restoration of the bridge lasted until 1973, when Hurricane Agnes completely destroyed it. The most recent replacement, begun in 1973, cost $321,000 and took a period of two years to complete. The locals did not seem to mind—they would have nothing other than a covered bridge. The setting is absolutely beautiful, and the structure, with natural vertical board and batten siding and red cedar shakes on the roof, is perfect in this location.

Jackson's Mill / West Octoraro 1 Bridge

Location: On Mt. Pleasant Road at the junction with Hollow Road, Bart Township. **Directions:** Between Quarryville and Christiana, at the junction of Valley Road (PA 372) and Mt. Pleasant Road (T 696), go south on Mt. Pleasant Road for 1.6 miles to the bridge.

Year: 1878 / **Truss:** Burr / **Waterway:** Octoraro Creek
In Use: Yes / **Number of Spans:** 1 / **Owner:** County
Builder: John Smith and Samuel Stauffer
Length: 147 ft. 5 in. / **Width:** 15 ft.
Condition: Very good / **Number:** PA-36-33
Register: Removed in 1986

This is one of the most attractive covered bridges in the county, yet it is reportedly seen by fewer people than any other, because it is not in a heavily traveled section of the county. The Jackson's Mill Bridge is the only Lancaster County covered bridge that doesn't lie straight across a waterway; the bridge is built "on a skew." Apparently, when the bridge was built, a saw mill was located on one side of the creek and a large rock formation lay on the other. These elements forced builders to place the bridge on a diagonal. It was damaged by a flood in July 1984 and rebuilt. It is now in fine condition, and covered with vertical board and batten siding. Shiplapped siding adorns the gable portions of the portals, and vertical boards cover the portals' legs. Cedar shakes cover the roof. The structure rests on new, concrete abutments, and there is an extended retaining wall on one side. There are no parapets, however, which are common on other county structures.

Kauffman's Distillery /
Sporting Hill Bridge

Location: On Sunhill Road (T 889), between Rapho and Penn Townships, Sporting Hill. **Directions:** In Sporting Hill, from the junction of PA 772 and Sunhill Road, go east on Sunhill Road to the bridge.

Year: 1874 / **Truss:** Burr / **Waterway:** Chickies Creek
In Use: Yes / **Number of Spans:** 1 / **Owner:** County
Builder: Elias McMellen / **Length:** 96 ft. 7 in. / **Width:** 14 ft. 5 in.
Condition: Good / **Number:** PA-36-32 / **Register:** December 11, 1980

When first constructed, this bridge was associated with a local distillery owned by the Kauffman family near the village of Sporting Hill. An account of this bridge in *Seeing Lancaster County's Covered Bridges*, by E. Gipe Caruthers, also calls this Whiskey Distillery Bridge. Caruthers reports that once a month, the Kauffman family traveled in a large loop selling whiskey in Mount Joy, Elizabethtown, Hershey, Lebanon, Brickerville, and Manheim. This bridge has the typical Lancaster County treatment of vertical board and batten siding and a shake roof. Another name documented in the *Statewide Covered Bridge Assessment* is the Big Chickies Bridge.

Kurtz's Mill / Baer's Mill / Keystone Mill Bridge

Location: On Kiwanis Road, Lancaster County Central Park.
Directions: Lancaster County Central Park is located approximately 2.5 miles from the center of Lancaster, just east of US 222. At the junction of US 222 and Golf Road, travel east on Golf Road into the park. Turn right on Kiwanis Road to the bridge.

Year: 1876 / **Truss:** Burr / **Waterway:** Mill Creek
In Use: Yes / **Number of Spans:** 1 / **Owner:** County
Builder: W. W. Upp / **Length:** 96 ft. 8 in. / **Width:** 12 ft. 7½ in.
Condition: Excellent / **Number:** PA-36-03 / **Register:**

During the Hurricane Agnes flood of 1972, the rising Conestoga River moved the Kurtz's Mill Bridge downstream a considerable distance, where it became hung up on a large maple tree. Following this calamity, the bridge was moved fifteen miles by trailer to Lancaster County Central Park. There, on new abutments, it crosses Mill Creek. The original cost of construction in 1876 was $1,407. Approximately 100 years later, the cost of moving the structure was $5,000, and the cost of restoration was $55,000. The bridge was rededicated on April 22, 1975. It is a charming structure in a picturesque setting. In its restored condition, the Kurtz's Mill Bridge is covered with vertical board and batten siding and a shake roof. Notice that the bridge has had several names; additional names that are not listed are Binder Tongue Carrier Bridge and Mill 2A.

Landis Mill / Little Conestoga 1 Bridge

Location: On the northwest edge of Park City Mall, between East Hempfield Township and the city of Lancaster. **Directions:** In northwest Lancaster, on Harrisburg Avenue, enter Park City Mall on Plaza Avenue. Go to the first traffic light and turn left to the bridge (no street names evident at traffic light).

Year: 1873 / **Truss:** Multiple kingpost
Waterway: Little Conestoga Creek
In Use: Yes / **Number of Spans:** 1 / **Owner:** County
Builder: Elias McMellen / **Length:** 52 ft 8½ in. / **Width:** 14 ft. 3½ in.
Condition: Good / **Number:** PA-36-16 / **Register:** December 10, 1980

The Landis Mill Bridge is the only example of a multiple kingpost truss style bridge found in Lancaster County. The bridge is heavily used because of its proximity to the shopping center and a modern housing development in the area. As a result, it has lost much of its original charm. At one time, the bridge was part of the farm property of John L. Landis, who also owned a mill in the area. It is covered with the familiar barn red vertical board and batten siding and is resting on stone-and-mortar abutments with stone-and-mortar wingwalls and parapets. The parapets are capped with concrete. One of the abutments has been reinforced with concrete, and heavy traffic has necessitated the erection of heavy, steel guardrails along the north side of the road approaches. Covered bridge society publications have indicated that the bridge is to be moved; however, on our visit in 2000 we found the bridge in its original location.

Leaman Place / Paradise / Eshelman's Mill Bridge

Location: On Belmont Road, between Paradise and Leacock Townships.
Directions: In the village of Paradise, go north on Belmont Road for 0.5 mile to the bridge.

Year: 1893 / **Truss:** Burr / **Waterway:** Pequea Creek
In Use: Yes / **Number of Spans:** 1 / **Owner:** County
Builder: Elias McMellen / **Length:** 113 ft. 4 in. / **Width:** 16 ft.
Condition: Excellent / **Number:** PA-36-20 / **Register:** December 11, 1980

This bridge is frequently visited by tourists traveling in the heart of Amish country. In 1991, the family living in the nearby stone house had placed a scroll-shaped sign at the end of the bridge. They are not in the tourist business but are proud of their heritage. The sign states: "PARADISE BRIDGE AT LEAMON PLACE SITUATED ON THE PEQUEA CREEK BETWEEN PARADISE AND LEACOCK TOWNSHIP BUILT IN 1894. SEPTEMBER OF 1712 MARY FERREE AND FAMILY SETTLED IN AREA HAVING BEEN GRANTED THIS LAND BY WILLIAM PENN. THE PEQUAW INDIANS WHO LIVED HERE THEN WERE FRIENDLY. AS THEN AND NOW THROUGH GOD'S HELP THE PEOPLE HAVE PROSPERED. EARL R. HOUCK." Mary Ferree was the first settler in this area, and lived on land given to William Penn by Queen Ann as part of the London Grant. This sign indicates 1894 as the year in which the bridge was built, though the *Statewide Covered Bridge Assessment* lists it as 1893. However, in 2000, we could not locate the sign.

The bridge has vertical board and batten siding on both the sides and the portals, a shake roof, and rests on concrete abutments with stone-and-mortar wingwalls and parapets. The parapets are capped with concrete. The abutments have been reinforced with concrete in recent years.

Lime Valley / Pequea 8 / Strasburg Bridge

Location: On Brenneman Road, Lime Valley, between West Lampeter and Strasburg Townships. **Directions:** In the village of Lime Valley, just south of Lime Valley Road, on Brenneman Road.

Year: 1871 / **Truss:** Burr / **Waterway:** Pequea Creek
In Use: Yes / **Number of Spans:** 1 / **Owner:** County
Builder: Elias McMellen / **Length:** 103 ft. 10 in. / **Width:** 14 ft. 1 in.
Condition: Good / **Number:** PA-36-23 / **Register:** December 10, 1980

This bridge is supported on stone-and-mortar abutments that extend to form long wingwalls and parapets. The sides of the bridge are covered with red board and batten siding, and the portals display white vertical boards without battens. The deck is covered with heavy lengthwise planking.

In 1972, Hurricane Agnes caused waters of eighteen inches to rise over the floor of the bridge, yet it remained standing. In the mid-1990s some restoration work was done, but at the time of our visit in 2000 there was noticeable damage to the portals caused by tall vehicles. Some damage to the siding was also apparent, probably caused by the high flood waters of the 1999 hurricane season. Otherwise, the bridge appears to be in good condition. Some years ago, a family living near the bridge raised tomatoes. As the story is told, they hauled one load of tomatoes weighing twenty-three tons over the bridge.

Neff's Mill / Pequea 7 Bridge

Location: On Penn Grant Road, between West Lampeter and Strasburg Townships. **Directions:** In Lampeter, go south on Bridge Road (T 714) for 0.9 mile to a "T" with Penn Grant Road. Turn left to the bridge.

Year: 1875 / **Truss:** Burr / **Waterway:** Pequea Creek
In Use: Yes / **Number of Spans:** 1 / **Owner:** County
Builder: James C. Carpenter / **Length:** 103 ft. 3 in. / **Width:** 12 ft. 10 in.
Condition: Good / **Number:** PA-36-22 / **Register:** December 11, 1980

In some accounts, this bridge is recorded as the narrowest bridge in the county. It only has a clear portal opening of twelve feet, ten inches. It rests on stone-and-mortar abutments reinforced with concrete and has long stone-and-mortar wingwalls and parapets. The parapets are capped with concrete. One of the wingwalls was partially washed away by the Hurricane Agnes flood, and a portion of it has been replaced with concrete. It has vertical board and batten siding that is painted the typical barn red on the sides and white on the portals. In addition to the lengthwise openings under the eaves, it has one narrow window located in the center of each side. Since our visit in 1991, the sheet metal roof has been replaced with cedar shakes. The high Burr arches are heavily reinforced with large timbers. These reinforcements were also evident when we visited the bridge in 1991.

Pinetown / Nolt's Point Mill Bridge

Location: On Bridge Road (T 620), northeast of Lancaster, between Manheim and Upper Leacock Townships. **Directions:** From the junction of PA 23, northeast of Lancaster, with Snake Hill Road (SR 1022 & T 620), go north on Snake Hill Road for 1.3 miles to Mondale Road (T 757). Turn left for 0.2 mile to Bridge Road; turn right on Bridge Road for 0.6 mile to the bridge.

Year: 1867 / **Truss:** Burr / **Waterway:** Conestoga Creek
In Use: Yes / **Number of Spans:** 1 / **Owner:** County
Builder: Elias McMellen / **Length:** 135 ft. 7 in. / **Width:** 12 ft. 9 in.
Condition: Good / **Number:** PA-36-05 / **Register:** December 11, 1980

As in many other parts of the state, the Hurricane Agnes flood of 1972 took its toll on Lancaster County's bridges. The Pinetown Bridge was one of its victims. This bridge, which originally cost $4,500 (making it the most expensive bridge in the area during the nineteenth century), was rebuilt at a cost of $40,000. Most of the repair and replacement work was done by Amish carpenters who worked diligently until the job was completed. Although the Pinetown Bridge had already been one of the highest above water level at seventeen feet, when it was rebuilt, it was raised several feet higher. Other than that change, the bridge retains its original appearance. Covered with vertical board and batten siding, it has a shake roof and rests on stone-and-mortar abutments. There are long, curving stone-and-mortar wingwalls and parapets. This is another bridge with several names; two additional ones are Big Conestoga 6 and Bushong's Mill.

Pool Forge Bridge

Location: Bypassed by Pool Forge Road, between Churchtown and Goodville, Caernarvon Township. **Directions:** From the junction of PA 23 and Pool Forge Road, between Churchtown and Goodville, go south on Pool Forge Road 0.1 mile to the bypassed bridge, on the left side of the road.

Year: 1859 / **Truss:** Burr / **Waterway:** Conestoga Creek
In Use: No / **Number of Spans:** 1 / **Owner:** Private
Builder: Levi Fink and Elias McMellen
Length: 99 ft. 3 in. / **Width:** 15 ft. 6 in.
Condition: Fairly good / **Number:** PA-36-01
Register: December 11, 1980

Pool Forge Bridge has been bypassed by contemporary Pool Forge Road, formerly Township Road 679, and left in the hands of the property owner adjoining the bridge. The barn red structure is covered with vertical board and batten siding on the sides and legs of the portals and cedar shakes on the gable ends. It has a sheet metal roof, and stone-and-mortar wingwalls and parapets. The parapets are capped with concrete. The bridge is now closed to all traffic and is being used as a storage area. Since our visit in 1991, it appears that the owner has made some effort to improve the bridge and its surroundings.

Red Run / Oberholtzer's Bridge

Location: In Red Run Campground, East Earl Township.
Directions: From Red Run, go southeast on Red Run Road (SR 1044) approximately 0.6 mile to the campground, located on the northeast side of the road.

Year: 1866 / **Truss:** Burr / **Waterway:** Muddy Creek
In Use: No / **Number of Spans:** 1 / **Owner:** Private
Builder: Elias McMellen / **Length:** 107 ft. / **Width:** 13 ft. 5½ in.
Condition: Fair / **Number:** PA-36-10 / **Register:** December 11, 1980

In 1961 this bridge was bypassed with the construction of a new bridge. Since it was on land adjoining the Red Run Grist Mill, it was assumed that it belonged to the mill; consequently, it was presented to the mill owners for a token fee. It now appears to be part of the Red Run Campground property. The vertical board and batten siding is in fair condition, but parts of the stone-and-mortar abutments and wingwalls were washed away in the Hurricane Agnes flood, and the portal timbers are deteriorating. It appears that the bridge is still being used only for storage. Between 1961 and the present, the Zimmermans, who operated a carriage house nearby, used it to refurbish wagons and carriages. The adjoining campground has also used it as a church. It, like the two other privately owned bridges in the county, appears to have been improved by its owner since our visit in 1991. This is most comforting, because frequently, lack of funds causes these historic structures to fall into disrepair and ruin.

Risser's Mill / Risser Mill / Horst's Mill Bridge

Location: On Mt. Pleasant Road, north of Mt. Joy, Mt. Joy Township.
Directions: From the Rheems-Elizabethtown exit of PA 283, go north on Cloverleaf Road (SR 4025) for 0.3 mile to Mt. Pleasant Road (SR 4010). Turn right (east) on Mt. Pleasant Road for 2.8 miles to the bridge, which is at the junction with Risser Mill Road.

Year: 1872 / **Truss:** Burr / **Waterway:** Little Chickies Creek
In Use: Yes / **Number of Spans:** 1 / **Owner:** State
Builder: Elias McMellen / **Length:** 81 ft. 10 in. / **Width:** 12 ft. 10 in.
Condition: Fairly good / **Number:** PA-36-36
Register: December 10, 1980

The report in *Seeing Lancaster County's Covered Bridges* (1974) indicated that this bridge was falling into disrepair. The principal of the Mount Joy Vo-Tech School had shown interest in using its preservation as a school project. Apparently he was successful, because the bridge is now in reasonably good condition. It is located close to the original Horst Mill, which has passed into the hands of Horst offspring by the name of Risser. The mill is still in the Risser family but is no longer functioning.

Like many of the other county spans, this bridge is covered with vertical board and batten siding painted barn red on the sides and white on the portals. It has a sheet metal roof. The Risser's Mill Bridge is not nearly as well preserved as some, but at least it is still standing and used regularly by a fair amount of traffic. While we have no reports of continued maintenance since our visit in 1991, in 2000 it still appears to be in fairly good condition.

Schenk's Mill / Shenk's Mill Bridge

Location: On Erisman Road (T 372), Rapho Township, where it meets
T 552, East Hempfield Township, just north of Landisville.
Directions: From the Landisville exit of PA 283, go north on Spooky
Nook Road (T 711) for 0.5 mile to Shenks Road (T 346). Turn left and go
0.7 mile to Erisman Road. The bridge is just to the left on Erisman Road.

Year: 1855 / **Truss:** Burr / **Waterway:** Chickies Creek
In Use: Yes / **Number of Spans:** 1 / **Owner:** County
Builder: Charles Malhorn / **Length:** 95 ft. 9 in. / **Width:** 14 ft. 9 in.
Condition: Good / **Number:** PA-36-30 / **Register:** December 10, 1980

Located in a beautiful, well-maintained, rural setting, the Schenk's
Mill Bridge is unusual in Lancaster County for several reasons: it
has horizontal clapboard siding, has two long horizontal windows
on either side of the eastern end of the structure, and the Burr
arch is only about half as high as similar structures in the county.
The *Statewide Covered Bridge Assessment* lists an additional name for
the bridge as the Big Chickies 4 Bridge, and lists Levi Fink as one
of the builders. It is built on stone-and-mortar abutments that
extend on either end into lengthy wingwalls and parapets. The
original Schenk farmhouse and mill are still standing. While this
is still a rural area, there are some very attractive contemporary
homes in the area. On our 2000 visit we found that the bridge is
still in good condition.

Shearer's Bridge

Location: In Manheim Memorial Park, between Penn and Rapho Townships, Manheim. **Directions:** In Manheim, follow East High Street to Laurel Street (follow sign to Manheim Central High School). Turn left to Adele Avenue. Turn right past the high school and go to parking area at end of Adele Avenue. The bridge is directly ahead.

Year: 1856 / **Truss:** Burr / **Waterway:** Chickies Creek
In Use: Pedestrian traffic only / **Number of Spans:** 1 / **Owner:** County
Builder: Jacob Clare / **Length:** 89 ft. 1 in. / **Width:** 15 ft. 1 in.
Condition: Fair / **Number:** PA-36-31 / **Register:** December 10, 1980

Shearer's Bridge was originally built in 1847 over Chickies Creek at a cost of about $600. In 1856, it was rebuilt for $1,200. In 1971 it was moved four miles to Manheim Memorial Park, across from the high school, at a cost of $12,000. In 1991, estimated costs of rehabilitation ranged from $14,000 to $32,700. While we have no reports of any restoration having been completed, we found the bridge in fair condition on our 2000 visit, though some of the siding is in need of replacement. The bridge seems to be used fairly extensively by the students of the adjoining high school, who seem to respect its historic value.

In its new location, this bridge still crosses Chickies Creek. Its style is similar to the Shenk's Mill Bridge, especially the horizontal siding and long, horizontal windows. The windows of the Shearer's Bridge are located just inside each portal.

Siegrist's Mill / Moore's Mill Bridge

Location: On Siegrist Road (T 360), Rapho Township, where it meets T 669, West Hempfield Township. **Directions:** In Silver Spring, go west on PA 23 for approximately 1 mile to Prospect Road (SR 4001). Turn right (north) on Prospect Road for 0.5 mile to Siegrist Road; turn left on Siegrist Road for 0.7 mile to the bridge.

Year: 1885 / **Truss:** Burr / **Waterway:** Chickies Creek
In Use: Yes / **Number of Spans:** 1 / **Owner:** County
Builder: James C. Carpenter
Length: 101 ft. 10 in. / **Width:** 13 ft. 11½ in.
Condition: Good / **Number:** PA-36-37 / **Register:** December 10, 1980

The local residents tell a story about two occupants of the county poorhouse, Bum Frank and John Weiskopf, who lived under this bridge during the summer months while they hired themselves out to work on the Siegrist family's farm. Mrs. Siegrist gave them soap about once every other week so they could bathe in the creek. In severe weather they slept in the barn; in the fall, they returned to the poorhouse.

This is one of the few bridges that withstood the wrath of Hurricane Agnes in 1972. It suffered only minor damage. Like many of the other Lancaster County bridges, it is in a charming setting. The structure has a slight camber, meaning that it arches upwards in the middle. It is supported on concrete abutments and has stone-and-mortar wingwalls and parapets. The bridge is covered with vertical board and batten siding, which is painted barn red on the sides and white on the portals. The roof is covered with cedar shakes. The *Statewide Covered Bridge Assessment* lists Big Chickies 6 Bridge as another documented name. Again, we have no reports of recent improvements, but the bridge remains in good condition.

Weaver's Mill / Isaac Shearer's Mill Bridge

Location: On Weaverland Road (T 773), north edge of Goodville, Caernarvon Township. **Directions:** In Goodville, at the junction of PA 23 and Water Street, go north on Water Street for 0.9 mile to Weaverland Road. Turn right on Weaverland Road for 1 mile to the bridge.

Year: 1878 / **Truss:** Burr / **Waterway:** Conestoga Creek
In Use: Yes / **Number of Spans:** 1 / **Owner:** County
Builder: B. C. Carter and J. F. Stauffer
Length: 88 ft. 7 in. / **Width:** 14 ft.
Condition: Very good / **Number:** PA-36-02
Register: December 11, 1980

Many of the Lancaster County bridges are located in the heart of Pennsylvania Dutch farming country. It is a common sight to see a horse-drawn buggy passing through the portals of this bridge, as well as those of many other bridges in the Amish section of Lancaster County. Reports received since the 1993 edition of this book indicate that the ends of the Burr arch truss system and some of the vertical posts in the multiple kingpost part of the truss have been replaced. In 2000, we felt the bridge was in very good condition. It is covered by vertical board and batten siding on both the sides and portals and rests on stone-and-mortar abutments which extend to stone-and-mortar wingwalls and parapets. The bridge has a deck of lengthwise planking.

White Rock Forge Bridge

Location: On White Rock Road (T 337) in White Rock, between Little Britain and Colerain Townships. **Directions:** From the junction of Noble Road (SR 2009) and Kirkwood Pike (PA 472), 0.8 mile northeast of Kirkwood, go south on Noble Road for 1.5 miles to White Rock Road. Turn left on White Rock Road and go 1.2 miles to the bridge.

Year: 1847 / **Truss:** Burr / **Waterway:** Octoraro Creek (West Branch)
In Use: Yes / **Number of Spans:** 1 / **Owner:** County
Builder: John Russell and Elias McMellen
Length: 113 ft. 1 in. / **Width:** 14 ft.
Condition: Good / **Number:** PA-36-18 / **Register:** December 10, 1980

This bridge is located in a peaceful, rural valley in the southeastern part of the county, and this setting does much to add to the charm of the White Rock Forge Bridge. According to the *Statewide Covered Bridge Assessment*, this bridge has also been called the West Octoraro 2 Bridge. It has typical board and batten siding and is painted barn red on the sides and white on the portals. There are two windows, one on either side, where the road makes a "T" with Township Route 490. The placement of the windows is probably meant to help people observe oncoming traffic. One of the more noticeable features of this span is its upwardly curved floor, known as a camber floor. The bridge was originally built this way by John Russell. After it was destroyed by a wind and rain storm in June 1884, it was rebuilt with the same floor contour by Elias McMellen in September of that same year. The White Rock Forge Bridge and the Jackson's Mill Bridge are a little distance from most of the bridges of the county, but relatively close to the bridges located on the border with Chester County—Mercer's Mill and Pine Grove.

Willow Hill Bridge

Location: Along PA 30, just west of PA 896, at the entrance to The Amish Farm, East Lampeter Township. **Directions:** The Amish Farm is on the north side of PA 30, west of PA 896, just west of the American Music Theater.

Year: 1962 / **Truss:** Burr / **Waterway:** Mill Creek (tributary)
In Use: Yes / **Number of Spans:** 1 / **Owner:** Private
Builder: Roy Zimmerman / **Length:** 72 ft. 6 in. / **Width:** 13 ft. 11½ in.
Condition: Excellent / **Number:** PA-36-43 / **Register:** Does not qualify

This bridge is a reconstruction of a historic covered bridge, the Miller's Farm Bridge, built in 1871 by Elias McMellen. The original bridge was presented to Adolph Neuber, owner of the Willows Restaurant, for preservation as a historic landmark. In 1991, the restaurant was located adjacent to the bridge. Mr. Neuber contracted a local builder, Roy Zimmerman of Strasburg, to restore the structure. Since the Miller's Farm Bridge was in poor condition, a second bridge was purchased to provide the timbers necessary for the rebuilding project. The second structure was the Goods Fording Bridge, which was built in 1855. Zimmerman used the best parts of the Miller's Farm Bridge for the basic project, replacing the deteriorated timbers with sound ones taken from the Goods Fording Bridge. He was even able to use some of the hardware and wooden pegs, or trunnels (tree-nails), to build the reconstructed span. Additional interesting information about the restoration is posted inside the bridge.

Since 1991, the Willows Restaurant has been replaced with a large theater structure—The American Music Theater—and the bridge, once part of that establishment, is now being used as the entrance to The Amish Farm, a Lancaster County tourist attraction.

Zook's Mill / Wenger's / Rose Hill Bridge

Location: On Log Cabin Road (T 797), west of Brownstown, between Warwick and Ephrata Townships. **Directions:** In Brownstown, from the junction of PA 272 and Rose Hill Road (T 797), go north on Rose Hill Road for 0.6 mile to Log Cabin Road. The bridge is just to the left on Log Cabin Road.

Year: 1849 / **Truss:** Burr / **Waterway:** Cocalico Creek
In Use: Yes / **Number of Spans:** 1 / **Owner:** County
Builder: Henry Zook / **Length:** 89 ft./ **Width:** 14 ft. 3½ in.
Condition: Good / **Number:** PA-36-14 / **Register:** December 11, 1980

As indicated above, this bridge, too, has had several names. The *Statewide Covered Bridge Assessment* lists an additional name of Cocalico 7. This is one of the county's earliest covered bridges, and it has been well maintained over the years. Reportedly, up until 1972, there was no need for major repairs. In that year, this very substantial bridge even withstood the high waters and strong currents created by Hurricane Agnes. The water filled the bridge to a depth of six and one-half feet. Some of the siding was damaged and part of the road washed away; however, this turned out to be a blessing in disguise, because it exposed some timbers that were beginning to rot, and they were quickly replaced. In addition, the horizontal clapboard siding was replaced with vertical boards and battens. The bridge now carries a load limit of seven tons. The average weight limit on covered bridges throughout the state is between two and five tons if steel reinforcements have not been added to the deck.

Although we have not received any reports of essential maintenance to the bridge, on our visit in 2000, we found it to be in good condition. The only noticeable structural damage was a few loosened boards on the downstream side of the bridge, which we assume was caused by the floodwaters of the 1999 hurricane season.

Banks Bridge

Location: On Covered Bridge Road, just north of Neshannock Falls, Wilmington Township. **Directions:** In Volant, at the junction of PA 168 and PA 208, go south on PA 168 for 1.2 miles to Gerber Road. Turn right on Gerber Road and go 1.4 miles to Covered Bridge Road (no name was visible), and turn right to the bridge. Or from the junction of PA 956 and Covered Bridge Road, north of Neshannock Falls, go north on Covered Bridge Road for 0.1 mile to the bridge.

Year: 1889 / **Truss:** Burr / **Waterway:** Neshannock Creek
In Use: Yes / **Number of Spans:** 1 / **Owner:** County
Builder: Unknown / **Length:** 133 ft. 1 in. / **Width:** 13 ft. 9½ in.
Condition: Excellent / **Number:** PA-37-02 / **Register:** June 27, 1980

This bridge has been heavily reinforced with steel beams under the deck of the Burr arch truss system. The steel reinforcements have allowed the bridge's load limit to increase to ten tons, which is considerably more than the three-ton limit typical of other covered bridges. In 1999, the Banks Bridge was remarkably improved by a $600,000 restoration project. Like the McConnell's Mill bridge, also in Lawrence County, the Banks Bridge benefited from federal funds made available for bridge restoration. (For more information about these funds, see the discussion of the Forry's Mill Bridge, Lancaster County.) The structure is covered with white vertical board and batten siding on both the sides and the portals, and the battens have unusual shapes. The roof is covered with asphalt shingles, and the deck consists of 1" x 6" boards set on edge and laminated into sections four feet wide. The bridge has large, lengthwise openings under the eaves, and the entire structure rests on cut stone abutments that appear to have been laid dry. There are road-level cut stone wingwalls. Although the bridge was in good condition when we visited it in 1991, we were delighted to see the results of the 1999 restoration when we visited it again in May 2000.

McConnell's Mill Bridge

Location: On McConnell's Mill Road, in McConnell's Mill State Park, Slippery Rock Township. **Directions:** Access to McConnell's Mill State Park is available from both PA 422 and PA 19. From the junction of PA 19 and PA 422, go west on PA 422 for 0.3 mile to the McConnell's Mill State Park entrance. Turn left and go 0.65 mile to the park direction signs at the crossroads. Or from the junction of PA 19 and PA 422, go south on PA 19 for 0.9 mile to Johnson Road (T 365); turn right on Johnson Road and go 0.8 mile to the park direction signs at the crossroads. Follow the signs to the covered bridge.

Year: 1874 / **Truss:** Howe / **Waterway:** Slippery Rock Creek
In Use: Yes / **Number of Spans:** 1 / **Owner:** County
Builder: Unknown / **Length:** 109 ft. 10 in. / **Width:** 13 ft. 6½ in.
Condition: Excellent / **Number:** PA-37-01 / **Register:** June 27, 1980

This bridge is in a splendid, picturesque setting in McConnell's Mill State Park, just downstream from the restored McConnell's Mill, and it is still used for traffic in the park. In 1998, the McConnell's Mill Bridge was beautifully restored and reopened to traffic during the week of December 13. The total cost of the restoration was $349,179. Ninety percent was federally funded, and the balance was supplied by the county. The bridge is covered with barn red vertical board and shaped batten siding on both the sides and portals. It has a roof of asphalt shingles, and a deck of 1" x 6" boards set on edge laminated into sections four feet wide. The structure rests on cut stone abutments which appear to have been laid dry. The only side openings are the typical, lengthwise, narrow ones directly under the eaves. This is one of only five Howe truss type covered bridges remaining in Pennsylvania, and one of only two in the western part of the state. The other Howe truss structures are located in Bucks, Indiana, Huntingdon, and Philadelphia counties. The combination of the restored mill and the restored covered bridge create a spectacular central focus for this lovely state park.

Bogert's Bridge

Location: Bypassed by Oxford Drive (South 24th Street, also SR 2007), Little Lehigh Park, Allentown. **Directions:** From I 78 East, take exit 18 (Lehigh Street). Turn right on Lehigh Street for 0.5 mile to traffic light at Oxford Drive; turn right on Oxford Drive for 0. 9 mile to the traffic light at Fish Hatchery Road. Turn right, then immediately left to the bridge. From I 78 West, take exit 18A (Lehigh Street). Turn left on Lehigh Street for 0.6 mile to traffic light at Oxford Drive. Turn right on Oxford Drive for 0.9 mile to the traffic light at Fish Hatchery Road. Turn right, then immediately left to the bridge.

Year: 1841 / **Truss:** Burr / **Waterway:** Little Lehigh River
In Use: Foot traffic only / **Number of Spans:** 1+ / **Owner:** City
Builder: Unknown / **Length:** 170 ft. 6 in. / **Width:** 20 ft. 2 in.
Condition: Fairly good / **Number:** PA-39-01
Register: December 1, 1980

The covered bridges of Lehigh County, like those of many other counties, have several features in common. They are all single-span bridges, they all use the Burr arch truss system, and, on average, they are among the widest bridges in the state. Their average width is 18 feet, 7 inches. Bogert's Bridge is one of the oldest of the remaining covered bridges in Lehigh County and one of the oldest in the nation. Today this bridge is located in Little Lehigh Park where it is maintained by the city of Allentown's Park Commission. In 1956, after being damaged by a truck, local residents saved it from demolition; the "Save the Bogert's Bridge Committee" was pictured in cartoons as a militant group defending the structure with a cannon. At the time of its reconstruction, two concrete piers were added to support the 170-foot structure. It has vertical board and batten siding on the sides and vertical boards on the portals. It rests on the original stone-and-mortar abutments that have been reinforced with concrete. The bridge has long, stone-and-mortar wingwalls and parapets and a slate roof. The structure has one small, square window located in the center of each side. The bridge is located in an area of the park that is a favorite of many Lehigh County residents. While this bridge has always been reasonably well maintained, it seems that maintenance has improved since it became a highlight in the city of Allentown's Christmas light tour.

Geiger's Bridge

Location: On Packhouse Road, northwest of Allentown, North Whitehall Township. **Directions:** From the Rex's Bridge, go west on Jordan Road for 1.1 miles to the junction with Ruheton Hill Road. Bear right on Jordan Road for 0.3 mile to the junction with Packhouse Road. Turn right on Packhouse Road and go 0.2 mile to the bridge. There is an area in which to park and turn around on the far side of the bridge, so that you can return through the bridge to Ruheton Hill Road to continue on to the Schlicher's Bridge.

Year: 1860 / **Truss:** Burr / **Waterway:** Jordan Creek
In Use: Yes / **Number of Spans:** 1 / **Owner:** County
Builder: Unknown / **Length:** 131 ft. 11 in. / **Width:** 18 ft. 4 in.
Condition: Very good / **Number:** PA-39-05
Register: December 1, 1980

This is one of five single-span Burr arch truss bridges that cross Jordan Creek in Lehigh County. Notice, in particular, the unusual stepped portal design; this is the only Lehigh County bridge with this design, and one of the few in the state with a similar facade. The bridge is covered with vertical board and batten siding on both the sides and the portals and has a deck of lengthwise planking laid over crosswise planking. It has long, concrete-faced, stone-and-mortar wingwalls. Both of the north wingwalls are of normal length, but one of the south wingwalls is shortened because of the surrounding topography. The portals of the Geiger's Bridge were replaced in 1998 in the original step design. Their freshly painted facade improves the appearance of this bridge, which continues to be in good condition.

Since Geiger's Bridge, Rex's Bridge, and Schlicher's Bridge are located within 3.5 miles of each other, directions to find these bridges will start at Rex's, proceed to Geiger's, and end with Schlicher's.

Manasses Guth Bridge

Location: On Lapp Road, just northwest of Allentown, South Whitehall Township. **Directions:** From the US 22 bypass (Cedar Crest Boulevard exit), go north on Cedar Crest Boulevard for 1.5 miles to Iron Bridge Road. Turn left on Iron Bridge Road for 0.8 mile to Lapp Road; turn right through the bridge. (There is a large parking area to the left of Lapp Road.

Year: 1868 / **Truss:** Burr / **Waterway:** Jordan Creek
In Use: Yes / **Number of Spans:** 1 / **Owner:** County
Builder: Unknown / **Length:** 128 ft. 4 in. / **Width:** 17 ft. 9 in.
Condition: Good / **Number:** PA-39-03 / **Register:** December 1, 1980

This is the second of five Lehigh County covered bridges, located within eight miles of each other, that cross the meandering Jordan Creek. All of these structures are in use and in good condition, and each one spans a distance of more than 116 feet. The Manasses Guth Bridge is covered with horizontal clapboard siding on the sides and shiplapped siding on the portals. It has no side openings other than the typical lengthwise ones under the eaves. The deck consists of lengthwise planking over crosswise planking, and the structure rests on stone-and-mortar abutments with long wingwalls and concrete-capped parapets. Like the other bridges in Lehigh County, the Manasses Guth Bridge has a slate roof. The Burr arch truss system, typically, sandwiches a multiple kingpost structure. During our visit in April 2000, we noticed that the sides could be refreshed with a new coat of paint.

Both the Manasses Guth Bridge and the Wehr's Bridge are located adjacent to Covered Bridge Park, a lovely, large, public park maintained by South Whitehall Township. Directions to the Wehr's Bridge use the Guth Bridge as a starting point. They are only 1 mile apart.

Rex's Bridge

Location: On Jordan Road, northwest of Allentown, North Whitehall Township. **Directions:** In Orefield, from the junction of PA 309 and Orefield Road, go west on Orefield Road for 1.1 miles to Jordan Road. Turn right and go 0.5 mile to the bridge, which is at the junction with Horseshoe Road.

Year: 1858 / **Truss:** Burr / **Waterway:** Jordan Creek
In Use: Yes / **Number of Spans:** 1 / **Owner:** County
Builder: Unknown / **Length:** 138 ft. 5 in. / **Width:** 17 ft. 4 in.
Condition: Good / **Number:** PA-39-04 / **Register:** December 1, 1980

This is the third of five covered bridges that span the Jordan Creek in Lehigh County. Like the other bridges in the county, it is painted barn red. The siding is horizontal clapboard on both the sides and portals, the roof is covered with slate, and the deck has lengthwise planking laid over crosswise planking. The high, double Burr arch reaches a little above the lengthwise openings under the eaves. Older accounts of this structure indicate that it has stone-and-mortar wingwalls and parapets; however, they appear to have been faced and capped with concrete in recent years. At the time of our visit in April 2000, we noticed that while the bridge was structurally sound, the interior paint was peeling However, on a return trip to the bridge in July 2000, we found the bridge closed because a crew was sandblasting the bridge's interior. We assume this was in preparation for repainting. All of the Lehigh County bridges are painted white on the interior.

Since Geiger's Bridge, Rex's Bridge, and Schlicher's Bridge are located within 3.5 miles of each other, directions to find these bridges will start at Rex's, proceed to Geiger's, and end with Schlicher's.

Schlicher's Bridge

Location: On Game Preserve Road (SR 4007), northwest of Allentown, North Whitehall Township. **Directions:** From the Geiger's Bridge, return on Packhouse Road for 0.2 mile to Jordan Road. Turn left on Jordan Road and go 0.3 mile to Ruheton Hill Road. Turn right on Ruheton Hill Road and go 0.9 mile to Game Preserve Road. Continue straight on Game Preserve Road for 1.3 miles to the bridge. An alternate approach to the bridge is from Schnecksville, at the junction of PA 309 and Game Preserve Road, go west on Game Preserve Road for 1.3 miles to the bridge.

Year: 1882 / **Truss:** Burr / **Waterway:** Jordan Creek
In Use: Yes / **Number of Spans:** 1 / **Owner:** County
Builder: Unknown / **Length:** 116 ft. 6 in./ **Width:** 18 ft. 11 in.
Condition: Fair / **Number:** PA-39-06 / **Register:** December 1, 1980

This is the shortest and newest of the covered spans in the county, and is also the fourth of the five bridges that cross the Jordan Creek. It has a relatively low overhead clearance and a wide opening which gives it a broader appearance than normal. It is covered with barn red, vertical board and batten siding on the sides and white, shiplapped siding on the portals. It rests on stone-and-mortar abutments that have been reinforced with concrete and it also has three, moderately long, stone-and-mortar wingwalls and parapets. The fourth wingwall and parapet are completely concrete, and all of the parapets are concrete-capped. This bridge is in a beautiful, rustic setting, close to the entrance of the Trexler-Lehigh County Game Preserve, a frequently visited tourist attraction. During our visit in April 2000, we noticed that while the bridge is structurally sound, some of the parapets are crumbling badly. Of the six bridges in Lehigh County, the Schlicher's Bridge appears to be in need of the most attention regarding maintenance. There is a rather severe sag at each end of the bridge, noticeable in the photo. This is unusual in comparison to other bridges throughout the state. We are not sure if the sag indicates a structural weakness, but, in any case, the bridge still carries reasonably heavy traffic, especially during the tourist season.

Since Geiger's Bridge, Rex's Bridge, and Schlicher's Bridge are located within 3.5 miles of each other, directions to find these bridges will start at Rex's, proceed to Geiger's, and end with Schlicher's. However, Schlicher's Bridge can also be reached from PA 309. (See the second set of directions on preceding page.)

Wehr's Bridge

Location: On Wehr Mill Road, northwest of Allentown, South Whitehall Township. **Directions:** From the Manasses Guth Bridge, go 0.2 mile north on Lapp Road to River Road, turn left on River Road for 0.8 mile to Wehr Mill Road, turn left through the bridge. There are parking areas on both the right of the road and in Covered Bridge Park to the left of the road.

Year: 1841 / **Truss:** Burr / **Waterway:** Jordan Creek
In Use: Yes / **Number of Spans:** 1+ / **Owner:** County
Builder: Unknown / **Length:** 138 ft. 4 in. / **Width:** 19 ft. 4 in.
Condition: Very good / **Number:** PA-39-02
Register: December 1, 1980

While there are no other names listed in our documented, state-wide sources, the Lehigh County tourist pamphlet, *Tracking Covered Bridges in the Lehigh Valley*, states: "Wehr's Bridge, also known as Sieger's Bridge, shares its claim to antiquity." This "claim to antiquity" refers to the fact that this bridge was built the same year as the Bogert's Bridge. Consequently, it can lay claim, also, to being one of the county's—and nation's—oldest remaining covered spans.

The Wehr's Bridge is located on a fairly heavily traveled township road adjacent to Covered Bridge Park, an attractive, public park maintained by South Whitehall Township. The bridge is covered with horizontal clapboard siding on the sides, shiplapped siding on the portals, has no side openings other than the typical lengthwise ones under the eaves. The bridge has a slate roof and a deck of lengthwise planking. It rests on stone-and-mortar abutments that have been reinforced with concrete and two stone-and-mortar piers located equidistant from each end. It also has long, sweeping, stone-and-mortar wingwalls and parapets. The parapets are capped with concrete. The high double Burr arch truss system was reinforced with steel beams in 1965, when some reconstruction was performed on the structure.

While we have no documented reports of improvements to the bridge, we are aware that the siding was replaced and painted in the mid-1990s. Its outward appearance is the best of the six county bridges.

Bittenbender's Bridge

Location: On the Bittenbender Farm, Huntingdon Mills. **Directions:** In Huntingdon Mills, from the junction of PA 239 and Waterton Road (SR 4006), go south on Waterton Road for 0.9 mile to the Bittenbender Farm (white house with blue shutters on left side of road). A dirt lane to the bridge is just beyond the house at the end of a stone wall.

Year: 1888 / **Truss:** Queenpost / **Waterway:** Huntingdon Creek
In Use: Yes, private only / **Number of Spans:** 1 / **Owner:** Private
Builder: Frank Monroe and Stephen Dodson
Length: 68 ft. 11 in. / **Width:** 11 ft. 9 in.
Condition: Fairly good / **Number:** PA-40-01
Register: December 1, 1980

This is the only remaining covered bridge in Luzerne County. It was repaired in 1936, including the addition of a center concrete pier and deck reinforcements. It presently rests on poured concrete abutments, which may also have been added during the 1936 improvement. The wingwalls appear to be the original stone walls that were laid dry. The structure is covered with a metal roof and vertical board siding that has been left to weather naturally. The deck consists of runners laid over crosswise planking The bridge was placed on the National Register of Historic Places in December of 1980. There are no reports of any recent work having been done on the bridge; however, on our visit in April 2000, we found it in fairly good condition.

Buttonwood Bridge

Location: On Covered Bridge Road (T 816), Jackson Township.
Directions: In Buttonwood, from the junction of PA 284 and SR 1009, go north on SR 1009 for 0.8 mile to Covered Bridge Road. Turn left (west) on Covered Bridge Road for 0.4 mile to the bridge.

Year: 1898 / **Truss:** Queenpost with kingpost
Waterway: Blockhouse Creek
In Use: Yes / **Number of Spans:** 1 / **Owner:** County
Builder: Unknown / **Length:** 74 ft. 4 in. / **Width:** 15 ft. 8½ in.
Condition: Excellent / **Number:** PA-41-01 / **Register:** July 24, 1980

This is another of the few Pennsylvania bridges designed with this variation of the kingpost truss system. Each side has a queenpost truss that sandwiches a kingpost truss. Efforts have been made to protect the portals and overhead structure of the bridge by placing a heavy steel frame at each portal to clearly indicate the overhead clearance. The portals are covered with vertical boards, and about three-quarters of each side are covered with the same material. The roof is covered with shakes, and the deck consists of runners laid over crosswise planking. The structure rests on poured concrete abutments, has no wingwalls, and there are no steel reinforcements.

In September 1995, a local newspaper article mentioned the need for some restoration to the bridge. By 1998, the bridge had been restored by Lycoming Supply, Inc., Williamsport, PA at a cost of $147,333. The bridge was reopened with a ribbon-cutting ceremony on October 30, 1998. At the time of our visit in April 2000, we found the bridge in excellent condition.

Cogan House / Buckhorn Bridge

Location: On Covered Bridge Road (T 784) (a dead end road) Cogan House Township. **Directions:** In Brookside, from the junction of PA 287 and PA 184, go east on PA 184 for 3.1 miles to Campbell Road (T 784), turn right (south) for 1.3 miles to Covered Bridge Road, turn right for 0.1 mile to the bridge.

Year: 1877 / **Truss:** Burr / **Waterway:** Larry's Creek
In Use: Yes / **Number of Spans:** 1 / **Owner:** County
Builder: Unknown / **Length:** 91 ft. 10 in. / **Width:** 17 ft. 3 in.
Condition: Excellent / **Number:** PA-41-02 / **Register:** July 24, 1980

The Cogan House Bridge is located on a public road that dead ends on the other side of the bridge. It has the typical Burr arch truss sandwiching a multiple kingpost structure, and has been kept in good condition. The portals are covered with horizontal clapboard siding, as are the lower two-thirds of the sides. The roof is covered with shakes. One-half of the deck has runners over crosswise planking, while the other half has lengthwise planking in the center laid over crosswise planking. The entire structure rests on dry, stone abutments with concrete reinforcements at the ends of the Burr arches. There are no parapets and no steel reinforcements.

The Cogan House bridge, like the Buttonwood Bridge, was restored in the 1990s, also by Lycoming Supply, Inc, Williamsport, PA. The cost of its restoration was $105,493. It was reopened on the same day, October 30, 1998, as the Buttonwood Bridge. Even though it is located in a rather remote area, it is worth the trip to see this beautifully restored historic treasure.

Lairdsville / Frazier / Moreland Bridge

Location: On Covered Bridge Road, southwest of Lairdsville.
Directions: In Lairdsville, from the iron bridge along PA 118 West, go 1.4 miles to Old Lairdsville Road (T 509). Turn left and go 0.1 mile to Dairy Farm Road (T 660), then turn left on Dairy Farm Road and go 0.8 mile to Covered Bridge Road (a narrow dirt road between farm buildings). Turn left and go 0.2 mile to the bridge.

Year: 1888 / **Truss:** Burr / **Waterway:** Little Muncy Creek
In Use: Yes / **Number of Spans:** 1 / **Owner:** County
Builder: Unknown / **Length:** 77 ft. 10 in / **Width:** 16 ft. 4½ in.
Condition: Fair / **Number:** PA-41-03 / **Register:** July 24, 1980

This bridge also appears to be fairly well maintained, though presently it only provides passage to a turn-around area next to a farm pasture. It is covered with vertical boards on both the sides and the portals. One portal has an angular arch opening, and the other has a curved arch opening. There is one window located at the end where the road curves. The bridge has a shake roof and a deck of runners laid over crosswise planking. The sides are open for the entire length of the bridge along, approximately, the upper four feet. The bridge rests on cut stone abutments that have concrete reinforcements. It has a typical Burr truss system.

The Lairdsville Bridge is a considerable distance from the other two bridges in Lycoming County, and while it is not in the excellent condition of the Buttonwood Bridge or the Cogan House Bridge, there is evidence that some maintenance is being done on the structure. While some of the paint is peeling, it does seem to be in fair condition. There is a pile of heavy, old timbers near the bridge which may simply be stored there, or may be old timbers from maintenance work on the bridge. We do not recall seeing them on our visit to the bridge in 1991.

Kidd's Mill Bridge

Location: Bypassed by Reynolds Industrial Park Road (SR 4012), between Victory Station and Reynolds Heights, Pymatuning Township. **Directions:** Just north of Victory Station, at the junction of PA 18 and Crestview Drive, go southeast on Crestview Drive for 0.8 mile to Reynolds Industrial Park Road. Turn left on Reynolds Industrial Park Road and go 0.3 mile to the bridge. It is located in a park-like setting on the right side of the road.

Year: 1868 / **Truss:** Smith truss, type 2 / **Waterway:** Shenango River
In Use: Foot traffic only / **Number of Spans:** 1 / **Owner:** County
Builder: Unknown / **Length:** 125 ft. 4 in / **Width:** 16 ft. 7 in.
Condition: Good / **Number:** PA-43-01 / **Register:** December 2, 1974

This is the only covered bridge remaining in Mercer County. It is also the only bridge in Pennsylvania to use any type of Smith truss (see the Introduction). This particular truss, Smith's second type, is shown in the photo of the bridge's interior. The original structure was restored in 1990 by Marcus H. Brandt and Crew, Bucks County, Pennsylvania. It is located in a park-like setting along the Shenango River. The structure is covered with unpainted, twelve-inch, vertical boards and battens on both the sides and the portals. It has a sheet metal roof, and a deck of runners laid over diagonally positioned planking. The runners do not extend over the entire length of the deck. They stop approximately twenty-two feet short of the east end. There are two small windows near the center of each side, in addition to wide, lengthwise openings under the eaves. The entire structure rests on stone-and-mortar abutments on the south side and stone abutments laid dry on the north side. The abutments extend to road-level wingwalls on each end.

The bridge's external appearance is quite attractive in its restored state; however, like several other bridges across the state, it has been extensively defaced with graffiti on the portal, interior sides, and truss structure.

Keefer Mill Bridge

Location: On Keefer Mill Road (TR 346), approximately 1 mile south-west of Washingtonville, Liberty Township. **Directions:** Approximately 1.5 miles south of Washingtonville, at the junction of PA 54 and Stecker-mill Road (SR 3010), go west on Steckermill Road for 0.6 mile to Keefer Mill Road. Turn right on Keefer Mill Road and go 0.5 mile to the bridge.

Year: 1853 / **Truss:** Burr / **Waterway:** Chillisquaque Creek
In Use: Yes / **Number of Spans:** 1 / **Owner:** County
Builder: William Butler / **Length:** 75 ft. 2 in. / **Width:** 16 ft. 6 in.
Condition: Excellent / **Number:** PA-47-03 / **Register:** November 29, 1979

This is the only covered bridge still standing within the Montour County borders, though there is one other covered span on the border with Northumberland County. Built in 1853 for $498 and rebuilt by the county in 1983, the bridge today is covered with vertical board and batten siding on both the sides and portals. The Burr truss arches sandwich a multiple kingpost structure, as is typical. The bridge has a shake roof and lengthwise floor plank-ing. Notice the unusual, square portal design, also known as a storefront portal, quite uncommon in Pennsylvania. The entire structure rests on stone-and-mortar abutments reinforced with concrete and has wingwalls extending only to road level.

In 1999, both the portals and the sides were recovered with new board and batten siding, and painted the typical barn red with white trim. By the time we visited the bridge in April 2000, it had also received a new cedar shake roof. The new roof was applied by ABC Roofing of Bloomsburg, PA, at a cost of $8,500. The Burr truss structure now stands in excellent condition with its new facade and roof. Our only disappointment was to find holes shot through the new siding by some thoughtless individual. However, the avid "bridger" should be sure to see this rather different covered bridge.

Gottlieb Brown / Gottlieb / Sam Wagner Bridge

Location: On Bridge Road (T 308), approximately 1 mile northeast of Pottsgrove, Northumberland County, in Liberty Township, Montour County and Chillisquaque Township, Northumberland County.
Directions: In Pottsgrove, at the junction of PA 642 and SR 1027, go east on PA 642 for 0.5 mile to the junction with Creek Road (SR 1029). Turn left (north) on Creek Road and go 0.7 mile to the bridge, which is immediately to the right on Bridge Road.

Year: 1881 / **Truss:** Burr / **Waterway:** Chillisquaque Creek
In Use: Yes / **Number of Spans:** 1 / **Owner:** Counties
Builder: George W. Keefer / **Length:** 85 ft. 10 in. / **Width:** 15 ft. 3 in.
Condition: Good / **Number:** PA-47-01; PA-49-11
Register: August 8, 1979

This bridge was originally built near the Gottlieb Brown Farm at a total cost of $939. George Keefer used a Burr arch truss system, which, like most Burr arches, sandwiches multiple kingpost framing. The bridge has wide vertical board and batten siding. The portals are also covered with vertical boards but without battens. The structure has stone-and-mortar abutments, stone-and-mortar wingwalls, concrete parapets, and a deck covered with crosswise planking. During our 1991 safari to the Montour/Northumberland border, we met the woman who was living on the farm near the bridge. She informed us that her neighbors consider her to be "keeper of the bridge." Upon our return in April 2000, we were unable to locate the "keeper of the bridge." However, we did find that the bridge is still in fine condition. It is, obviously, still being well maintained by the two counties that claim ownership.

Kreidersville Bridge

Location: On Covered Bridge Road, Kreidersville, Allen Township.
Directions: In Kreidersville, at the junction of Kreidersville Road and Howertown Road, go north for 0.3 mile on Kreidersville Road to Covered Bridge Road. Turn right and go 0.2 mile on Covered Bridge Road to the bridge.

Year: 1839 / **Truss:** Burr / **Waterway:** Hokendauqua Creek
In Use: Foot traffic only / **Number of Spans:** 1 / **Owner:** County
Builder: Unknown / **Length:** 115 ft. 6 in. / **Width:** 18 ft. 3 in.
Condition: Excellent / **Number:** PA-48-01
Register: December 1, 1980

This is the only remaining covered bridge in Northampton County and is also among the oldest remaining covered spans in the state. Shiplapped siding covers the structure, and, unlike many other covered bridges in the state, the sides have no openings at all, not even under the eaves. This creates a very dark interior. The bridge rests on stone-and-mortar abutments set on concrete and has stone-and-mortar wingwalls capped with concrete. The bridge has also had steel reinforcements, which were added during the twentieth century. Even though the bridge appears to be in excellent condition, it is currently closed to vehicular traffic. The present condition of the bridge, which we observed in April 2000 , is largely due to the interest of the residents of Allen Township and Northampton County. According to 1999 publications of the Theodore Burr Covered Bridge Society, these people are "working hard to keep the last covered bridge in this county in good shape." A biennial festival was held at the bridge on June 5, 1999, and since that date, it's been reported that local Boy Scout Troop 40 has repainted the bridge. The roadway leading into the bridge from the south side, formerly made of older asphalt, has been replaced with cobblestone pavers laid in a decorative pattern. All the improvements have been made by local residents and contractors without charge. These efforts have resulted in quite an impressive improvement to the bridge since our last trip.

Himmel's Church / Rebuck Bridge

Location: On T 442, just east of Rebuck, Washington Township.
Directions: In Rebuck, at the junction of SR 3010 and Crissinger Road
(T 426—Rebuck Post Office is at this intersection), go east on SR 3010 for
0.5 mile to Himmel's Church. Turn left on the road past the church
(T 442) and go 0.3 mile to the bridge.

Year: 1874 / **Truss:** Multiple kingpost / **Waterway:** Schwaben Creek
In Use: Yes / **Number of Spans:** 1 / **Owner:** County
Builder: Peter Keefer / **Length:** 42 ft. 3 in. / **Width:** 14 ft. 1 in.
Condition: Good / **Number:** PA-49-06 (2) / **Register:** August 8, 1979

While there are four covered spans still standing within Northumberland County, only three of them were built in the 1800s. Other
examples of nineteenth-century covered bridges can be found
in areas where Northumberland borders Montour and Columbia
Counties. (See Montour/Northumberland Counties and Colum-
bia/Northumberland Counties.)

The Himmel's Church Bridge is situated in an idyllic, rustic, rural
setting in a rather remote area of the county. It uses a short, multiple kingpost truss structure. Both the portals and the sides are
covered with wide, barn red vertical boards and white battens.
Only the lower three-fourths of the sides are covered, however,
leaving fairly wide, lengthwise openings under the eaves. The
bridge rests on concrete abutments with short, stone-and-mortar,
road-level wingwalls. It has a sheet metal roof, and the floor is
decked with crosswise planks set on edge. During both of our visits to this bridge we found it to be a charming, historic structure.
However, on our last visit in April 2000, it had lost a few of its
battens. Hopefully they will be replaced before our next visit.

Keefer Station Bridge

Location: On Mill Road (T 699), approximately 5 miles east of Sunbury, Upper Augusta Township. **Directions:** In Sunbury, from the junction of PA 147 and PA 61, go south on PA 61 for 2 miles to Black Mill Road (SR 4009). Turn left on Black Mill Road and go 0.7 mile to Saw Mill Road (T 509). Continue straight on Saw Mill Road for 1.8 miles to Mill Road (T 699), turn left on Mill Road and go 0.3 mile to the bridge.

Year: 1888 / **Truss:** Burr / **Waterway:** Shamokin Creek
In Use: Closed for repair / **Number of Spans:** 1 / **Owner:** County
Builder: George W. Keefer / **Length:** 96 ft. 2 in. / **Width:** 15 ft. 5½ in.
Condition: Under restoration/ **Number:** PA-49-02
Register: August 8, 1979

The cost of this structure in 1888 was a mere $882. In 1991, narrow, vertical, tongue-and-groove siding covered both the sides and the portals. The portal has a different overhanging gable design, and the sides have lengthwise openings under the eaves that are wider than usual. The roof is covered with sheet metal, and the deck is covered with lengthwise planking. The bridge rests on stone-and-mortar abutments that have been reinforced with concrete, and the stone-and-mortar wingwalls appear to be original to the bridge. At the time of our visit in April 2000, attempts to restore the bridge were underway. Siding on the downstream side had been removed for replacement, and the upstream side was already refurbished with new, tongue-and-groove siding. However, according to a nearby resident, as soon as the bridge is repaired, it is vandalized by youths in the area who hold regular parties on or near the bridge. While the bridge is not located in a particularly attractive area, it is too bad that its historic value is not respected to a greater extent. The renovated, upstream side is already extensively covered with graffiti.

Mertz / Northwood Bridge

Location: On Mirkwood Road, approximately 3 miles north of Northumberland, Point Township. **Directions:** Approximately 3 miles north of Northumberland, at the junction of PA 147 and Ridge Road (T 703), go east for 0.5 mile on Ridge Road to Mirkwood Road. Turn left on Mirkwood Road for 0.2 mile to the bridge.

Year: 1976 / **Truss:** Multiple kingpost / **Waterway:** Unnamed brook
In Use: Yes, private only / **Number of Spans:** 1 / **Owner:** Private
Builder: Unknown / **Length:** 44 ft. 11 in. / **Width:** 12 ft. 5 in.
Condition: Fair / **Number:** PA-49-14 / **Register:** Does not qualify

This is another bridge that is not listed in Zacher's *The Covered Bridges of Pennsylvania* or on the 1989 list of Pennsylvania bridges prepared by The Theodore Burr Covered Bridge Society. The Mertz Bridge is included in our collection because it is listed in the *World Guide to Covered Bridges,* 1989 edition. It was built in 1976 using the multiple kingpost truss design. The bridge is located at the entrance to a private area labeled "Northwood," which is the property of Steve and Katie Mertz. It is sided with vertical boards on the lower half of the sides and on the gable end of the portal. The roof is covered with corrugated metal, and the deck consists of runners laid over diagonal crosswise planking. The deck is reinforced with two, lengthwise, steel I-beams. It rests on poured concrete abutments and a center pier. There are no wingwalls. At the time of our visit in April 2000, we considered the bridge to be in fair condition in comparison to the other bridges that we have visited. Mrs. Mertz informed us that the bridge is used daily as she and her husband enter and leave their property, which is located beyond the bridge.

Rishel / Montandon Bridge

Location: On Covered Bridge Road (T 573), approximately 3 miles east of Chillisquaque, between West Chillisquaque and East Chillisquaque Townships. **Directions:** From PA 147 North, exit to Montandon. Turn right (east) on PA 45 and go 0.7 mile to Covered Bridge Road. Turn right on Covered Bridge Road and go 1 mile to the bridge. (Remain on Covered Bridge Road; where it meets Ridge Road, bear left. Covered Bridge Road is marked T 573 at PA 45 but T 576 at Ridge Road.)

Year: 1830 / **Truss:** Burr / **Waterway:** Chillisquaque Creek
In Use: Yes / **Number of Spans:** 1 / **Owner:** County
Builder: John Shriner and Zacheus Braley / **Length:** 110 ft. 3½ in. /
Width: 17 ft. 6 in.
Condition: Good / **Number:** PA-49-05 / **Register:** August 8, 1979

Some consider this to be the oldest remaining covered bridge in Pennsylvania; however, the *Statewide Covered Bridge Assessment* of 1990 asserts that the Hassenplug Bridge in Union County was built in 1825. Considering that the Hassenplug Bridge was rebuilt in 1959, though, this might be considered the oldest remaining original covered bridge. Except for the lengthwise, narrow openings under the eaves, the Rishel Bridge is completely covered with vertical board siding. The floor decking is composed of runners laid on top of crosswise planks. A Theodore Burr Covered Bridge Society publication of 1998 indicates that the runners were replaced during the summer of that year. The wingwalls and parapets were also repaired during the same season. The Burr arches, in a typical design, sandwich a multiple kingpost truss structure. The roof is made of sheet metal. Notice the rectangular, steel arch that has been erected beyond each portal to control the height of vehicles that use the span; the overhead clearance is a low six feet, three inches. During our visit in 2000, we noticed that the Burr arch on the west end of the bridge has been repaired with eight-ply, laminated, two-by-six inch timbers. Some of the siding on the downstream side has been loosened by flood waters, possibly during the 1999 hurricane season.

Adairs / Cisna Mill Bridge

Location: On SR 3008, just south of Cisna Run, Southwest Madison Township. **Directions:** In Cisna Run, at the junction of PA 274 and SR 3008, go south on SR 3008 for 0.4 mile to the bridge.

Year: 1864 / **Truss:** Burr / **Waterway:** Sherman's Creek
In Use: Yes / **Number of Spans:** 1+ / **Owner:** State
Builder: Unknown / **Length:** 160 ft. 2½ in. / **Width:** 15 ft. 2 in.
Condition: Fair / **Number:** PA-50-04 / **Register:** August 25, 1980

Perry County has fourteen covered bridges that are still standing. Eight of them span Sherman's Creek, which flows in an easterly direction in a valley between two ridges of the Allegheny Mountain range—Tuscarora Mountain and Blue Mountain. Eight of the county's covered bridges were in full use at the time of our 2000 visit; one was closed awaiting determination of repair or restoration possibilities; another was closed because a concrete bridge, just beyond it on the same road, had been washed away; three are located on private property, having been bypassed by a new highway; and the remaining bridge has been moved to Little Buffalo State Park. All of the county's structures have a style typical of other covered bridges in the state—triangular, gable ends on the portals; lengthwise, narrow openings under the eaves; and barn red paint.

During our visit in 1991, we found the Adairs Bridge closed because repairs were being made on the stone-and-mortar wingwalls and the abutment at the north end of the bridge. Since its original construction, the bridge has been reinforced with steel I-beams and an additional, vertical, steel superstructure. This is positioned on concrete foundations in the streambed, located midway between each abutment and a center concrete pier. The bridge is covered with a corrugated metal roof, has beaded, vertical, tongue-and-groove siding, and is decked with lengthwise planking laid over crosswise planking. There are no windows. The only side openings are the typical ones immediately under the eaves. Other than the work that was underway in 1991, we have only one documented mention of additional repairs. In 1997, repairs were made to one of the knee braces. The bridge is still in use, but is in only fair condition. New paint would do much to improve its appearance and preserve the life of the siding material.

Bistline / Flickinger's Mill Bridge

Location: On Red Rock Road (TR 397), 1.5 miles south of Andersonburg, Southwest Madison Township. **Directions:** In Andersonburg, at the junction of PA 274 and SR 3005, go south on SR 3005 for 0.5 mile to Madison Road (T 399). Turn right on Madison Road and go 0.85 mile to Red Rock Road; turn left on Red Rock Road to the bridge.

Year: 1871 / **Truss:** Burr / **Waterway:** Sherman's Creek
In Use: Yes / **Number of Spans:** 1 / **Owner:** State
Builder: Unknown / **Length:** 106 ft. 1 in. / **Width:** 15 ft. 6 in.
Condition: Poor / **Number:** PA-50-03 / **Register:** August 25, 1980

This bridge is covered with barn red, weather-beaten, vertical boards on the sides and vertical boards with battens on the portals. All of the siding is in poor condition. The Bistline Bridge has a corrugated metal roof and a deck of lengthwise planking laid over crosswise planking. It rests on concrete abutments with short, road-level, stone-and-mortar wingwalls on the north end only. Prior to 1991, it had been strengthened with steel reinforcements. The Burr arches, in a typical design, sandwich the multiple kingpost structure. While we considered the bridge to be in fair condition in 1991, we could only evaluate its condition as poor in June 2000. Even some of the major truss timbers are showing signs of deterioration. However, it is still open to traffic and may be scheduled for improvement as part of the state's overall maintenance program.

Book's / Books / Kaufman Bridge

Location: On SR 3003, approximately 2.8 miles east of New Germantown, Jackson Township. **Directions:** Approximately 2.6 miles east of New Germantown, at the junction of PA 274 and SR 3003, go south on SR 3003 for 0.2 mile to the bridge.

Year: 1884 / **Truss:** Burr / **Waterway:** Sherman's Creek
In Use: Closed / **Number of Spans:** 1 / **Owner:** State
Builder: Unknown / **Length:** 87 ft. 6 in. / **Width:** 14 ft. 3 in.
Condition: Very poor / **Number:** PA-50-13 / **Register:** August 25, 1980

This is another one of the eight bridges that span Sherman's Creek in Perry County. The Burr arches sandwich multiple kingpost structures, and the sides and portals are covered with vertical board and batten siding that is in poor condition. The truss timbers are reinforced with steel plates. The roof is covered with sheet metal, and the deck consists of lengthwise planking laid over crosswise planking, all of which is covered with macadam. The only side openings are those under the eaves. This bridge was closed shortly after our visit in 1991, and it has remained closed because of severe damage caused by an overweight vehicle.

Publications of the Theodore Burr Covered Bridge Society have traced the lack of progress regarding repair to this bridge, which is owned by the state. In 1994, it was recommended that repair of the Books Bridge become a priority, and work be rescheduled during the first four years of an updated twelve year plan. In 1997 it appeared that the bridge had dropped 5 or 6 inches and needed to be repaired soon if it was not to be totally lost. In 1999, the bridge was scheduled for rehabilitation under the twelve year road improvements plan of the Harrisburg Area Transportation Study. Yet in the winter of 2000, debate continued about the bridge's fate. The choices seem to be: to do nothing, and let the bridge continue to deteriorate; to rehabilitate the bridge with materials similar to the original; to rehabilitate the bridge with steel I-beams as reinforcements underneath; to rehabilitate the bridge and bypass it with a modern span downstream; or to remove the covered bridge and construct a modern, open span in its place. To the dismay of many persons, both locally and statewide, as this guide went to press, no decision had been made.

Clays / Wahneta Bridge

Location: In Little Buffalo State Park, just north of Juniata Furnace, Centre Township. **Directions:** Little Buffalo State Park is located just north of Juniata Furnace, on SR 1011 (south of SR 4010). There are two entrances to the park. The southernmost entrance leads to the small parking area near Shoaff's Mill, and the northern one leads to the main parking lot. The bridge is easily accessible from either parking area.

Year: 1890 / **Truss:** Burr / **Waterway:** Little Buffalo Creek
In Use: Foot traffic only / **Number of Spans:** 1 / **Owner:** State
Builder: George Harting / **Length:** 80 ft. 11 in. / **Width:** 12 ft. 10 in.
Condition: Very good / **Number:** PA-50-18 / **Register:**

This bridge was moved to Little Buffalo State Park from its original site near New Bloomfield, several miles south of the park. In its new location, it was placed on new concrete abutments where it spans Little Buffalo Creek just a short distance from the restored Shoaff's Mill. On January 26, 1994, the bridge collapsed under heavy snows. Main truss timbers and siding were salvaged and stored under cover at the bridge site until the bridge could be restored. In the spring of 1995 a sign posted at the site stated: "COVERED BRIDGE RESTORATION BEING DONE WITH THE COOPERATION OF THE DEPT. OF ENVIRONMENTAL RESOURCES, BUREAU OF STATE PARKS, SETCO, SIDE, PA MUSEUM COMMISSION, AND PA TRAPPERS ASSOCIATION." A report in Theodore Burr Covered Bridge Society publications of 1997 indicated that the bridge was completely restored and visited by society members.

In June 2000, we visited the restored bridge and found it in very good condition. It has many elements typical of the Perry County bridges, such as barn red vertical board siding, white-trimmed portals, a roof of cedar shakes, and a deck of random-width, lengthwise planks reinforced with steel. The bridge has no wingwalls, and the only openings on the sides are the lengthwise ones under the eaves. Visitors who come to the park to see the bridge are rewarded, also, with the opportunity to see the beautifully restored Shoaff's Mill, complete with stone and clapboard siding and a huge, steel mill wheel. It is just a short walk from the covered bridge.

Dellville Bridge

Location: On Pine Hill Road, Dellville, Wheatfield Township.
Directions: In Dellville, where SR 2002 makes a ninety degree turn, Pine Hill Road goes to the southwest. The bridge is visible from this intersection on Pine Hill Road.

Year: 1889 / **Truss:** Burr / **Waterway:** Sherman's Creek
In Use: Yes / **Number of Spans:** 1+ / **Owner:** County
Builder: Andrew Clouser / **Length:** 174 ft. 7 in. / **Width:** 16 ft.
Condition: Fairly good / **Number:** PA-50-16
Register: August 25, 1980

This is the most easterly bridge that spans Sherman's Creek. It is the longest and widest bridge in Perry County, and outward appearances would lead one to think it is a two-span bridge. However, examination of the truss structure inside the bridge indicates that it is a single-span bridge that consists of high, double Burr arches—reinforced with additional diagonal bracing—that sandwich the multiple kingpost structures. The bridge has vertical board and batten siding on both the sides and the portals and a shake roof. The deck consists of crosswise planking which, in the center sixty percent of the deck, is overlaid with lengthwise planking. In addition to the normal openings under the eaves, there are three windows on the southeast side and two on the northwest side. The entire structure is strengthened with steel beams and tie rods under the deck. It rests on concrete abutments and a center concrete pier. The stone-and-mortar wingwalls and parapets at the northeast end have been rebuilt; the ones at the southwest end appear to be the original ones reinforced with concrete. Publications in the spring of 1999 indicated that some work was done on the bridge in that year. At the time of our visit in June 2000, we noticed that the roof, in particular, could use some additional repair. The cedar shakes displayed many holes which, if left untreated, will gradually expose the truss and deck to inclement weather.

Enslow / Turkey Tail Bridge

Location: On an unnamed, unmarked road, approximately 1 mile southeast of Blain, Jackson Township. **Directions:** Just south of Blain, at the junction of PA 274 and SR 3006, go south on SR 3006 for 0.8 mile. Turn left on an unnamed road and go 0.15 mile; turn left on another unnamed road and go 0.3 mile to the bridge.

Year: 1904 / **Truss:** Burr / **Waterway:** Sherman's Creek
In Use: Yes / **Number of Spans:** 1+ / **Owner:** County
Builder: Unknown / **Length:** 116 ft. 5½ in. / **Width:** 14 ft. 1 in.
Condition: Fair / **Number:** PA-50-14 / **Register:**

This is another typical example of a Burr truss structure. It, too, spans Sherman's Creek. This bridge has random-width vertical board siding on both sides and portals, a rusty metal roof, and a deck of crosswise planking. It rests on concrete abutments and a center pier of concrete, and it has stone-and-mortar wingwalls. Its undercarriage is reinforced with steel I beams.

The Enslow Bridge suffered damage during Hurricane Fran in September 1996. The bridge was closed in that year, but by the spring of 1997 it had been straightened and repaired. The structure received new portals, new beams, and new side boards, and the end posts were mended. The county then awarded a contract for additional repairs to the Enslow Bridge, the Mount Pleasant Bridge, and the Rice Bridge. At the time of our visit in June 2000, we noticed that some work had been completed on the approaches to the three bridges, but the Enslow Bridge itself had again suffered some damage. One of the corner posts has partially shifted off of its foundation, and the portal on the west end had been fractured, resulting in missing boards. This bridge, like several other Perry County bridges, could be additionally improved with a coat of paint.

Fleisher's Bridge

Location: On Fairground Road, on the northwest edge of Newport, Oliver Township. **Directions:** In Newport, at the junction of the north end of Fourth Street and Fairground Road, go west on Fairground Road for 1 mile to the bridge.

Year: 1887 / **Truss:** Burr / **Waterway:** Big Buffalo Creek
In Use: Yes / **Number of Spans:** 1+ / **Owner:** County
Builder: Yohn and Ritter / **Length:** 123 ft. 8½ in. / **Width:** 14 ft. 6 in.
Condition: Good / **Number:** PA-50-17 / **Register:** August 25, 1980

Improvements have definitely been made to this bridge since our visit to it in 1991. A portal that was leaning severely has been straightened, new vertical board siding has been applied, and a new sheet metal roof has been installed. The bridge has been recently repainted the typical barn red color, and trimmed with white. The seven-ton load limit has been increased to fourteen tons. Three parapets, each approximately two and one-half feet high, have been built along the approaches to the bridge. In the place of a fourth parapet, a steel guardrail has been erected. The original stone-and-mortar abutments have also been reinforced with concrete. The only side openings are immediately under the eaves and run the length of the bridge. We were quite pleased by the extensive repairs to this bridge we saw in June 2000.

Kochenderfer Bridge

Location: Bypassed by Fritz Road (T 332), approximately 1 mile south of Saville, Saville Township. **Directions:** Approximately 1 mile south of Saville, at the junction of PA 17 and Fritz Road, go south on Fritz Road for 0.2 mile to the bridge.

Year: 1919 / **Truss:** Queenpost with kingpost
Waterway: Big Buffalo Creek
In Use: Foot traffic only / **Number of Spans:** 1 / **Owner:** Private
Builder: Adair Brothers / **Length:** 71 ft. 1½ in. / **Width:** 15 ft. 8½ in.
Condition: Fair / **Number:** PA-50-08 / **Register:** August 25, 1980

This privately owned bridge was being used for storage of farm equipment in 1991, but was completely empty in June 2000. The basic truss structure is a multiple kingpost which is overlaid with a queenpost truss. The sides and portals are covered with narrow, vertical boards. The roof is corrugated metal, the deck is crosswise planking, and the bridge rests on concrete abutments. Short, concrete wingwalls rise to form parapets along the approaches, approximately two feet above road level. The only side openings are the typical narrow ones under the eaves. Additional steel reinforcing appears under the deck. Except for a few missing siding boards and one portal that is unpainted, the bridge seems to be in fair condition.

Mount Pleasant Bridge

Location: On Mt. Pleasant Road (TR 391), Mt. Pleasant, Jackson Township. **Directions:** In Mt. Pleasant, at the junction of PA 274 and Mt. Pleasant Road, go south on Mt. Pleasant Road for 0.35 mile to the bridge.

Year: 1918 / **Truss:** Queenpost with kingpost
Waterway: Sherman's Creek
In Use: Closed / **Number of Spans:** 1 / **Owner:** County
Builder: L. M. Wentzel / **Length:** 73 ft. 2 in. / **Width:** 15 ft. 3½ in.
Condition: Fair / **Number:** PA-50-12 / **Register:** August 25, 1980

This bridge is another example of the combination of kingpost and queenpost trusses. Like the New Germantown Bridge (also in Perry County), the Mount Pleasant Bridge has a kingpost truss sandwiched between two queenpost trusses. The sides and portals are sided with narrow, vertical, tongue-and-groove boards, and the roof is metal. The deck consists of wide runners, which appear to have been recently replaced, laid over wide, crosswise planking. The bridge rests on concrete abutments and has road-level, stone-and-mortar wingwalls covered with concrete. The entire structure has been reinforced with steel. There are no windows, but there are typical side openings under the eaves. This is one of the bridges in Perry County that has been under contract for improvements since 1997. There is evidence of some new, freshly painted, siding, but the bridge needs to be entirely repainted. The roadway approaches to the bridge have been repaved. At the time of our visit in June 2000, the road to the bridge was closed, not because of the condition of the Mount Pleasant Bridge, but because the bridge a short distance to the south was no longer there.

New Germantown Bridge

Location: On Lower Buck Ridge Road, New Germantown, Toboyne Township. **Directions:** In New Germantown, at the junction of PA 274 and Lower Buck Ridge Road, go south on Lower Buck Ridge Road for 0.3 mile to the bridge.

Year: 1891 / **Truss:** Multiple kingpost with queenpost
Waterway: Sherman's Creek
In Use: Yes/ **Number of Spans:** 1 / **Owner:** County
Builder: John W. Fry / **Length:** 74 ft. 8½ in. / **Width:** 13 ft. 9 in.
Condition: Fairly good / **Number:** PA-50-11
Register: August 25, 1980

This is one of the more attractive bridges in Perry County. It, too, has a rather unusual truss treatment in which a multiple kingpost truss structure is sandwiched between two queenpost trusses. The sides and portals are covered with vertical board and batten siding, the roof is made of corrugated metal, and the deck consists of lengthwise planking laid over crosswise planking. The structure rests on concrete abutments with moderately long, stone-and-mortar wingwalls that rise to parapets approximately two feet above the approaches. Like several other bridges in the county, the New Germantown Bridge has been damaged by flood waters over the past nine years. Although Hurricane Fran caused damage to the bridge in September 1996, it was not closed. Since then, repairs have been made.

Red Bridge

Location: Bypassed by SR 1005, approximately 1.5 miles west of Liverpool, Liverpool Township. **Directions:** In Liverpool, at the junction of PA 17 and SR 1010 (just west of junction of PA 17 and US 11/15), go south on SR 1010 for 1.3 miles (SR 1010 turns right after 0.2 miles) to SR 1005. Turn right and go 0.2 mile to the bypassed bridge.

Year: 1886 / **Truss:** Multiple kingpost with queenpost
Waterway: Wildcat Creek
In Use: Foot traffic only / **Number of Spans:** 1 / **Owner:** Private
Builder: Unknown / **Length:** 55 ft. 3 in. / **Width:** 15 ft. 7 in.
Condition: Fair / **Number:** PA-50-05 / **Register:** August 25, 1980

This bridge has been bypassed by a new highway, and when we visited the bridge in 1991, it was being restored by a Perry County historical society. A local, retired mason was rebuilding the stone-and-mortar wingwalls and parapets. We were pleased that people in the county were concerned about the preservation of this bridge even though it is no longer used for traffic. We also have reports that members of the Theodore Burr Covered Bridge Society cleared the heavy, wild growth near the portals in 1994. In 1991, much of the siding was covered with heavy vine growth. On our visit in April 2000, the vines had been cleared from the sides of the bridge, and the area immediately surrounding the bridge had been recently mowed. Otherwise, the bridge was in basically the same, fair condition.

The Red Bridge's truss design is similar to that of the New Germantown Bridge. Again, here, a multiple kingpost truss is sandwiched between two queenpost trusses. The bridge is covered with vertical boards and battens on the sides and horizontal clapboard on the portals. While most of the other bridges in Perry County have only white trim on their portals, the portals on the Red Bridge are completely white. The bridge has no windows. The roof is made of sheet metal, the deck is laid in a diagonal herringbone pattern, and the structure rests on stone-and-mortar abutments that extend to moderately long wingwalls and fairly low parapets.

Rice / Landisburg Bridge

Location: On Kennedy Valley Road (T 331), on the south edge of Landisburg, Tyrone Township. **Directions:** In Landisburg, at the junction of PA 233, PA 850, and Carlisle Street, go south on Carlisle Street for 0.1 mile to Kennedy Valley Road. Turn right on Kennedy Valley Road and go 0.5 mile to the bridge.

Year: 1869 / **Truss:** Burr with two queenposts
Waterway: Sherman's Creek
In Use: Yes / **Number of Spans:** 1+ / **Owner:** County
Builder: Unknown / **Length:** 132 ft. 4 in. / **Width:** 16 ft. 3 in.
Condition: Fairly good / **Number:** PA-50-10 / **Register:** August 25, 1980

This bridge, too, has an unusual truss structure. In the Rice Bridge, single Burr arches sandwich a multiple kingpost structure that runs the length of the bridge, and queenpost trusses overlay the kingpost truss for what appears to be two spans. The Burr arches rest on the abutments, and the queenpost trusses rest on the abutments at each end and on the pier in the center. Some of the "old-timers" among our "bridging" associates seem to think that the bridge was originally a single span Burr truss bridge and that the pier and the queenpost truss overlays were later revisions. We have no documentation to prove or disprove this assumption. The bridge is covered with barn red, vertical boards and battens on the sides and portals. It has a sheet metal roof and a deck of lengthwise planking laid over crosswise planking. There are two windows on each side located near the end where the road bends, and there are additional steel reinforcements under the deck. During our visit in June 2000, we found the bridge in fairly good condition, except that some of the siding boards had been either intentionally removed or washed away by flood waters of the 1999 hurricane season. Replacement of these boards would greatly improve the appearance of the bridge, as well as preserve the interior.

Saville Bridge

Location: On SR 4001, in Saville, Saville Township. **Directions:** The bridge is in Saville, on SR 4001, just south of SR 4002.

Year: 1903 / **Truss:** Burr / **Waterway:** Big Buffalo Creek
In Use: Yes / **Number of Spans:** 1 / **Owner:** State
Builder: L. M. Wentzel / **Length:** 72 ft. 1 in. / **Width:** 13 ft. 11½ in.
Condition: Fair / **Number:** PA-50-07 / **Register:** August 25, 1980

This bridge, although built later than many others in the county, was badly in need of repair when we visited it in 1991. There were many boards and battens missing on the sides. The portals, covered with similar material, were in much better condition. On our return trip in June 2000, we found that the missing boards and battens had been replaced, apparently recently. The material seems to be quite new, and much of it is still unpainted. The truss structure of the bridge consists of Burr arches which, in a typical manner, sandwich a multiple kingpost structure. The truss is reinforced with vertical, steel I-beams placed on concrete footings at three locations under this relatively short bridge. There are also supporting steel structures placed at the abutments. These are rusted to an extensive degree, and some are missing entirely. The original stone-and-mortar abutments and wingwalls are still standing. The bridge has a sheet metal roof and a deck of lengthwise planking laid over crosswise planking. The only openings are the typical, narrow ones under the eaves.

Waggoner Mill / Waggoner's Mill / Thompson Bridge

Location: Bypassed by PA 274, approximately 0.5 mile east of Fort Robinson, Northeast Madison Township. **Directions:** In Fort Robinson, at the junction of PA 274 and PA 850, go east on PA 274/PA 850 for 0.5 mile. Watch carefully for the bridge on the left side of the road. The covered bridge can be seen from the concrete bridge which has bypassed it.

Year: 1889 / **Truss:** Burr / **Waterway:** Bixler's Run
In Use: Closed / **Number of Spans:** 1 / **Owner:** Private
Builder: Joseph D. Lightner/ **Length:** 84 ft. 10 in. / **Width:** 14 ft. 9 in.
Condition: Poor / **Number:** PA-50-15 / **Register:** August 25, 1980

Much of the beauty of the Waggoner Mill Bridge lies in its proximity to an old stone gristmill with the dam and portions of the mill race still present. We understand that the gristmill is currently being restored, but during our visit to the bridge in June 2000, we were not able to see any of the renovations. The access road to the mill is now completely closed at the end of the bridge near PA 274.

The bridge is in basically poor condition. It rests on stone-and-mortar abutments with moderate length stone-and-mortar wingwalls that rise to moderate height parapets. The sides and portals are covered with vertical board and batten siding, but most of the battens are missing. The roof is covered with corrugated metal, and the deck consists of lengthwise planking. The only openings in the sides are the narrow ones immediately under the eaves.

Thomas Mill Bridge

Location: On Thomas Mill Road, in Fairmount Park, Philadelphia.
Directions: From the Pennsylvania Turnpike (I 276), take exit 25 (Norristown) to Germantown Pike East. Go east on Germantown Pike for 4.8 miles to Chestnut Hill Avenue. Turn right on Chestnut Hill Avenue for 0.6 mile to Towanda Avenue; turn right on Towanda Avenue for 0.3 mile to dead end. Park along Towanda Avenue. Follow the walking trail, downhill, straight ahead, along a high stone wall for several hundred feet (trail turns right along the wall). The trail meets Thomas Mill Road (gravel road), at the end of the wall. Turn left and follow Thomas Mill Road, bearing left downhill where the road forks. Continue to the bridge. Total walking distance is approximately 0.5 mile.

Year: 1855 / **Truss:** Howe / **Waterway:** Wissahickon Creek
In Use: Foot traffic only / **Number of Spans:** 1 / **Owner:** City
Builder: Unknown / **Length:** 97 ft. / **Width:** 16 ft. 4 in.
Condition: Excellent / **Number:** PA-51-01
Register: December 1, 1980

This is the oldest—and one of the longest—of Pennsylvania's five remaining historic Howe truss type covered bridges. Although there were a number of covered bridges in the Philadelphia area during the nineteenth century, this is the only one still standing. It is comforting to know that there are still persons concerned enough to preserve this one. Its portals have unusual sawtooth decorations. Its sides and portals are covered with barn red vertical board and batten siding. It has a deck of crosswise planks, stone and mortar abutments and wingwalls, and a sheet metal roof. It is open only to foot traffic, horses, and unmotorized vehicles, since it is located within the Wissahickon Park section of Fairmont Park, which is closed to all motorized vehicles. Accessible by foot, the bridge is approximately three-quarters of a mile from Chestnut Hill Avenue in Chestnut Hill, Philadelphia. Our satisfaction at having found the bridge, as well as the opportunity to photograph it, were well worth the efforts of reaching this bridge.

During our visit to the bridge in 1991, we considered the bridge to be only in fair condition. However, when we returned in May 2000, we were most pleased with the rehabilitated appearance of the bridge. In the summer of 1999, the Stepnoski Bros., Inc., of Philadelphia replaced the original shingle roof with sheet metal, replaced the four corners of the bridge that rest on the abutments, replaced and painted the siding, and replaced floor boards as required. The total cost of the renovation was $400,000. It is now in excellent condition.

Rock Bridge

Location: On T 542 (name and Township Route number not posted), just east of Rock, Washington Township. **Directions:** In Rock, at the "Village of Rock" sign, at the east end of the village, go east on PA 895 for 0.5 mile to a road going north. Go north on that road for 0.1 mile to the bridge.

Year: 1870 / **Truss:** Burr / **Waterway:** Little Swatara Creek
In Use: Yes / **Number of Spans:** 1 / **Owner:** County
Builder: Unknown / **Length:** 55 ft. 7 in. / **Width:** 16 ft. 2 in.
Condition: Good / **Number:** PA-54-02 / **Register:**

The original stone abutments of the Rock Bridge have been strengthened with concrete, and steel I-beam supports have been placed next to the abutments to add extra support to the structure. Inside, steel guardrails protect the truss system from traffic. This is a modern addition we saw a few times during our travels. While these huge I-beams protect the truss structure and add rigidity to the bridge deck, they do little for the overall appearance of this historic structure. An article in a 1996 newsletter of the Theodore Burr Covered Bridge Society quoted a local newspaper which said that "the bridge has been closed far too long for the people who live south of the Little Swatara Creek." Our information does not relate why the bridge was closed prior to 1996. A publication released later in 1996 indicated that the bridge had been opened again. When we visited the bridge in May 2000, we found it in good condition except for the necessary interior I-beams, and a large amount of graffiti covering the inner walls.

Zimmerman's Bridge

Location: On T 661, just west of Rock, Washington Township.
Directions: At the east end of Rock, starting at the "Village of Rock" sign, go west on PA 895 for 1.3 miles to a road going south (there are no road markings in the area). Turn left (south) for 0.1 mile to the bridge.

Year: 1880 / **Truss:** Burr / **Waterway:** Little Swatara Creek
In Use: Closed / **Number of Spans:** 1 / **Owner:** County
Builder: Unknown / **Length:** 64 ft. 10 in./ **Width:** 12 ft. 8 in.
Condition: Good / **Number:** PA-54-01 / **Register:**

Like the Rock Bridge, the Zimmerman's Bridge is covered with wide, vertical boards without battens. The deck is covered with floorboards laid at a forty five degree angle. This bridge, too, has a heavy, steel guardrail on the inside of the bridge to protect the truss structure. However, this rail is not as large or unattractive as the one on the Rock Bridge. We have reports from 1996 that indicate that J. D. Eckman Construction, Inc., of Atglen, PA, lifted the entire structure from its abutments. They placed it, intact, on the roadway while the abutments were being rebuilt. Repairs were delayed by "red tape" typical to government agencies, but finally, in the summer of 1998, the bridge was returned to the refurbished abutments. Its basic structure had also been rebuilt during this time, including the replacement of the lower cords. When we visited the bridge in May 2000, we found it in good condition except for a moderate amount of graffiti on the inside. It is unfortunate that there is a lack of respect for these historic structures in some areas of the state. We became aware of an even more recent indication of disrespect for this particular bridge through an announcement made at a covered bridge society meeting on July 9, 2000. There, we learned that the Zimmerman's Bridge has again been closed because of extensive damage done by an overweight vehicle. At the time of this writing, nothing is known of anticipated repairs.

Aline / Meiserville Bridge

Location: Bypassed by Aline Church Road (TR 333), Aline, between Chapman and Perry Townships. **Directions:** In Aline, just southwest of the junction of PA 104 and Aline Church Road.

Year: 1884 / **Truss:** Burr / **Waterway:** Mahantango Creek (North Branch)
In Use: Foot traffic only / **Number of Spans:** 1 / **Owner:** County
Builder: Unknown / **Length:** 69 ft. 11 in. / **Width:** 18 ft. 8½ in.
Condition: Very poor / **Number:** PA-55-04 / **Register:** August 10, 1979

This bridge was bypassed in 1982 by a new bridge over the North Branch of the Mahantango Creek. The area around the Aline Bridge is becoming overgrown, and the structure is used only for foot traffic. It still appeared to be in fair condition until, upon closer examination of the truss structure in April 2000, we found that the arch of the Burr truss was cracked. The bridge has no steel reinforcements. It rests on stone-and-mortar abutments which have been reinforced with concrete and has low, stone-and-mortar wingwalls. It is covered with vertical board and batten siding on both the sides and the portals. The barn red paint has faded since our 1991 visit. The roof is metal, and the deck, like those of the other two Snyder County bridges, consists of runners down the center of the bridge laid over crosswise planking. The Aline Bridge has fairly wide, lengthwise openings under the eaves. There are no other side windows.

Dreese's / Dreese / Beavertown Bridge

Location: Bypassed by Covered Bridge Road (T 600), approximately 2 miles east of Beavertown. **Directions:** In Beavertown, from the junction of PA 522 and SR 4007, go north on PA 522 for 1.5 miles to Covered Bridge Road. Turn left on Covered Bridge Road and go 1 mile to the bridge.

Year: 1870 / **Truss:** Burr / **Waterway:** Middle Creek
In Use: Foot traffic only / **Number of Spans:** 1 / **Owner:** County
Builder: Unknown / **Length:** 103 ft. 6 in. / **Width:** 15 ft. 9 in.
Condition: Fair / **Number:** PA-55-02 / **Register:** August 10, 1979

This bridge was bypassed by a new highway in 1979. The area surrounding it is heavily overgrown, and the old roadway into the bridge appears to be used as a storage area for township or county road maintenance equipment. We were gratified to see, however, that the structure was still standing and in fair condition. It is covered with vertical board and batten siding on both the sides and the portals, and has a sheet metal roof. The deck consists of runners in the center laid over crosswise planking. There are side openings only under the eaves. The truss system is Burr arch with multiple kingpost. The entire structure rests on stone-and-mortar abutments reinforced with concrete, and there are stone-and-mortar wingwalls and parapets. The parapets are capped with concrete. There were no obvious changes to the bridge since our visit in 1991.

Klinepeter's / Gross / Overflow Bridge

Location: On Railroad Street, Beaver Springs, Spring Township.
Directions: In Beaver Springs, at the junction of PA 235 and PA 522, go south on PA 522 for 0.1 mile to Spring Street. Turn left on Spring Street for 0.1 mile to Railroad Street; turn right on Railroad Street for 0.1 mile to the bridge.

Year: 1871 / **Truss:** Burr / **Waterway:** Middle Creek (tributary)
In Use: Yes / **Number of Spans:** 1 / **Owner:** Township
Builder: Unknown / **Length:** 105 ft. 5 in. / **Width:** 17 ft. 1 in.
Condition: Excellent / **Number:** PA-55-03 / **Register:** August 29, 1977

Originally built across Middle Creek, one mile northwest of its present location, this bridge was rebuilt in the town of Beaver Springs in 1982. The typical Burr truss structure is covered with vertical board and batten siding on both the sides and the portals. The roof is sheet metal, and the deck has runners down the center laid over crosswise planking. The bridge presently spans a creekbed that is a tributary of Middle Creek. It rests on poured concrete abutments that extend to short wingwalls. The stone-and-mortar parapets are approximately two feet high and rise above the wingwalls. The only side openings are fairly wide, lengthwise ones directly under the eaves. We have no information regarding specific maintenance work on the bridge since our visit in 1991, but it is apparent that the bridge is being well maintained. It may have had a coat of paint since our last visit. We considered it to be in excellent condition, which is far better than we recalled from our earlier visit.

Barronvale Bridge

Location: Bypassed by SR 3014 in Barronvale, Middlecreek Township.
Directions: In New Lexington, at the junction of PA 218 and PA 653, go
west on PA 653 for 2 miles to junction with SR 3035. Go north on
SR 3035 for 1 mile to a "T" with SR 3014. Turn right on SR 3014 and go
0.1 mile to the bypassed bridge.

Year: 1902 / **Truss:** Burr / **Waterway:** Laurel Hill Creek
In Use: Foot traffic only / **Number of Spans:** 2 / **Owner:** Private
Builder: Cassimer Cramer / **Length:** 162 ft. 1½ in. / **Width:** 13 ft.
Condition: Fair / **Number:** PA-56-03 / **Register:** December 11, 1980

The Burr truss bridges in Somerset County have two interesting
features. The Burr arches are constructed with six to nine lami-
nates of approximately two-by-four inch lumber, and the wide side
openings expose part of the truss structure. With the exception of
the New Baltimore Bridge, the Pack Saddle Bridge, and the Kings
Bridge, every bridge in this county has at least one-quarter to one-
half of the truss structure open to view and the weather.

The date of construction for the Barronvale Bridge as shown on
the name plate is 1830; however, the *Statewide Covered Bridge Assessment* lists it as 1846, and the *World Guide to Covered Bridges* and
Zacher's book list it as 1902. If you look carefully at the photo of
this bridge, you will notice that the two spans are of different
lengths, and consequently have Burr arches of different heights.
Both Burr trusses, however, consist of seven-ply laminated arches.
Vertical boards cover only the lower half of the sides, exposing a
portion of the higher Burr arch and the upper half of the multiple

kingpost truss structure. The bottom of the bridge's interior is covered with one, eight-inch high board. The portals are also covered with vertical boards and are attractively painted. They are identical in design to the portals of the King's Bridge, which is located only one mile downstream. The Barronvale Bridge has a metal roof laid over old shakes, and it has lengthwise deck planking. It rests on cut stone-and mortar-abutments without wingwalls. It appears to be used for private farm traffic, but this information is not posted in any way. There was little change in the condition or appearance of the bridge when we visited it in 2000.

Burkholder / Beechdale Bridge

Location: On Burkholder Bridge Road (T 548), approximately 2.2 miles northeast of Garrett, Brothers Valley Township. **Directions:** Just northeast of Garrett, and north of Garrett Slope Station, at the junction of PA 219 and Burkholder Bridge Road, go west for 0.1 mile on Burkholder Bridge Road to the bridge.

Year: 1870 / **Truss:** Burr / **Waterway:** Buffalo Creek
In Use: Yes / **Number of Spans:** 1 / **Owner:** County
Builder: Unknown / **Length:** 52 ft. 4 in. / **Width:** 12 ft. 9½ in.
Condition: Fair / **Number:** PA-56-01 / **Register:** December 10, 1980

The Burkholder Bridge has a mixture of six-ply and nine-ply laminated Burr arches, which sandwich the multiple kingpost structure in a typical manner. The siding on both sides and the portals is of vertical boards. The top half of each side is open, exposing part of the multiple kingpost structure. The Burr arch is below the side openings. The roof is metal, and the deck is made of random-width crosswise planking. The structure rests on cut stone-and-mortar abutments, has road-level wingwalls on one end only, and is heavily reinforced with four I-beams under the deck. While most of the Somerset County bridges appear to be well maintained, it does not appear that much has been done to this bridge since we visited it in 1991. In May 2000, we found peeling paint and a rusting metal roof. Perhaps in the near future, the Burkholder Bridge will see the kind of restoration that has been done to three of the other county bridges in recent years—the Glessner, the New Baltimore, and the Pack Saddle Bridges.

Glessner Bridge

Location: On Covered Bridge Road (T 565), 0.8 mile north of Shanksville, Stony Creek Township. **Directions:** In Shanksville, at the junction of SR 1001 and SR 1007, go north on SR 1007 for 0.1 mile. Bear left on SR 1007 for 0.15 mile, bear right on SR 1007, and go 0.65 mile to Covered Bridge Road. Turn left on Covered Bridge Road and go 0.5 mile to the bridge.

Year: 1881 / **Truss:** Burr / **Waterway:** Stony Creek
In Use: Yes / **Number of Spans:** 1+ / **Owner:** County
Builder: Tobias Glessner/ **Length:** 96 ft. 2 in. / **Width:** 12 ft. 8½ in.
Condition: Excellent / **Number:** PA-56-08
Register: December 10, 1980

This bridge, like two other bridges owned by Somerset County, has been recently restored. It had been closed to traffic in 1995, but was completely restored and rededicated on July 18, 1998 (the same day as the other two restored bridges, the New Baltimore and the Pack Saddle Bridges, were rededicated). Random-width, vertical boards cover the lower two-thirds of the exterior and lower one-third of the interior. The portals are also covered with vertical boards. The bridge is attractively painted in a typical scheme of barn red with white trim. The roof is new, corrugated metal and the deck has runners laid over crosswise planking. The Burr truss structure, again, consists of six-ply laminated arches. The entire structure rests on concrete abutments and a center concrete pier built on a concrete foundation in the middle of the stream. One abutment extends to form short wingwalls below road level. Even though the bridge has heavy, steel reinforcements under the deck, it is posted with a three-ton load limit.

King's Bridge

Location: Bypassed by PA 653, 1.8 miles west of New Lexington,
Middlecreek Township. **Directions:** In New Lexington, at the junction of
PA 281 and PA 653, go west on PA 653 for 1.9 miles to a gravel road on
the left. Turn left on the gravel road, and the bridge is just to the right.

Year: 1906 / **Truss:** Burr / **Waterway:** Laurel Hill Creek
In Use: No (restoration under way) / **Number of Spans:** 1
Owner: Private / **Builder:** Unknown
Length: 127 ft. 10 in. / **Width:** 12 ft. 8 in.
Condition: Poor / **Number:** PA-56-06 / **Register:** December 11, 1980

The year of construction posted on the gable end of this bridge is
1802. This date is questionable because most bridges in this area
were not built until considerably later in the nineteenth century.
Another sign indicates that the bridge was rebuilt in 1906, and the
World Guide to Covered Bridges lists this year for the bridge's origin.
The bridge has been bypassed by a contemporary road. At the time
of our visit in 1991, the bridge was privately owned and used for
storage. Since 1992, efforts have been underway to preserve and
restore the bridge. An item in a 1992 Theodore Burr Society peri-
odical indicated that money was being sought from the America's
Industrial Heritage project to renovate the bridge. In spring 1997,
the Burr Society donated $350 toward its restoration. The King
family, on whose property the bridge was situated, requested that

Rockwood Historical Society assume responsibility for it. In the fall of 1997, there was indication that the Rockwood Historical Society had made restoration of the bridge one of its goals. At the time of our visit in May 2000, we found that the bridge had been stabilized with steel superstructure by Arnold M. Graton Associates, Ashland, NH, a bridge restoration company. Additional funds for the restoration of the King's Bridge are still being sought by the Rockwood Historical Society.

Lower Humbert / Faidley Bridge

Location: On Covered Bridge Road (T 312), approximately 2 miles northeast of Ursina, Lower Turkeyfoot Township. **Directions:** In Kingwood, at the junction of PA 281 and SR 3007, go south on SR 3007 for 6.1 miles to Covered Bridge Road, and the bridge is just to the right. Or (for better road conditions), follow PA 281 toward Ursina, then, approximately 1.3 miles northeast of Ursina, at the junction of PA 281 and SR 3007, go north on SR 3007 for 1 mile to Covered Bridge Road, and the bridge is just to the left on Covered Bridge Road.

Year: 1891 / **Truss:** Burr / **Waterway:** Laurel Hill Creek
In Use: Yes / **Number of Spans:** 1+ / **Owner:** County
Builder: Unknown / **Length:** 126 ft. 4 in. / **Width:** 12 ft. 4 in.
Condition: Good / **Number:** PA-56-12/ **Register:** December 10, 1980

At the time of our 1991 visit to this bridge, we found that contractors were taking considerable measures to divert the flow of Laurel Hill Creek from the east abutment. Extensive work was being done to reinforce both the abutment and the approaches to the bridge. Obviously, the bridge was closed at that time. During our visit in 2000, we found the restored bridge open and in fine condition. It has been reinforced with four steel I-beams resting on both the stone-and-mortar abutments and a central stone and mortar pier which has been erected in the middle of Laurel Hill Creek. However, the bridge still supports only a three-ton vehicular load. Approximately two-thirds of the sides are covered with barn red, random-width vertical board siding, and the portals are similarly covered, and trimmed in white. The deck consists of lengthwise planks, and the roof is made of sheet metal. The bridge is located in a quiet, peaceful valley in the southwestern corner of the county, approximately ten miles from the Maryland border.

New Baltimore Bridge

Location: On Findley Street (T 812), New Baltimore, Allegheny Township. **Directions:** Northwest of New Baltimore, at the junction of SR 1015 and SR 1017, go east on SR 1015 for 1 mile (watch for sign on telegraph pole to "New Baltimore Bridge"). Turn left on Findley Street and go 0.1 mile to the bridge.

Year: 1879 / **Truss:** Multiple kingpost
Waterway: Raystown Branch, Juniata River
In Use: Yes / **Number of Spans:** 1 / **Owner:** County
Builder: Unknown / **Length:** 86 ft. 1½ in. / **Width:** 11 ft. 9 in.
Condition: Excellent / **Number:** PA-56-09 (2)
Register: December 10, 1980

This bridge is located on the northern edge of New Baltimore, where it appears to be used fairly frequently for vehicular traffic. It is one of three bridges in the county that has had extensive, recent restoration. The New Baltimore Bridge required major renovations because January 1996 flood waters washed it from its abutments. A temporary foot bridge was erected by the Army Corps of Engineers to provide passage to the family living on the opposite side of the bridge. Reconstruction started in the summer of 1997 when Lone Pine Construction, Inc. was awarded the $538,621 contract to rebuild the bridge. A Theodore Burr Society publication indicated that the main load carrying members would be steel beams; "however, timber members will be assembled to replicate the original structure to restore the bridge appearance." The restoration was completed by the summer of 1998, and the bridge was one of three rededicated on July 18, 1998. Neilan Engineers, Inc., of Somerset were the engineers entrusted with overseeing the project. Review was conducted by the Pennsylvania Department of Transportation in coordination with the Pennsylvania Historic and Museum Commission. This lovely restoration is covered with barn red, random-width, vertical board siding on both the sides and the portals, and the portals are trimmed in white. The bridge has a sheet metal roof and a deck of lengthwise planking. It rests on new, concrete abutments that extend to road-level wingwalls, all of which have been faced with cut stone. The structure no longer has reinforcing piers to support the three-ton vehicular load.

Pack Saddle / Doc Miler Bridge

Location: On Packsaddle Road (T 407), 4.3 miles northwest of Fairhope, Fairhope Township. **Directions:** Approximately 4.5 miles southwest of New Baltimore, at the junction of PA 31 and Dividing Ridge Road (SR 1015), go south on Dividing Ridge Road for 4.5 miles to a "T" with SR 2019. Turn right on SR 2019 and go 3 miles to Pine Valley Road, turn right on Pine Valley Road, and go 0.3 mile to Packsaddle Road. Turn left and go 0.1 mile to the bridge.

Year: 1870 / **Truss:** Multiple kingpost / **Waterway:** Brush Creek
In Use: Yes / **Number of Spans:** 1 / **Owner:** County
Builder: Unknown / **Length:** 47 ft. 11½ in. / **Width:** 13 ft 10½ in.
Condition: Excellent / **Number:** PA-56-02
Register: December 10, 1980

This bridge is located in an attractive, quiet, wooded setting where it spans a rocky glen through which the Brush Creek tumbles. It, too, was badly damaged by flood waters in January 1996. A $5,000 grant from the Federal Emergency Management Agency was used to make minor repairs that same year; however, an engineering study recommended reconstruction of the stone masonry abutments, installation of steel stringers, new timber floor beams, a new plank deck, and a new galvanized corrugated steel roof. While the state wanted to close the bridge and replace it with a concrete bridge upstream, the townspeople protested. In 1998, Kee-Ta Quay Construction of Hustontown, PA, restored the bridge at a cost of

$382,263. Eighty percent of this amount came from the Billion Dollar Bridge Bill, and twenty percent came from Act 26 funds. The reconstructed bridge was rededicated on July 18, 1998 (the same day that the Glessner and the New Baltimore Bridges were rededicated). This lovely span now stands proudly over the rapidly cascading waters of the Brush Creek. It rests on new, concrete, stone-faced abutments that extend to short, road-level wingwalls. It is covered with barn red, random-width, vertical board siding and trimmed in white. The deck consists of crosswise planking, and the roof is made of corrugated metal. It is worth a trip to this remote, southeastern corner of the county to see this restored, historic structure and its spectacular setting.

Shaffer / Bens Creek Bridge

Location: On Covered Bridge Road (T 634), approximately 2 miles west of Bens Creek, Conemaugh Township. **Directions:** At the east end of Bens Creek, at the junction of PA 403 and PA 985, go west on PA 985 for 1.95 miles to Covered Bridge Road. Turn left on Covered Bridge Road and go 0.1 mile to the bridge.

Year: 1877 / **Truss:** Burr / **Waterway:** Bens Creek
In Use: Yes / **Number of Spans:** 1 / **Owner:** County
Builder: Unknown / **Length:** 67 ft. 10 in. / **Width:** 13 ft. 3½ in.
Condition: Good / **Number:** PA-56-11 / **Register:** December 10, 1980

This covered bridge is located in the extreme northern part of the county, at least nineteen miles from the closest bridge. The Shaffer Bridge, like most of the other county bridges, appears to have been well maintained. Vertical board and batten siding covers the lower half of the exterior sides, and vertical boards cover the lower three feet of the interior. The upper half of the sides are open, exposing just the top edge of the fairly low, six-ply laminated Burr arch truss and the upper part of the sandwiched, multiple kingpost structure. The portals are covered with vertical boards. The roof is sheet metal, and the deck consists of crosswise planking. The structure rests on cut stone-and-mortar abutments and has no wingwalls. This bridge, like others in Somerset County, is in a rustic, sylvan setting.

Trostletown / Kantner Bridge

Location: In Stoystown Lions Club Park, Stoystown, Quemahoning Township. **Directions:** In Stoystown, at the junction of US 30 and PA 403, go west on US 30 for 0.15 mile to Stoystown Lions Club Park Road. Turn left and go 0.2 mile to parking area. The bridge is to the left as you approach the parking area.

Year: 1845 / **Truss:** Multiple kingpost with queenpost
Waterway: Stony Creek
In Use: Foot traffic only / **Number of Spans:** 3 / **Owner:** Private
Builder: Unknown / **Length:** 104 ft. 1 in. / **Width:** 12 ft. 8½ in.
Condition: Very good / **Number:** PA-56-10
Register: December 11, 1980

In 1965, the Stoystown Lions Club undertook the project of restoring and preserving the Trostletown Bridge. The club has a park immediately adjoining the bridge, and the bridge is now used for foot traffic only. The Lion's Club sought additional funds for restoration from the America's Industrial Heritage Project. The resulting refurbishing took place over a three-year period from 1993–1996. The recent restoration was rededicated on September 28, 1996. The structure still stands on its original cut stone abutments and stone-and-mortar piers. The roof is covered with regular roof shingles, and the deck consists of crosswise planking. Since our visit in 1991, short, decorative, stone walls, of approximately seven feet long have been added inside the extended portals of the bridge. The sides and portals are covered with random-width vertical boards. The top one-third of the sides are open, exposing the rather distinctive truss structure, which has additional, diagonal supports of both steel rods and wooden timbers. The *World Guide* lists the truss as a multiple kingpost with queenpost; however, the *State-wide Covered Bridge Assessment*, the Burr Society, and Zacher's *The Covered Bridges of Pennsylvania* list it as a multiple kingpost. Our on-site examination of the structure led us to the conclusion that it is a three-span bridge. Starting at the parking lot approach, a kingpost truss spans from the abutment to the first pier, another kingpost truss spans from pier to pier, and a queenpost truss spans from the second pier to the far abutment. The photo shows the upper portion of each truss.

Walter's Mill / Cox Creek Bridge

Location: In Somerset Historical Center, approximately 4 miles north of Somerset, Middlecreek Township. **Directions:** Approximately 4 miles north of Somerset at the junction of PA 601 and PA 985, go north on PA 985 for 0.1 mile to the entrance to Somerset Historical Center. Turn left into the parking lot. The bridge is located in the historic display area.

Year 1859 / **Truss:** Burr / **Waterway:** Haupts Run
In Use: Foot traffic only / **Number of Spans:** 1 / **Owner:** State
Builder: Christian Ankeny and Jacob Walter
Length: 62 ft. 3 in. / **Width:** 12 ft. 10 in.
Condition: Fair / **Number:** PA-56-05 / **Register:** December 10, 1980

This bridge was originally located over Cox Creek, approximately four miles south of Somerset, but is now located in the Somerset Historical Center, which is operated by the state. There is some uncertainty concerning the date of its origin. The *Statewide Covered Bridge Assessment* lists it as 1859 with 1830 as "Other Doc. Date." The *World Guide to Covered Bridges* and the pamphlet, *Somerset Historical Center,* list 1859. Susan Zacher's *The Covered Bridges of Pennsylvania* lists 1830. Taking into consideration the date of origin of the other Somerset County bridges and those of surrounding counties, we are inclined to believe that 1859 is the more plausible date.

The Walter's Mill Bridge now spans Haupts Run and rests on poured concrete abutments. Random-width vertical boards cover the portals and the lower half of the exterior sides. The lower three feet of the interior sides are also covered. The roof is overlaid with cedar shakes, and the deck consists of crosswise planking. The Burr arches are made of seven-ply laminated, rough cut two-by-four timbers, and the entire structure is heavily reinforced with steel I-beams.

Forksville Bridge

Location: On Bridge Street, Forksville. **Directions:** In Forksville, along PA 154, look for the bridge on Bridge Street. The street directly across PA 154 from the bridge, however, is Huckle Street.

Year: 1850 / **Truss:** Burr / **Waterway:** Loyalsock Creek
In Use: Yes / **Number of Spans:** 1 / **Owner:** State
Builder: Sadler Rodgers / **Length:** 163 ft. 3 in. / **Width:** 18 ft. 10½ in.
Condition: Good / **Number:** PA-57-01 / **Register:** July 24, 1980

This bridge is heavily traveled since it is the shortest route from PA 154 to the general store in the town of Forksville, just north of World's End State Park. The Forksville Bridge is covered with vertical board siding on both the sides and the portals. It has a sheet metal roof and a deck of very narrow crosswise planks. The entire structure is heavily reinforced with steel girders. Its typical Burr truss structure rests on stone and concrete abutments. It has three long, narrow windows on the north side and four on the south side. It also has the typical lengthwise opening under the eaves.

There have been no announcements regarding improvements to this bridge since 1991. At the time of our 2000 visit we considered the bridge to be in good condition with the exception of one piece of missing siding on the downstream side. This is another affirmation of the exceptional durability of covered bridges. Many of them continue to survive with little or no maintenance.

Hillsgrove / Rinkers Bridge

Location: On Covered Bridge Road (T 357), northeast of Hillsgrove.
Directions: Between Hillsgrove and Loyalsock Creek, from the junction of PA 87 with Splash Dam Road (T 359), go north for 0.1 mile to Covered Bridge Road. Turn left to the bridge.

Year: 1850 / **Truss:** Burr / **Waterway:** Loyalsock Creek
In Use: Yes / **Number of Spans:** 1 / **Owner:** County
Builder: Sadler Rodgers / **Length:** 185 ft. 7 in. / **Width:** 15 ft. ½ in.
Condition: Good / **Number:** PA-57-02 / **Register:** July 2, 1973

This bridge and the Forksville Bridge were both built by Sadler Rodgers in 1850. They are similar in design and use the same truss system. The Hillsgrove Bridge has vertical board and batten siding on the sides and vertical boards without battens on the portals. It has a sheet metal roof laid over the original shakes and very narrow crosswise planking for the deck. There are three narrow windows on the south side and two on the north side. The bridge also has the typical, lengthwise openings under the eaves. It rests on stone-and-mortar abutments which have been reinforced with concrete, and there are no parapets.

We have received no information regarding extensive repair work to the Hillsgrove Bridge since 1991. However, when we visited the bridge in April 2000, it was obvious that some of the board and batten siding had been replaced on the northeast side. Other than a few missing battens, the bridge is in good condition and continues to carry vehicular traffic.

Sonestown Bridge

Location: On Champion Hill Road (T 310), just south of Sonestown.
Directions: Along US 220, approximately 1 mile south of Sonestown, the bridge is located on Champion Hill Road, just to the east of US 220.

Year: 1850 / **Truss:** Burr / **Waterway:** Muncy Creek
In Use: Yes / **Number of Spans:** 1 / **Owner:** County
Builder: Unknown / **Length:** 118 ft. 11 in. / **Width:** 14 ft. 6 in.
Condition: Good / **Number:** PA-57-03 / **Register:** July 24, 1980

This bridge was built using the typical Burr truss system, but the Burr truss is angular rather than the usual, smoothly shaped arch. The structure is covered with vertical boards on both the sides and the portals, and it rests on stone-and-mortar abutments with wing walls that are below road-level. The bridge has a shake roof, and the deck consists of runners laid over crosswise planking. There are no steel reinforcements and no windows other than the openings under the eaves.

The Sonestown bridge was closed in 1996 because of damage caused by flooding in January of that year. The Lycoming Supply Co. of Williamsport, PA, repaired the damage within a sixty-day period at a cost of $89,000, and the bridge was promptly reopened. At the time of our 2000 visit, we found the bridge in good condition

Old Mill Village / L. C. Beavan Bridge

Location: In Old Mill Village. **Directions:** From I 81 North, take Exit 66 (Gibson Exit). Follow PA 848 west for 3.5 miles to the village on the right side of the highway.

Year: 1965 / **Truss:** Town / **Waterway:** Unnamed stream
In Use: No / **Number of Spans:** 1 / **Owner:** State
Builder: Unknown / **Length:** 29 ft. 5½ in. / **Width:** 8 ft. 11 in.
Condition: Good / **Number:** PA-58-01 / **Register:** Does not qualify

In 1850, a Town truss covered bridge was built in Delaware County, New York. One truss of that bridge was moved to Old Mill Village in 1965, where it was used to build this structure. Old Mill Village is a reconstructed, early American village, reminiscent of the late eighteenth and early nineteenth centuries. This bridge has been included in this guide because it is one of the 221 Pennsylvania covered bridges included in the most recent copy of the *World Guide to Covered Bridges*. While it is not an authentic, historic, Pennsylvania bridge, it does add charm to the Old Mill Village. It is an unpainted structure, covered with vertical board and battens on the sides. The portals are covered with vertical boards cut in a sawtooth pattern. The bridge has a shingled roof and a deck of lengthwise planking. It rests on rock and concrete abutments without wingwalls.

Factory / Horsham Bridge

Location: On Gray Hill Road (T 514), White Deer, White Deer Township.
Directions: In White Deer, from the junction of SR 1011 and SR 1010, go west on SR 1010 for 1.6 miles to Gray Hill Road. Turn left (south) on Gray Hill Road for 0.1 mile to the bridge.

Year: 1880 / **Truss:** Queenpost with kingpost
Waterway: White Deer Creek
In Use: Yes / **Number of Spans:** 1 / **Owner:** County
Builder: Unknown / **Length:** 68 ft. 2 in. / **Width:** 16 ft. 2 in.
Condition: Fairly good / **Number:** PA-60-04
Register: February 8, 1980

This is one of the five authentic, historic covered bridges remaining in Union County. Notice the exceptionally high load limit indicated on the sign in the photo—thirty-four tons. (The average load limit for a covered bridge is between two and five tons.) This high limit is made possible by eight large I-beams placed under the deck of the original structure. These rest on concrete reinforcements to the original stone-and-mortar abutments. The original, low, stone-and-mortar wingwalls still stand behind the heavy, steel guardrails. Both the sides and the portals are covered with vertical board and batten siding, the roof is made of sheet metal, and the deck is covered with lengthwise planking. The only openings are the lengthwise, narrow ones under the eaves. This bridge has a kingpost truss system sandwiched between two queenpost trusses. Since our visit in 1991, the only reported work done on the bridge was the deck replacement in the summer of 1992. During our visit in 2000, we considered the bridge to be in fairly good condition.

Gordon Hufnagle Memorial Park Bridge

Location: On Sixth Street, in the Gordon Hufnagle Memorial Park, Lewisburg. **Directions:** In Lewisburg, on Sixth Street, just north of PA 45.

Year: 1982 / **Truss:** Town / **Waterway:** Bull Run
In Use: Foot traffic only / **Number of Spans:** 1 / **Owner:** Community
Builder: Randy Cassidy and Brian Hassinger
Length: 46 ft. 6 in. / **Width:** 5 ft. 5 in.
Condition: Good / **Number:** PA-60-06 / **Register:** Does not qualify

The construction of this bridge was completed in 1982; therefore, it cannot be considered an authentic historical structure. It is included in our collection because it is listed in the *World Guide to Covered Bridges*; however, it is not included in Zacher's *The Covered Bridges of Pennsylvania* or on the list of Pennsylvania covered bridges prepared by the Theodore Burr Covered Bridge Society of Pennsylvania. This attractive covered footbridge was an engineering project of student engineers Randy Cassidy and Brian Hassinger from Bucknell University, working under the supervision of R. J. and R. L. Brungraber. The entire structure is a wooden Town truss completely open on the sides and left to weather naturally.

Hassenplug Bridge

Location: On Fourth Street, Mifflinburg, Buffalo Township.
Directions: In Mifflinburg, at the junction of PA 45 and PA 304, go north on Fourth Street to the bridge. (South Fourth Street is PA 304.)

Year: 1825 / **Truss:** Burr / **Waterway:** Buffalo Creek
In Use: Yes / **Number of Spans:** 1 / **Owner:** County
Builder: Unknown / **Length:** 80 ft. 4 in. / **Width:** 16 ft. 9 in.
Condition: Good / **Number:** PA-60-03 / **Register:** February 8, 1980

This bridge is essentially a modern steel bridge that has been built within the shell of the original wooden structure. It has an open steel mesh deck with broad steel guardrails. The steel structure rests on concrete abutments and vertical steel girders positioned on a concrete foundation in midstream. It has red board and batten siding on the sides and horizontal white clapboard siding on the portals. The original truss structure consisted of Burr arches sandwiching a multiple kingpost structure. The stone-and-mortar wingwalls and concrete-capped parapets were repaired in the summer of 1998 according to bridge society publications. The only side openings are the very narrow, lengthwise ones under the eaves. It was pleasing to see that there is still interest in retaining the original historic facade of the covered bridge for this otherwise modern, steel structure.

During our visit to the bridge in April 2000, we noticed that the area around the bridge has been greatly improved since 1991. Some of this improvement may have taken place during the refurbishing of the wingwalls and parapets in 1998. The stream, too, has been redirected since our 1991 visit, possibly to eliminate some of the erosion that was taking place near the abutments and wingwalls.

Hayes Bridge

Location: On Hoover Road (T 376), approximately 2 miles west of Mifflinburg, West Buffalo Township. **Directions:** In Mifflinburg, from the junction of PA 45 and PA 304, go west on PA 45 for 2.4 miles to Hoover Road. Turn right (north) on Hoover Road and go 0.6 mile to the bridge.

Year: 1882 / **Truss:** Multiple kingpost / **Waterway:** Buffalo Creek
In Use: Yes / **Number of Spans:** 1 / **Owner:** County
Builder: Unknown / **Length:** 70 ft. 2 in. / **Width:** 17 ft. 7½ in.
Condition: Good / **Number:** PA-60-02 / **Register:** February 8, 1980

When we visited this bridge on our first "bridging" safari, during the first week of May 1991, some restoration work was underway. At that time, the contractors indicated that they intended to replace only the timbers that were deteriorating, and they did not intend to add any steel reinforcements. At the time of our visit in April 2000, the bridge appeared in good condition. It is covered with barn red vertical boards and battens on both the sides and the portals. It has a sheet metal roof and a deck of lengthwise planking laid over crosswise planking. The multiple kingpost structure rests on abutments of cut stone-and-mortar reinforced with concrete, and the wingwalls and parapets are made of stone-and-mortar. The only side openings are the typical, lengthwise ones under the eaves. Notice the angled, iron overhead clearance structures at each entrance to the bridge. They limit passage over the bridge to vehicles of six feet, six inches or less.

Hubler / Lewisburg Penitentiary Bridge

Location: On a private farm lane and the end of William Penn Drive, Lewisburg Penitentiary, Lewisburg. **Directions:** (Penitentiary access) In Lewisburg, from the junction of US 15 and PA 192, go north 0.4 mile on US 15 to William Penn Drive. Turn left on William Penn Drive and go 2.8 miles to the bridge. After entering William Penn Drive, Buffalo Creek will be to the left. Keep the creek on the left, making left turns where necessary. This drive enters the penitentiary property. Passage beyond the large recreation hall may be questioned. Or (farm lane access) in Lewisburg, from the junction of US 15 and PA 192, go west on PA 192 for 1.7 miles to Strawbridge Road (TR 451). Turn right (north) and go 1.5 miles to the dirt lane to the right after crossing the iron bridge. The property is owned by the farm just ahead on Strawbridge Road. Enter only after acquiring permission.

Year: 1850 / **Truss:** Multiple kingpost (modified)
Waterway: Little Buffalo Creek
In Use: No, Closed / **Number of Spans:** 1 / **Owner:** Federal/Private
Builder: Unknown / **Length:** 41 ft. 7 in. / **Width:** 17 ft. 6 in.
Condition: Excellent / **Number:** PA-60-05 / **Register:**

This bridge is located at the end of a farm lane where it meets the property of the Federal Penitentiary in Lewisburg, Pennsylvania. During our visit to this bridge in 1991, we reached it from a farm lane off of Strawbridge Road, by permission of the owner of the farm. In 2000, through the courtesy of Richard Donovan, third vice-president of the Theodore Burr Covered Bridge Society, we were able to visit the bridge through the Federal Penitentiary facility. The bridge is actually located on both the farm property and the penitentiary property. The bridge has an interesting truss structure, which is a modification of the Burr truss. Two diagonal timbers rest on cut stone-and-mortar abutments and meet in the form of an inverted "V" approximately in the middle of the sandwiched multiple kingpost structure. The bridge is covered with horizontal, clapboard siding on both the sides and the portals, has a shake roof, and has a deck of crosswise planking. The only side openings are the narrow, lengthwise ones under the eaves. The original cut stone-and-mortar wingwalls and parapets are still standing. While we considered the bridge to be in only fair condition in 1991, in 2000 we found it to be in excellent condition. It received extensive repairs in the fall of 1993.

Millmont Red / Glen Iron Bridge

Location: On TR 320, approximately 1.5 miles southwest of Millmont, Hartley Township. **Directions:** In Hartleton, at the junction of PA 45 and Millmont Road (SR 3003), go south on Millmont Road for 1.7 miles to the junction with SR 3004. Turn right (west) on SR 3004 for 0.8 miles to the bridge, which is just to the left.

Year: 1855 / **Truss:** Burr / **Waterway:** Penns Creek
In Use: Closed / **Number of Spans:** 1 / **Owner:** County
Builder: Unknown / **Length:** 157 ft. 10 in. / **Width:** 14 ft. ½ in.
Condition: Very poor / **Number:** PA-60-01 / **Register:** February 8, 1980

The horizontal, shiplapped siding on both the portals and the side walls make this 157 feet, 10 inch structure appear even longer. The roof is covered with sheet metal, and the deck is lengthwise planking in the center laid over crosswise planking. There are no windows, but the typical openings under the eaves run the length of the bridge. The interesting, sloping portals, which were open in earlier photographs, are now closed, and the clearance dimension is plainly marked as six feet. This is an exceptionally long Burr arch structure with a few reinforcing tie rods, all of which rest on stone-and-mortar abutments with stone-and-mortar wingwalls. Both the abutments and wingwalls appear to have been rebuilt. When we visited the Millmont Bridge in 1991, it was still open to traffic. Publications of the Theodore Burr Covered Bridge Society indicate that it has been closed since about 1994. At the time of this writing, we have no information concerning the future of this structure. While the photograph does not show it graphically, there is a sag in the entire structure. If this historic structure is to survive, it will definitely require some repair.

Bailey Bridge

Location: On Bailey Road (T 686), a dead end road, approximately 1.5 miles southeast of Amity, Amwell Township. **Directions:** From I 79 south, Marianna/Prosperity Exit (Exit 5), at the end of the exit ramp, go west on Ten Mile Road for 1.3 miles to Bailey Road. Turn left and go 0.1 mile to the bridge.

Year: 1889 / **Truss:** Burr / **Waterway:** Ten Mile Creek
In Use: Yes / **Number of Spans:** 1+ / **Owner:** County
Builder: Daniel Smith for Bailey Brothers
Length: 70 ft. 3 in. / **Width:** 15 ft. 5 in.
Condition: Excellent / **Number:** PA-63-08 (2)
Register: June 22, 1979

The Bailey Covered Bridge is one of twenty-four bridges still standing within the boundaries of Washington County. Twenty-three of these bridges are almost identical in design, color, and structural material. At the time of this writing in June 2000, seventeen still carry vehicular traffic. Of the seven bridges closed to traffic, one, the Ralston Freeman Bridge, is on private property and closed to the public, and another, the Pine Bank Bridge, is located in a recreated early American farm village. Two are located in park areas and do not carry vehicular traffic—the Devil's Den Bridge and the Hughes Bridge. Three bridges, the Longdon L. Miller Bridge, the Wyit Sprowls Bridge, and the Sprowls Bridge, are being restored. The former two have anticipated completion dates in the end of 2000, and the latter should be completed by the end of 2001.

At the time of our visit to the bridge in 1991, we considered the bridge to be in excellent condition. However, we learned that it was destroyed by fire in July 1994, when a truck was driven on the bridge and set on fire. By 1999, the bridge had been completely rebuilt using all new materials except for the Burr arches and central cross timbers of each truss. In May 2000, we again found the bridge in excellent condition. It is still located on a gravel township road and now rests on beautifully stone-faced abutments with wingwalls and a center pier. The entire bridge structure is supported on eight steel girders. The wingwalls rise above road level to form fairly short stone-and-mortar parapets. The Executive Director of the County Planning Commission informed us that the Burr truss bridge has been reconstructed exactly as it was when the county assumed possession of it. The barn red vertical board siding and portals are typical of many of the well-maintained bridges in this county.

Brownlee / Scott Bridge

Location: On Templeton Run Road (T 414), approximately 2.5 miles north of East Finley, East Finley Township. **Directions:** In East Finley, at the junction of PA 231 (East Finley Drive) and Rocky Run Road (SR 3035), go north on PA 231 for 2.2 miles to Templeton Run Road. Turn left on Templeton Run Road and go 0.2 mile to the bridge.

Year: Unknown / **Truss:** Kingpost
Waterway: Templeton Fork, Wheeling Creek
In Use: Yes / **Number of Spans:** 1 / **Owner:** County
Builder: Unknown / **Length:** 40 ft. 3½ in. / **Width:** 12 ft. 9 in.
Condition: Good / **Number:** PA-63-09 / **Register:** June 22, 1979

This bridge is covered with vertical boards on both the sides and portals and is painted barn red inside and outside. It has a sheet metal roof and a deck with heavy, canvas runners laid over crosswise planking. There are two rectangular windows on each side in addition to the lengthwise openings under the eaves. The entire structure is supported with additional wooden timbers that are positioned at equal intervals resting in the streambed. It rests on cut stone-and-mortar abutments built on concrete foundations. Stone-and-mortar wingwalls extend into moderate length parapets approximately two feet above road level at each approach. In May 2000, we found that the Brownlee Bridge, like many others in the county, had recently been painted, and it was in better condition than we recalled from our previous visit. Through the Executive Director of the County Planning Commission, we learned that there has been considerable interest and progress in covered bridge restoration in Washington County during the past nine years. This was quite obvious to us as we traveled through the county.

Crawford Bridge

Location: On a gravel road (no road name or Township Route number visible), approximately 1 mile north of West Finley, West Finley Township. **Directions:** In West Finley, at the junction of West Finley Road (SR 3037) and Burnsville Ridge Road, go west on West Finley Road for 1.05 miles (after 0.25 mile bear right) to a gravel road. Turn left on gravel road and go 0.1 mile to the bridge.

Year: Unknown / **Truss:** Queenpost
Waterway: Robinson Fork, Wheeling Creek
In Use: Yes / **Number of Spans:** 1 / **Owner:** County
Builder: Unknown / **Length:** 48 ft. 5 in. / **Width:** 12 ft. 7½ in.
Condition: Very good / **Number:** PA-63-10 / **Register:** June 22, 1979

The Crawford Bridge is typical of other Washington County bridges. It has vertical board siding on both the sides and portals, and both the exterior and interior walls are painted barn red. The bridge has a sheet metal roof and a deck of crosswise planking. There are two rectangular windows on each side in addition to the eave openings. The structure rests on cut stone-and-mortar abutments laid on concrete foundations, and the abutments extend to form short, stone-and-mortar wingwalls. Moderate length parapets rise approximately two feet above road level at each approach. The Crawford Bridge is also reinforced with heavy timbers that are positioned in the streambed at equal intervals under the cross members of the deck. Publications of the Theodore Burr Covered Bridge Society indicate that the bridge was closed early in 1996 and placed on the twelve year plan for restoration. However, a local resident told us that the bridge was repaired and reopened after being closed for about six months. She also told us that it is re-painted annually. Its appearance, when we visited it in May 2000, was very good.

Danley Bridge

Location: On Dogwood Hill Road (T 379), 1.2 miles north of Good Intent, West Finley Township. **Directions:** In Good Intent, at the junction of Good Intent Road (SR 3025) and Robinson Run (T 343), go north on Good Intent Road for 1.2 miles to Dogwood Hill Road (T 379). Turn right on Dogwood Hill Road and go 0.1 mile to the bridge.

Year: Unknown / **Truss:** Queenpost
Waterway: Robinson Fork, Wheeling Creek
In Use: Yes / **Number of Spans:** 1 / **Owner:** County
Builder: Unknown / **Length:** 48 ft. 2 in. / **Width:** 13 ft. 1 in.
Condition: Good / **Number:** PA-63-11 / **Register:** June 22, 1979

The Danley Bridge is another span that is located along a gravel township road in a hidden valley of Washington County. Like many of the other county bridges, it is covered with vertical board siding on both the sides and portals, is painted barn red inside and outside, has a sheet metal roof, and has a deck of crosswise planking. There are two rectangular windows on each side and the typical eave openings. The Danley Bridge rests on stone-and-mortar abutments. On one end, the wingwalls and parapets are made of stone-and-mortar, one of which is quite long; and on the other end they are made concrete. The deck is supported with two sets of wooden timbers that rest in the streambed.

Theodore Burr Society publications indicate that the bridge was closed in 1996 but was not placed on the twelve year plan for restoration. However, in May 2000, the bridge was open and had recently been repainted, possibly as part of the ongoing efforts of the Washington County Planning Commission to keep the local covered bridges in good condition.

Day Bridge

Location: On T 339, 1.3 miles east of Sparta, Morris Township.
Directions: In Sparta, at the junction of PA 18 and SR 3033, go north on PA 18 for 1.3 miles to a road leading to the right. The bridge is just off of PA 18.

Year: 1875 / **Truss:** Queenpost / **Waterway:** Short Creek
In Use: Foot traffic only / **Number of Spans:** 1 / **Owner:** County
Builder: Unknown / **Length:** 41 ft. 3 in. / **Width:** 13 ft. 2½ in.
Condition: Good but closed / **Number:** PA-63-12
Register: June 22, 1979

This is another typical Washington County covered bridge. It is barn red inside and outside, has vertical board siding on both the sides and the portals, has a sheet metal roof, has a deck of crosswise planking, and has two windows on each side in addition to the narrow eave openings. The queenpost truss structure rests on one abutment made of stone-and-mortar reinforced with concrete and a second abutment that appears to be all concrete. The wingwalls extend into short parapets approximately two feet above road level at each approach. Three of the parapets are stone-and-mortar, the fourth is concrete.

In May 2000, the bridge was closed, which is obvious in the photo. Upon contacting the Washington County Planning Commission, we were informed that the bridge is scheduled for some restoration work in 2001. Recently, however, the Day Bridge (like all the other bridges we visited in this county) has been painted. Its appearance in 2000 was quite good, which is another indication of the county's attempt not only to maintain, but to improve the condition of its bridges.

Ebenezer / Ebenezer Church Bridge

Location: In Mingo Creek County Park, just northeast of Kammerer, Nottingham Township. **Directions:** From the park access road, approximately 1 mile east of Kammerer, at the junction of PA 136 and Chapel Road, go north on Chapel Road for 0.65 mile. Turn left on the park road (Mingo Creek Road) for 0.3 mile. Bear left for 0.1 mile to the bridge and parking area.

Year: Unknown / **Truss:** Queenpost / **Waterway:** Mingo Creek
In Use: Yes / **Number of Spans:** 1 / **Owner:** County
Builder: Unknown / **Length:** 38 ft. 4 in. / **Width:** 12 ft. 9 in.
Condition: Very good / **Number:** PA-63-14 / **Register:** June 22, 1979

This bridge was moved to its present location in Mingo Creek County Park in 1977 and altered to rest on abutments remaining from another structure. From the side, the revised structure resembles an old-style train caboose; otherwise, it is similar in style to the other county bridges. A side view of this bridge is found in some of Washington County's tourist promotion literature and is very prominent on Washington County Tourism Promotion Agency internet site. The bridge has a sheet metal roof and a deck of crosswise planking. It is covered with vertical board siding on both the sides and portals, and is painted barn red both inside and outside. Two rectangular windows are cut into each side, and the openings under the eaves are fairly wide. The deck is heavily reinforced with five steel I-beams. These, in turn, rest on the original abutments reinforced with concrete. Fairly long, cut stone-and-mortar wingwalls extend into parapets that are capped with concrete at each approach. The Ebenezer Bridge is an attractive addition to the county park.

Erskine Bridge

Location: On Erskine Road, approximately 3 miles south of West Alexander, West Finley Township. **Directions:** In West Alexander, at the junction of Main Street and Maple Ave. (SR 3023), go south on Maple Ave. for 2.75 miles to Middle Creek Road (SR 3018), turn right on Middle Creek Road and go 0.55 mile to Erskine Road. The bridge is just to the left on Erskine Road.

Year: 1845 / **Truss:** Queenpost / **Waterway:** Middle Wheeling Creek
In Use: Yes / **Number of Spans:** 1 / **Owner:** County
Builder: William Gordon / **Length:** 48 ft. / **Width:** 12 ft. 10 in.
Condition: Good / **Number:** PA-63-15 / **Register:** June 22, 1979

This bridge has the most westerly location of any covered bridge in Pennsylvania, less than one mile from the Ohio/Pennsylvania state line. It is the oldest remaining covered bridge in Washington County, and is typical of most of the Washington County structures. It has vertical board siding on both the sides and the portals, is painted barn red inside and outside, has a sheet metal roof, a deck of crosswise planking, and two windows on each side in addition to the narrow eave openings. The queenpost truss structure rests on stone-and-mortar abutments reinforced with concrete. Further support is provided by heavy timbers resting in the streambed that have been replaced since our 1991 visit. The bridge has short, concrete wingwalls and parapets on the north end and attractive, short, stone-and-mortar wingwalls and parapets on the south end. The Erskine Bridge has been recently painted, probably in the past year.

Henry Bridge

Location: In Mingo Creek County Park, just northeast of Kammerer, Nottingham Township. **Directions:** Approximately 1 mile east of Kammerer, at the junction of PA 136 and Chapel Road (the park access road), go north on Chapel Road for 0.65 mile. Turn right on the park road (Mingo Creek Road) and go 0.4 mile to Parkview Road. Turn right on Parkview Road and go 1.1 miles to Mansion Road; turn right on Mansion Road to the bridge.

Year: 1881 / **Truss:** Queenpost / **Waterway:** Mingo Creek
In Use: Yes / **Number of Spans:** 1 / **Owner:** County
Builder: Unknown / **Length:** 45 ft. 4 in. / **Width:** 12 ft 9 in.
Condition: Good / **Number:** PA-63-16 / **Register:** June 22, 1979

This is the more easterly of the two bridges that are standing in Mingo Creek County Park. It appears to be used quite heavily, perhaps because of its location in the park. Its deck, consequently, has been heavily reinforced with five steel I-beams that rest on concrete abutments. A sign on the bridge posts a two-ton limit; however, a sign on the road at the approach posts a three-ton limit. The structure is covered with vertical board siding on both the sides and portals and is painted barn red inside and outside. The roof is sheet metal, and the deck consists of lengthwise planking. The presence of two rectangular windows on each side beneath the eave openings is typical of this county's bridges. The structure has moderate length stone-and-mortar wingwalls and concrete-capped parapets. During our visit in May 2000, we noticed that the mortar joints in two of the wingwalls are beginning to separate, and the parapets are beginning to lean—one toward the approach and one toward the creek.

Hughes Bridge

Location: Bypassed by Montgomery Run Road (T 688), approximately 1 mile west of Ten Mile, Amwell Township, in a park-like setting.
Directions: From I 79 south, Marianna/Prosperity Exit (Exit 5), at the end of the exit ramp, turn left on Ten Mile Road and go 0.2 mile to Montgomery Run Road (first road past I 79 north ramp). Turn left and go 0.3 mile to gated entrance of park area.

Year: 1889 / **Truss:** Queenpost / **Waterway:** Ten Mile Creek
In Use: Foot traffic only / **Number of Spans:** 1 / **Owner:** Township
Builder: Unknown / **Length:** 64 ft. 4 in. / **Width:** 12 ft. 10 in.
Condition: Fair / **Number:** PA-63-17 / **Register:** June 22, 1979

The Hughes Bridge is located in a park-like setting and appears to be used only for intermittent foot traffic. It is still maintained by Amwell Township and is typical of most of the other county covered spans. It has barn red vertical board siding on both the portals and the exterior sides, and is painted the same color on the inside. The bridge has a sheet metal roof, a deck of crosswise planking, and three rectangular windows on each side in addition to the narrow eave openings. There are no steel or wood reinforcements; the bridge rests on a concrete abutment at the north end and a cut stone-and-mortar abutment at the south end. It has short, cut stone-and-mortar wingwalls and parapets that are capped with concrete at both ends.

During our visit in 2000, we observed that while the grounds around the bridge are maintained, the bridge itself, other than annual repainting, may not receive much regular maintenance. There is a noticeable sag in the bridge deck, there are several holes in the sheet metal roof, and some of the trim on the gable ends is beginning to deteriorate. This bridge is owned and maintained by the township, while twenty one of the other bridges in the county are owned and maintained by the county.

Jackson's Mill Bridge

Location: On Kingscreek Road, approximately 1.4 miles north of Hamilton, 4.5 miles west of Florence, Hanover Township.
Directions: Starting at the Hanover Township Building (location of the McClurg/Devil's Den Bridge), go west on Steubenville Road (SR 4004) for 2.2 miles to Phillips Road. Turn right on Phillips Road for 1 mile to Kingscreek Road. Continue straight on Kingscreek Road for 0.4 mile to the bridge.

Year: Unknown / **Truss:** Queenpost / **Waterway:** King's Creek
In Use: Yes / **Number of Spans:** 1 / **Owner:** County
Builder: Unknown / **Length:** 46 ft. 2 in. / **Width:** 12 ft. 10½ in.
Condition: Good / **Number:** PA-63-18 / **Register:** June 22, 1979

This bridge is located in a remote county valley, and is another typical Washington County bridge. It has a sheet metal roof, vertical board siding on both the sides and the portals, and barn red paint on both the exterior and interior, and two windows are located at each end in addition to the eave openings. The deck is made of crosswise planking and is reinforced with wooden, trestle-type supports that rest in the streambed. The bridge rests on cut stone-and-mortar abutments laid on concrete footings that extend to form stone-and-mortar wingwalls and parapets. One wingwall and one parapet have been replaced with concrete.

By contacting the Washington County Commissioner's Office in June 2000, we learned that this bridge, too, is scheduled for restoration work during 2001. The bridge did appear, however, to have been recently painted in May 2000.

Krepps Bridge

Location: On Covered Bridge Road, approximately 1 mile southeast of Cherry Valley, Pleasant Township. **Directions:** In Hickory, at the junction of PA 50 and Wabash Ave., go north on Wabash Ave. for 0.4 mile to Waterdam Road. Turn right on Waterdam Road and go 3.3 miles to the bridge on Covered Bridge Road (stay on the main road—other, more secondary roads turn off). The bridge is just to the left.

Year: Unknown / **Truss:** Kingpost / **Waterway:** Raccoon Creek
In Use: Yes / **Number of Spans:** 1 / **Owner:** County
Builder: Unknown / **Length:** 29 ft. 11 in. / **Width:** 13 ft. 1 in.
Condition: Very good / **Number:** PA-63-19 / **Register:** June 22, 1979

After seeing about half of the Washington County covered bridges, we noted that, except for location and very minor differences in certain features, all of the structures are similar. Our comments reflect those similarities. Krepps Bridge, like the others, has vertical board siding on both portals and sides, is painted barn red inside and outside, has a sheet metal roof, a deck of crosswise planking, and two rectangular windows on each side in addition to the eave openings. The entire structure is reinforced with treated timber supports that sit in the streambed; otherwise, the structure rests on a concrete abutment at one end and a stone-and-mortar abutment at the other. The stone-and-mortar abutment has been extended to form moderate length wingwalls and parapets that are capped with concrete.

A Theodore Burr Society publication dated Spring 1995 indicated that some of the siding boards were missing from the bridge. However, when we visited the bridge in May 2000, every board was in place and the bridge had been recently painted. We considered it, like many other bridges in the county, to be in very good condition.

Leatherman Bridge

Location: On Letherman Bridge Road (NBT 449), 1.4 miles northeast of Odell, North Bethlehem Township. **Directions:** In Odell, at the junction of US 40 and Dague Hollow Road (NBT 447), go north on Dague Hollow Road for 1.15 miles to Letherman Bridge Road. Turn right on Letherman Bridge Road and go 0.25 mile to the bridge. The road name is not spelled the same as the bridge name.

Year: Unknown / **Truss:** Queenpost
Waterway: South Branch, Pigeon Creek
In Use: Yes / **Number of Spans:** 1 / **Owner:** County
Builder: Unknown / **Length:** 43 ft. 5 in. / **Width:** 12 ft. 10 in.
Condition: Excellent / **Number:** PA-63-20 / **Register:** June 22, 1979

The Leatherman Bridge, which has features typical of most of the Washington County bridges, was in far better condition when we saw it in 2000 than in 1991. We are sure that the improved condition is the result of restoration work which was done in 1998. The basic structure has retained its original historic integrity, and remains a barn red bridge with vertical board siding on both the sides and the portals. There are narrow openings under the eaves and two windows on each side. The bridge now has a new, cedar shake roof. The deck, made of crosswise planking, is no longer supported by the previous framework of heavy timbers which once rested in the center of the streambed. Instead, it has been reinforced with a steel substructure. The entire structure rests on reconstructed concrete abutments faced with stone-and-mortar. The stone-and-mortar wingwalls and parapets are capped with concrete. We were amazed at the drastic changes that had been made to improve the structure we saw in 1991. The overall appearance is greatly enhanced and the bridge, which supported a 5-ton limit in 1991, now carries a 15-ton load.

Longdon L. Miller Bridge

Location: On Miller Creek Road (T 414), approximately 3.5 miles southeast of West Finley. **Directions:** In West Finley, at the junction of West Finley Road (SR 3037) and Burnsville Ridge Road, go south on West Finley Road for 2.4 miles to Enon Church Road. Turn left on Enon Church Road and go 0.7 mile to Miller Creek Road. Turn left on Miller Creek Road and go 0.3 mile to the bridge site.

Year: Unknown / **Truss:** Queenpost
Waterway: Templeton Fork, Wheeling Creek
In Use: No (construction under way) / **Number of Spans:** 1+
Owner: County / **Builder:** Unknown
Length: 67 ft. 7 in. (1991) / **Width:** 11 ft. 10 in. (1991)
Condition: Under restoration / **Number:** PA-63-22
Register: June 22, 1979

The Longdon L. Miller Bridge, located in the extreme southwestern part of the county, is another bridge that is well secluded along a gravel township road. Because this bridge is in the midst of restoration, we will first recount the information we gathered about this bridge for our 1993 book. The bridge has a rather long queenpost truss structure that has four wooden trestle supports under its sixty-seven foot long deck. Barn red vertical board siding covers the sides and the portals. It has a sheet metal roof and a deck of crosswise planking, and there are three rectangular windows on each side in addition to the narrow eave openings. The bridge rests on cut stone-and-mortar abutments that have been extended to form short, stone-and-mortar wingwalls, one of which is capped with concrete.

At the time of our visit in May 2000, we were surprised to find the bridge site totally devoid of a bridge structure. There was nothing at the site but construction equipment and evidence that a central pier was being constructed in the middle of Templeton Fork. After a telephone call to the Executive Director of the Washington County Planning Commission, we learned that the bridge is being completely restored. It was anticipated that restoration will be completed by fall of 2000. Consequently, we returned to the bridge in August 2000, and found the bridge in the condition shown in the photo, with freshly primed lumber and a new cedar shake roof. The new vertical board siding will probably be finished with a deep barn red paint, typical of the Washington County bridges. It should be completely finished in time for the annual Washington–Greene County Covered Bridge Festival in September.

Lyle Bridge

Location: On Kramer Road (T 861), approximately 5 miles northeast of Florence, Hanover Township. **Directions:** In Florence, at the junction of PA 18 and Steubenville Road (SR 4004) go east on Steubenville Road for 2.3 miles to Knowlton Hill Road. Turn left on Knowlton Hill Road and go 1.5 miles to Kramer Road; turn left on Kramer Road and go 1.4 miles to the bridge.

Year: Unknown / **Truss:** Queenpost / **Waterway:** Brush Run
In Use: Yes / **Number of Spans:** 1 / **Owner:** County
Builder: Unknown / **Length:** 39 ft. 2½ in. / **Width:** 12 ft. 10½ in.
Condition: Excellent / **Number:** PA-63-21 / **Register:** June 22, 1979

This is another Washington County bridge that is tucked away in a remote, quiet valley along a gravel township road. It is located in the northernmost part of the county. When we visited the bridge in 1991, we considered it to be in fair condition. Upon our return to the bridge in May 2000, we were pleasantly surprised at the improvements to the bridge resulting from restoration done in 1999. The deck of the queenpost truss span had formerly been supported with two heavy timber trestles, which rested in the streambed at intervals equidistant from each end. The bridge now rests on six steel I-beam stringers, which enable it to carry a fifteen-ton limit. The new vertical board siding on both the sides and the portals has been freshly painted barn red. The roof, which had been covered with rusted sheet metal, is now covered with cedar shakes, and the deck is covered with wide, crosswise planking. There are three windows on each side in addition to the fairly wide eave openings. The entire structure rests on stone-and-mortar abutments laid on concrete foundations. The abutments have been extended to form short wingwalls and parapets that rise about two feet above the roadway approach. The improvements to this bridge, once again, indicate the county's objective to improve and preserve these historic landmarks for future generations to see and enjoy.

Mays / May's Blaney / Blaney Bridge

Location: On Waynesburg Road, approximately 1 mile southeast of West Alexander, Donegal Township. **Directions:** Just north of West Alexander, at the junction of PA 40 and W. Liberty Street (SR 3005), go south on W. Liberty Street for 0.35 mile to Main Street. Turn left on Main Street and go 0.45 mile to Lynn Street; turn right on Lynn Street and go 1.4 miles to the bridge. (Note: after 0.6 mile Lynn Street becomes Waynesburg Road.)

Year: Unknown / **Truss:** Queenpost
Waterway: Middle Wheeling Creek
In Use: Yes / **Number of Spans:** 1 / **Owner:** County
Builder: Unknown / **Length:** 39 ft. 9½ in. / **Width:** 12 ft. 10 in.
Condition: Good / **Number:** PA-63-23 / **Register:** June 22, 1979

This bridge is typical of the other county covered bridges, and located along a remote, gravel township road in a quiet, secluded valley. It is covered with vertical boards on both the sides and the portals and is painted barn red inside and outside. The bridge has a sheet metal roof and a deck of crosswise planking. It has two windows on each side as well as the narrow eave openings and rests on stone-and-mortar abutments that extend into short, stone-and-mortar wingwalls and parapets. It has additional timber trestles that rest in the streambed and support the deck. In 1991 we considered the bridge to be in fair condition; however, when we returned nine years later, the appearance of the recently painted interior and exterior affected us enough that we improved our rating to good. This improvement, again, is due to the county's efforts to keep all of the county owned bridges in the best condition possible.

McClurg / Devil's Den Bridge

Location: In Hanover Township Park, approximately 1 mile west of Florence, Hanover Township. **Directions:** In Florence, at the junction of PA 18 and Steubenville Road (SR 4004), go west on Steubenville Road for 1 mile to Hanover Township Park on the left side of the road. If the park gate is locked, acquire permission to enter the park from the clerk in the Hanover Township Building on the right side of the road.

Year: 1880 / **Truss:** Kingpost / **Waterway:** Small gully
In Use: Foot traffic only / **Number of Spans:** 1 / **Owner:** County
Builder: Unknown / **Length:** 31 ft. 9½ in. / **Width:** 12 ft. 11 in.
Condition: Good / **Number:** PA-63-13 / **Register:** June 22, 1979

The McClurg or Devil's Den Covered Bridge was originally located over King's Creek, just north of Paris in the northwest corner of the county. It was moved to its present location over a small, dry gully in 1987. The bridge is a typical county structure—sides and portals covered with vertical, barn red boards, a roof of cedar shakes, a deck of crosswise planking, and four rectangular windows on each side along with the eave openings. It rests on stone-and-mortar abutments with short stone-and-mortar wingwalls and parapets, and has an additional, U-shaped vertical timber that rests in the gully to lend support to the middle of the deck. At the time of our visit in May 2000, it was one of a few county owned bridges that had not been painted recently. The exterior, especially, was faded and beginning to peel.

Pine Bank Bridge

Location: In Meadowcroft Village, approximately 2.5 miles west of Avella, Jefferson Township. **Directions:** In Avella, at the junction of PA 50 and SR 4029, look for the sign to Meadowcroft Village. Go west on SR 4029 for 2.6 miles to the entrance gate of Meadowcroft Village. Turn right on to the entrance road and follow it to the parking area. The bridge is several hundred yards from the Visitors Center. Acquire directions and/or map at the Visitors Center.

Year: 1870 / **Truss:** Kingpost / **Waterway:** Avella Ravine
In Use: Foot traffic only / **Number of Spans:** 1 / **Owner:** Private
Builder: Unknown / **Length:** 38 ft. 3 in. / **Width:** 12 ft. 9 in.
Condition: Good / **Number:** PA-63-35 / **Register:** June 22, 1979

This bridge was formerly located in Greene County where it spanned Toms Run in Gilmore Township. It was moved to the Meadowcroft Village property in 1962 to become part of the re-created early American farm scene. Although it has been painted barn red, like the other bridges of the county, it is not similar in style. It has a different portal design, a roof of asphalt shingles, and no paint on the interior. In fact, the inside walls still display some old advertisements. The bridge rests on stone abutments that have been laid dry, and it has large, cut stone slabs at each end where parapets would usually be. It also has two unusual, heavy, diagonal timbers on each side that go from the base of the abutments to the center of the bridge deck. Like most of the other bridges in the county, the privately owned Pine Bank Bridge is being well maintained.

Plant's Bridge

Location: On Skyview Road (T 408), approximately 2.5 miles west of East Finley, East Finley Township. **Directions:** In East Finley, at the junction of PA 231 (East Finley Road) and Rocky Run Road (SR 3035), go west on Rocky Run Road for 1.3 miles to Fairmount Church Road. Turn right on Fairmount Church Road and go 0.1 mile to Skyview Road. Continue straight on Skyview Road for 1 mile to the bridge. Or from the Sprowl's Bridge (see Sprowl's Bridge), continue northeast on Rocky Run Road for 0.3 mile to Fairmount Church Road (T 450). Turn left on Fairmount Church Road and go 0.1 mile to Skyview Road; continue straight on Skyview Road for 1 mile to the bridge.

Year: Unknown / **Truss:** Kingpost
Waterway: Templeton Fork, Wheeling Creek
In Use: Yes / **Number of Spans:** 1 / **Owner:** County
Builder: Unknown / **Length:** 34 ft. 1½ in. / **Width:** 12 ft. 8½ in.
Condition: Good / **Number:** PA-63-26 / **Register:** June 22, 1979

The Plant's Bridge is a rather short kingpost truss structure that has many stylistic similarities to most of the other county bridges. The sides and the portals are covered with barn red, vertical board siding on both sides and portals, and the interior is painted the same color. There is a sheet metal roof, a deck of crosswise planking, and two rectangular windows on each side. The stone-and-mortar abutments extend into short wingwalls and relatively low parapets, and there are no additional reinforcements under the deck. The bridge is supported entirely by the kingpost truss system. In May 2000, we found that this bridge, too, was in better condition than in 1991. It appeared to have fresh paint and a new sheet metal roof. The abutments, wingwalls, and parapets had been repointed, and the road name obelisk adjacent to the bridge had been painted.

Ralston Freeman Bridge

Location: On private land, approximately 4 miles north of Hamilton, Hanover Township. **Directions:** (See Jackson's Mill Bridge) From the Jackson's Mill Bridge, continue through the bridge on Kingscreek Road for 0.05 mile to McCracken Hill Road. Turn left on McCracken Hill Road and go 1.3 miles to a "T" at Meadow Road. Turn right on Meadow Road and go 0.3 mile to Ralston Road. Make a hard left on to Ralston Road and go 0.5 mile to the end of the improved gravel road at a private home. The road to the bridge is gated just to the left. The walk to the bridge, down the old lane, is approximately 150 yards.

Year: 1915 / **Truss:** Kingpost
Waterway: Aunt Clara's Fork, Kings Creek
In Use: Foot traffic only / **Number of Spans:** 1 / **Owner:** Private
Builder: Unknown / **Length:** 36 ft. 1 in. / **Width:** 12 ft. 3 in.
Condition: Good / **Number:** PA-63-27 / **Register:** June 22, 1979

This bridge is truly located in the most remote corner of the county, at the end of a road that is in very poor condition. It is now on private property and is being maintained by the owner. The bridge is posted with "No Trespassing" signs because of difficulty the owner has had with "partying" visitors. Otherwise, it is typical of the other county bridges—similar siding, roof, deck, abutments, wingwalls, and parapets. The owner has tried hard to maintain it in a condition equal to most of the other Washington County covered bridges. In 2000, we considered its condition to be equal to, if not better than, what we had observed in 1991.

Sawhill Bridge

Location: On Buffalo Camp Road, approximately 3.5 miles northwest of Taylorstown, Blain Township. **Directions:** In Taylorstown, at the junction of PA 221 and SR 4024, where PA 221 is named Buffalo Creek Road, go north on Buffalo Creek Road (PA 221) for 3.1 miles to Buffalo Camp Road. The Bridge is just to the left on Buffalo Camp Road.

Year: 1915 / **Truss:** Queenpost / **Waterway:** Buffalo Creek
In Use: Yes / **Number of Spans:** 1 / **Owner:** County
Builder: Unknown / **Length:** 57 ft. 3½ in. / **Width:** 12 ft. 11½ in.
Condition: Fair / **Number:** PA-63-34 / **Register:** June 22, 1979

This is another of the few Washington County covered bridges that is not hidden away in a remote area. Just off SR 221, which carries a fairly large amount of traffic, the bridge structure is quite similar to the others in the county. It has vertical board siding, barn red paint inside and outside, three rectangular windows on each side, a roof of sheet metal, and a deck of crosswise planking. The queenpost truss structure rests on one concrete abutment and one of stone-and-mortar. The stone-and-mortar abutment extends to form attractive, curved wingwalls on the Route 221 end of the bridge. The deck requires no additional reinforcement. In May 2000, we noticed that the bridge leans a little toward the downstream side, has some new, unpainted siding, and has some holes in the metal roof. Consequently, we considered it to be in only fair condition.

Sprowl's Bridge

Location: On Newland School Road (T 450), 1.5 miles southwest of East Finley, East Finley Township. **Directions:** In West Finley, at the junction of West Finley Road (SR 3037) and Burnsville Ridge Road (SR 3035), go northeast on Burnsville Ridge Road for 0.7 mile to Rocky Run Road (SR 3035—white Presbyterian Church at the crossroads). Turn right on Rocky Run Road and go 4.1 miles to Newland School Road. Turn right and go 0.1 mile to the bridge. Or in East Finley, at the junction of PA 231 (East Finley Road) and Rocky Run Road (SR 3035), go west on Rocky Run Road for 1.6 miles to Newland School Road; turn left and go 0.1 mile to the bridge.

Year: 1875 / **Truss:** Kingpost / **Waterway:** Rocky Run
In Use: Yes / **Number of Spans:** 1 / **Owner:** County
Builder: Unknown / **Length:** 36 ft. 2 in. / **Width:** 12 ft. 6½ in.
Condition: Good / **Number:** PA-63-03 / **Register:** June 22, 1979

The Sprowl's Bridge is a kingpost truss structure covered with vertical board siding on both the sides and the portals. It has a sheet metal roof, a deck of crosswise planking, and two square windows cut into each side in addition to the narrow, lengthwise openings under the eaves. The bridge is painted barn red on both the inside and outside and rests on stone-and-mortar abutments reinforced with concrete. It also has stone-and-mortar wingwalls and parapets that are capped with concrete. Like most of the Washington County covered bridges, the Sprowl's Bridge is located in a secluded, rural valley on a gravel township road. In the summer of 1996, publications of the Theodore Burr Covered Bridge Society reported that the bridge was closed; however, when we visited the bridge in May 2000, we found it open and in good condition. At the August 2000 meeting of the Theodore Burr Covered Bridge Society, however, it was announced that the bridge had been closed again. This encouraged us to revisit the bridge. When we arrived later that month, we found the bridge closed due to damage done by mining operations in the area. The truss structure was quite severely twisted, and rather wide cracks were developing in the abutments. The bridge will remain closed until blasting by the mining company is concluded later in 2000. The mining company has assured the county that it will restore the bridge to its original, usable condition.

Wilson's Mill Bridge

Location: In Cross Creek County Park, approximately 2.5 miles east of West Middleton, between Cross Creek and Hopewell Townships.
Directions: In Woodrow, at the junction of PA 50 and Old Ridge Road, go south on Old Ridge Road for 1.9 miles to the park entrance on the right. Turn right and go 0.1 mile to a parking area to the left; the bridge is just ahead.

Year: 1889 / **Truss:** Queenpost / **Waterway:** Cross Creek
In Use: Yes / **Number of Spans:** 1 / **Owner:** County
Builder: Unknown / **Length:** 39 ft. 4½ in. / **Width:** 13 ft. 4½ in.
Condition: Fair / **Number:** PA-63-28 / **Register:** June 22, 1979

This is one of the five Washington County covered bridges that are being preserved in county park areas. The Wilson's Mill Bridge was moved to its present location in 1978 as part of a flood control project. Compared to the other bridges of the county, it is a rather high structure. This may be due, in part, to the heavy steel I-beams that have been added to support the deck and the additional siding material that has been used to conceal the steelwork. Otherwise, it is similar to the other covered spans in the county. While most of the county bridges appeared to have a relatively fresh coat of paint in May 2000, we were surprised to find that the Wilson's Mill Bridge had not been painted recently and that some of the siding material and structural members of the queenpost truss were showing signs of deterioration.

Wright / Cerl Bridge

Location: On Ridge Road (T 802), approximately 1.5 miles south of Kammerer, Somerset Township. **Directions:** In Kammerer, at the junction of PA 136 and Sumney Road, go south on Sumney Road for 0.5 mile to the junction with Holman Road. Bear left on Sumney Road for 1.1 miles until Sumney Road becomes Ridge Road (at a crossroads with Carlton Road). Cross over I 70 and go 0.15 mile to the bridge.

Year: Unknown / **Truss:** Kingpost
Waterway: North Branch, Pigeon Creek
In Use: Yes / **Number of Spans:** 1 / **Owner:** County
Builder: Unknown / **Length:** 33 ft. 9 in. / **Width:** 13 ft. 8½ in.
Condition: Excellent / **Number:** PA-63-30 (2) / **Register:** June 22, 1979

This is another one of the few Washington County covered bridges that is not located in a hidden valley. Rather, it is in an open pasture area just south of the township road overpass of Interstate 70. The design, siding, deck, abutments, wingwalls, and parapets are typical of Washington County. However, during our 2000 visit, we found that the bridge had been completely restored, reportedly with all new lumber. Like several other bridges in the county, the Wright Bridge has been rebuilt on refurbished, stone-faced abutments and supported with steel I-beams under its deck. The abutments extend into moderately long cut stone-and-mortar wingwalls and parapets. The parapets are capped with concrete. This reconstruction is a marked improvement over the bridge's condition in 1991.

Wyit Sprowls Bridge

Location: In East Finley Park, East Finley Township. **Directions:** From Plant's Bridge (see Plant's Bridge), go north on Templeton Run Road (T 414) for 0.4 mile. Where Templeton Run Road turns right, continue on it for 1 mile. Where the road turns right again, continue for 1.1 miles to East Finley Park. The bridge is to the right.

Year: Unknown / **Truss:** Queenpost
Waterway: Robinson Fork, Wheeling Creek
In Use: Being moved to East Finley Park / **Number of Spans:** 1
Owner: County
Builder: Unknown / **Length:** 43 ft. (1991) / **Width:** 11 ft. 6 in. (1991)
Condition: Under restoration / **Number:** PA-63-29
Register: June 22, 1979

The description given for most of the other Washington County covered bridges quite adequately describes this bridge also. However, the photo displayed here was taken in 1991 at the bridge's original location. Like several other county bridges, the Wyit Sprowls Bridge is being moved. Its new location will be in East Finley Park. At the time of our visit in 2000, only the abutments were completed in the new location, and the bridge had been removed from its former site and placed in storage until the new site is prepared. We assume that it will be restored to its original state with barn red vertical board siding, paint inside and outside, a sheet metal roof, crosswise deck planking, and three rectangular windows on each side.

Bells Mills / Bell's Mills Bridge

Location: On Bell's Mills Road (SR 3061), approximately 2 miles north of Wyano and 1 mile west of Milbell, between Sewickley and South Huntingdon Townships. **Directions:** From I 70, take Exit 24, (PA 31 West toward West Newton). Go west on PA 31 for 0.4 mile to Strickertown Road; turn right on Strickertown Road and go 0.85 mile to Bell's Mills Road. Turn left on Bell's Mills Road and go 1.7 miles to the bridge.

Year: 1850 / **Truss:** Burr / **Waterway:** Sewickley Creek
In Use: Yes / **Number of Spans:** 1 / **Owner:** County
Builder: Daniel McCain / **Length:** 106 ft. 4½ in. / **Width:** 13 ft. 1½ in.
Condition: Good / **Number:** PA-65-01 / **Register:** June 27, 1980

This is the only remaining covered bridge in Westmoreland County. Notice, in particular, the different styling of the portal support posts and gable ends. They are reminiscent of the ancient Greek and Roman styles of columns and pediments. The sides are covered with barn red horizontal clapboard siding, and the interior is painted the same color. The portal gables are covered with barn red horizontal boards, the roof consists of cedar shakes, and the deck has rather wide runners that are laid over crosswise planking. There are no side openings other than the rather wide, typical, lengthwise eave openings. The entire structure rests on stone-and-mortar abutments that are reinforced with concrete at both ground level and road level. The bridge also has stone-and-mortar wingwalls and low parapets that are protected with heavy wooden guardrails. A large, heavy, arch-type structure built outside of each portal limits the overhead clearance to six and one-half feet. The bridge has been well maintained. There was nothing noticeably different in the condition of the bridge in 2000 from what we observed in 1991. There was evidence, however, that an attempt is being made to keep the bridge free of graffiti. One of the portal legs that had been covered with graffiti has been freshly painted.

Bibliography

Books

Allen, Richard Sanders. *Covered Bridges of the Middle Atlantic States*. Brattleboro, Vt.: The Stephen Greene Press, 1959.

Barton, Edwin M. *The Covered Bridges of Columbia County, Pennsylvania*. Orangeville, Pa.: Columbia County Historical Society, 1974.

Caruthers, E. Gipe. *Seeing Lancaster County's Covered Bridges*. Lancaster, Pa.: E. Gipe Caruthers, 1974.

Evans, Benjamin D. and June R. Evans. *Pennsylvania's Covered Bridges, A Complete Guide*. Pittsburgh, Pa., and London: University of Pittsburgh Press, 1993.

Hammer, Arthur F. *Romantic Shelters*. Marlboro, Mass.: The National Society for the Preservation of Covered Bridges, Inc., 1989.

Helsel, Bill. *World Guide To Covered Bridges*. Marlboro, Mass.: The National Society for the Preservation of Covered Bridges, Inc., 1989.

Horst, Mel, and Elmer L. Smith. *Covered Bridges of Pennsylvania Dutchland*. Lebanon, Pa.: Applied Arts Publishers, 1988.

Krekeler, Brenda. *Covered Bridges Today*. Canton, Oh.: Daring Publishing Group, Inc., 1988.

Zacher, Susan. *The Covered Bridges of Pennsylvania*. Harrisburg, Pa.: The Pennsylvania Historical and Museum Commission, 1989.

Data

Wilson, Robert. *State Image Files* (CD-ROM—Digital Pennsylvania Map Files). Indiana, Pa.: Spatial Science Research Center, Indiana University of Pennsylvania, 2000.

Maps

General Highway Map, Adams County, Pennsylvania. Harrisburg, Pa.: Department of Transportation, 1980.

General Highway Map, Bedford County, Pennsylvania. Harrisburg, Pa.: Department of Transportation, 1990.

General Highway Map, Bucks County, Pennsylvania. Harrisburg, Pa.: Department of Transportation, 1986.

General Highway Map, Chester County, Pennsylvania. Harrisburg, Pa.: Department of Transportation, 1978.

General Highway Map, Columbia County, Pennsylvania. Harrisburg, Pa.: Department of Transportation, 1982.

General Highway Map, Greene County, Pennsylvania. Harrisburg, Pa.: Department of Transportation, 1990.

General Highway Map, Indiana County, Pennsylvania. Harrisburg, Pa.: Department of Transportation, 1978.

General Highway Map, Juniata County and Mifflin County, Pennsylvania. Harrisburg, Pa.: Department of Transportation, 1990.

General Highway Map, Lancaster County, Pennsylvania. Harrisburg, Pa.: Department of Transportation, 1972.

General Highway Map, Montour County and Northumberland County, Pennsylvania. Harrisburg, Pa.: Department of Transportation, 1990.

General Highway Map, Perry County, Pennsylvania. Harrisburg, Pa.: Department of Transportation, 1990.

General Highway Map, Snyder County and Union County, Pennsylvania. Harrisburg, Pa.: Department of Transportation, 1981.

General Highway Map, Somerset County, Pennsylvania. Harrisburg, Pa.: Department of Transportation, 1990.

General Highway Map, Washington County, Pennsylvania. Harrisburg, Pa.: Department of Transportation, 1990.

Lancaster County Central Park. Lancaster, Pa.: Lancaster County Department of Parks and Recreation, 1988.

Pennsylvania Atlas and Gazetteer, Second Edition. Freeport, Maine: DeLorme Mapping Co., 1987.

Pennsylvania Atlas and Gazetteer, Fifth Edition. Freeport, Maine: DeLorme Mapping Co., 1999.

Pamphlets

Covered Bridges of Bedford County. Bedford, Pa.: Bedford County Travel Agency.

Covered Bridges of Columbia and Montour Counties of Pennsylvania. Columbia and Montour Counties, Pa.: Columbia-Montour Tourist Promotion Agency, Inc.

Covered Bridges of Snyder, Union, and Northumberland Counties. Sunbury and Selinsgrove, Pa.: Northumberland County TPA and Susquehanna Valley Visitors Bureau.

Pennsylvania Covered Bridge List. Carlisle, Pa.: The Theodore Burr Covered Bridge Society of Pennsylvania, Inc., 1991.

Somerset Historical Center. Somerset, Pa.: Somerset Historical Center, Pennsylvania's Rural Heritage Museum.

Standards for Rehabilitation & Guidelines for Rehabilitating Historic Buildings. Harrisburg, Pa.: Pennsylvania Historical and Museum Commission, Commonwealth of Pennsylvania.

Tracking Covered Bridges in the Lehigh Valley. Lehigh Valley, Pa.: The Lehigh Valley Convention and Visitors Bureau, Inc.

Washington County Covered Bridges. Charleroi, Pa.: Pictorial America.

Periodicals

"Covered Bridges." In *Lancaster County Parks and Recreation Department Newsletter* VIII, no. 4 (Winter 1986).

Pennsylvania Crossings. The Theodore Burr Covered Bridge Society of Pennsylvania, Inc., Vol. 14, no. 2 through Vol. 23, no. 2 (Spring 1991 through Spring 2000).

Wooden Covered Spans. The Theodore Burr Covered Bridge Society of Pennsylvania, Inc., Volume 14, Number 2 through Volume 23, Number 1 (Spring 1991 through Winter 2000).

Reports

Pennsylvania Covered Bridges, Rebuilding-Rehabilitations-Repairs-Painting. Compiled by Abe Ludy and Thomas Walczak, Theodore Burr Covered Bridge Society of Pennsylvania, Inc.

Statewide Covered Bridge Assessment for the Pennsylvania Department Of Transportation. Media, Pa.: Ortega Consulting, 29 November 1991.

Web sites

Washington County Tourism Promotion Agency, Washington, Pa. Home Page. Fall 2000 <http://www.washpatourism.org/>

Index

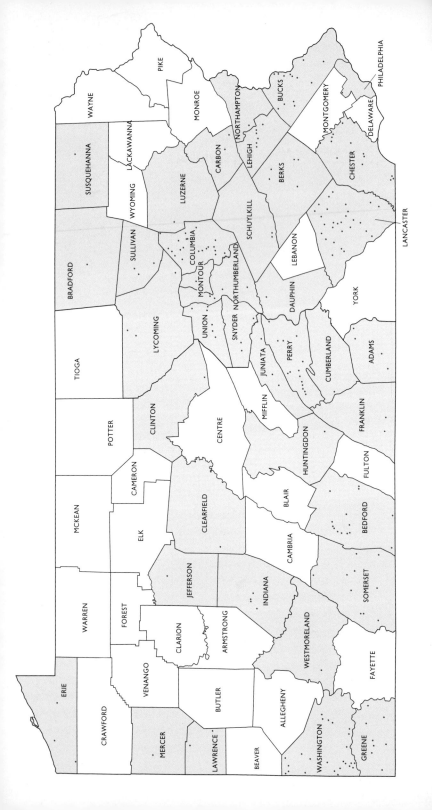